Lecture Notes in Electrical Engineering

Volume 1218

The book series *Lecture Notes in Electrical Engineering* (LNEE) publishes the latest developments in Electrical Engineering—quickly, informally and in high quality. While original research reported in proceedings and monographs has traditionally formed the core of LNEE, we also encourage authors to submit books devoted to supporting student education and professional training in the various fields and applications areas of electrical engineering. The series cover classical and emerging topics concerning:

- Communication Engineering, Information Theory and Networks
- Electronics Engineering and Microelectronics
- Signal, Image and Speech Processing
- Wireless and Mobile Communication
- Circuits and Systems
- Energy Systems, Power Electronics and Electrical Machines
- Electro-optical Engineering
- Instrumentation Engineering
- Avionics Engineering
- Control Systems
- Internet-of-Things and Cybersecurity
- Biomedical Devices, MEMS and NEMS

For general information about this book series, comments or suggestions, please contact leontina.dicecco@springer.com.

To submit a proposal or request further information, please contact the Publishing Editor in your country:

China

Jasmine Dou, Editor (jasmine.dou@springer.com)

India, Japan, Rest of Asia

Swati Meherishi, Editorial Director (Swati.Meherishi@springer.com)

Southeast Asia, Australia, New Zealand

Ramesh Nath Premnath, Editor (ramesh.premnath@springernature.com)

USA, Canada

Michael Luby, Senior Editor (michael.luby@springer.com)

All other Countries

Leontina Di Cecco, Senior Editor (leontina.dicecco@springer.com)

**** This series is indexed by EI Compendex and Scopus databases. ****

Santanu Chaudhury · Anand Mishra ·
Anoop M. Namboodiri · Dinesh Babu Jayagopi ·
Neelam Sinha · Rajendra Nagar
Editors

Computer Vision, Pattern Recognition, Image Processing, and Graphics

Proceedings of the 8th National Conference, NCVPRIPG 2023

Springer

Editors
Santanu Chaudhury
IIT Jodhpur
Jodhpur, Rajasthan, India

Anand Mishra
IIT Jodhpur
Jodhpur, Rajasthan, India

Anoop M. Namboodiri
IIIT Hyderabad
Hyderabad, Telangana, India

Dinesh Babu Jayagopi
IIIT Bangalore
Bengaluru, Karnataka, India

Neelam Sinha
IIIT Bangalore
Bengaluru, Karnataka, India

Rajendra Nagar
IIT Jodhpur
Jodhpur, Rajasthan, India

ISSN 1876-1100 ISSN 1876-1119 (electronic)
Lecture Notes in Electrical Engineering
ISBN 978-981-97-5211-9 ISBN 978-981-97-5212-6 (eBook)
https://doi.org/10.1007/978-981-97-5212-6

This Springer imprint is published by the registered company Springer Nature Singapore Pte Ltd.
The registered company address is: 152 Beach Road, #21-01/04 Gateway East, Singapore 189721, Singapore

Preface

The Eighth National Conference on Computer Vision, Pattern Recognition, Image Processing and Graphics (NCVPRIPG 2023) was held at the beautiful IIT campus at Bluecity Jodhpur, Rajasthan, from 21 to 23 July 2023. NCVPRIPG 2023 was organized by the Indian Institute of Technology Jodhpur in association with the Indian Unit for Pattern Recognition and Artificial Intelligence (IUPRAI). NCVPRIPG aims to bring together researchers and practitioners from the allied areas of computer vision, graphics, image processing, and pattern recognition to promote community-wide discussions of ideas that will influence and foster continued research in the field. Over the years, the conference has grown into a vibrant national conference with participation from many students and researchers.

The number of physical participants was about 152, an excellent physical restart to such a significant event. NCVPRIPG 2023 centered around the technical program in areas of computer vision, pattern recognition, image processing, and graphics. Specifically, our program included three plenary lectures, four challenges, three workshops, four tutorials, Industry, and a demo session. Within this compilation, you will find meticulously chosen and rigorously double-blind peer-reviewed eight papers from the Workshop on High-Throughput Vision-based Phenotyping (HTVP'23) alongside six papers from the Workshop on Contactless Hand Biometrics and Gesture Recognition (CHBGR-23), both conducted in conjunction with NCVPRIPG. Additionally, it includes summaries of four challenge papers.

The sponsorship from SERB (Department of Science and Technology, Government of India), Google, Robert-Bosch, and Elancer Pvt. Ltd. for NCVPRIPG 2023 is greatly appreciated. Our gratitude extends to IIT Jodhpur for its exceptional academic, infrastructure, and hospitality arrangements that ensured the smooth execution of all sessions. We trust that akin to previous editions, this conference has delivered enriching experiences and forged new connections, fostering growth in computer vision, image processing, and computer graphics across India's associated research areas.

Jodhpur, India — Santanu Chaudhury
Hyderabad, India — Anoop M. Namboodiri
Bengaluru, India — Dinesh Babu Jayagopi
Bengaluru, India — Neelam Sinha
Jodhpur, India — Anand Mishra
Jodhpur, India — Rajendra Nagar

Contents

About the Editors

Prof. Santanu Chaudhury is an esteemed academician and researcher known for his significant contributions to Electrical Engineering, Computer Science, and Engineering Education. He currently serves as the Director of the Indian Institute of Technology Jodhpur (IITJ) and is a professor in the Department of Computer Science and Engineering at IITJ. With a rich academic background, Prof. Chaudhury earned his B.Tech. in Electronics and Electrical Communication Engineering, followed by a Ph.D. in Computer Science and Engineering from IIT Kharagpur. His academic journey commenced in 1992 when he joined the Department of Electrical Engineering, IIT Delhi faculty. Over the years, he has demonstrated exceptional leadership, serving as the Dean of Undergraduate Studies at IIT Delhi and later as the Director of CSIR-CEERI, Pilani, from 2016 to 2018. Professor Chaudhury's expertise and scholarly contributions have been widely recognized. He is a recipient of the Distinguished Alumnus Award from IIT Kharagpur. He has been honored as a Fellow by esteemed organizations such as the Indian National Academy of Engineers (INAE), the National Academy of Sciences (NAS), and the International Association Pattern Recognition (IAPR). In recognition of his early research endeavors, he was awarded the INSA Medal for Young Scientists in 1993 and later received the ACCS-CDAC award for his research contributions in 2012. His extensive research profile boasts approximately 300 publications in peer-reviewed journals and conference proceedings, 15 patents, and the authorship/editing of four books.

Dr. Anand Mishra serves as an Assistant Professor at the Department of Computer Science and Engineering and an affiliate faculty member at the School of AI and Data Science at IIT Jodhpur. He leads the Vision, Language, and Learning Group (VL2G) at IIT Jodhpur, which focuses on problems intersecting vision and language. Previously, Anand had the opportunity to work at the Indian Institute of Science, focusing on Knowledge-aware Computer Vision. Anand's doctoral work is on understanding text in scene images, and he received the Microsoft Research India Ph.D. fellowship. Recently, Anand has been recognized as an outstanding reviewer at ICCV 2021 and CVPR 2023.

Prof. Anoop M. Namboodiri is a professor at the International Institute of Information Technology, Hyderabad, India. He is associated with the Centre for Visual Information Technology and heads the Biometrics and Secure Identity Lab. He holds a B.Tech. and Ph.D. in Computer Science and Engineering. His research interests include Biometrics, Machine Learning, Computational Imaging, and Computer Vision. He also serves as the Chief Science Officer of DreamVu Inc.

Dr. Dinesh Babu Jayagopi is currently an Associate Professor at IIIT Bangalore, where he heads the Multimodal Perception Lab. His research interests are Audio-Visual Signal Processing, Machine Learning, and Social Computing. He obtained his doctorate from Ecole Polytechnic Federale Lausanne (EPFL), Switzerland, beginning of 2011. He received the National Teachers Award in 2023. He received the Outstanding Paper Award at the International Conference on Multimodal Interaction (ICMI) 2012 and the Idiap Best Ph.D. student Research Award in 2009. More recently, his Ph.D. student's work was nominated for Best Student Paper in ICMI 2016 Tokyo. He received the Department of Science and Technology (DST) Young Scientist Start-up Grant 2016. He has successfully collaborated and executed sponsored research projects with CAIR, DRDO (Defence Research and Development Organization), and NI Systems. He was a visiting professor at the University of Lausanne in the summer of 2019 and the University of Oulu in the summer of 2023.

Dr. Neelam Sinha is an associate professor at the Centre for Brain Research at IISc Bangalore. Dr. Sinha's interests lie in applying machine learning techniques for multi-modal neuroimaging. She obtained Ph.D. at IISc for her work on strategies for rapid MR imaging in 2008. She worked in the MR Imaging group at GE Healthcare for a year and then joined IIIT-Bangalore. At IIIT-Bangalore, her research focused on healthcare problems, including surgical video, fundal images, and neuro-data analysis. She executed a DST-funded project on resting-state fMRI for brain characterization. She has worked on problems such as age estimation using Diffusion MR, analysis of atypical PD variants, and chromosomal mutation detection in Low-Grade Glioma using structural MR images in collaboration with NIMHANS. As part of an industry-sponsored project, she has worked on visual functioning networks in the brain, utilizing fMRI time series. She was part of a state-funded center (MINRO) with projects on EEG analysis for quantifying abstract notions, such as creativity.

Dr. Rajendra Nagar is an Assistant Professor in the department of Electrical Engineering at the Indian Institute of Technology Jodhpur, India. He received his B.Tech. degree from Indian Institute of Technology Jodhpur in 2013. He received his Ph.D. degree in Electrical Engineering from Indian Institute of Technology Gandhinagar. He was awarded a gold medal for the best academic performance in B.Tech. Electrical Engineering at IIT Jodhpur, 2013. He was awarded NCC 2019 best Ph.D. thesis award. His research interests include 3D Computer Vision, Digital Geometry Processing, and Deep Learning. Dr. Rajendra Nagar is an assistant professor at IIT Jodhpur. Before joining IIT Jodhpur, he was an Assistant Research Professor in Electrical Engineering at the Indian Institute of Technology Gandhinagar from 24

December 2018 to 19 July 2019. He completed his Ph.D. in Electrical Engineering under the supervision of Dr. Shanmuganathan Raman at the Indian Institute of Technology Gandhinagar. Before joining the Ph.D. program, Dr. Nagar was a system engineer at TCS Innovation Lab, Gurgaon, for nearly one year. He completed his B.Tech. in Electrical Engineering from the Indian Institute of Technology Jodhpur.

Cross-domain Image Translation and Feature Extraction for Large FoV Aerial Crop NIR Image Creation

Sudeep Rathore, Ankit Shukla, Avinash Upadhyay, Manoj Sharma, and Ajay Yadav

Abstract Near-Infrared Spectroscopy (NIR) is valuable for getting thorough information the human eye cannot capture in agricultural operations and investigations. A special multispectral camera is required to get NIR spectral data, which provides low-resolution images compared to RGB (Red–Green–Blue) data. NIR spectral data contains low contrast and no colour information making it difficult to identify and match features in the NIR domain. We require more features for image stitching to achieve large FoV (Field of View) NIR images. We use Cycle Generative Adversarial Network (CycleGAN) for image-to-image translation to synthesise an RGB image from a NIR spectral band image to take advantage of both RGB and NIR bands for the feature extraction. Features are extracted from NIR and synthetic RGB images. Then, we stitch the different NIR views using concatenated features of both domains to create large Field of View (FoV) NIR images. This augmented feature set yields superior stitching results compared to NIR features alone. The effectiveness of the proposed framework is demonstrated through experiments, showcasing the improvements in stitching quality.

Keywords NIR image stitching · CycleGAN · Deep learning · Feature matching · Image blending

1 Introduction

For agricultural operations and studies, near-infrared (NIR) imaging spectroscopy is a potent tool since it can identify and measure crop health, nutrient levels and other crucial factors. Since water, chlorophyll and other components in plants absorb NIR light, NIR images can be utilised to provide in-depth maps of crop health and development. Using this knowledge, crop yields can be increased, pesticide

S. Rathore (✉) · A. Shukla · A. Upadhyay · M. Sharma · A. Yadav
Bennett University, Greater Noida, UP, India
e-mail: sudeep.nehu@gmail.com

S. Chaudhury et al. (eds.), *Computer Vision, Pattern Recognition, Image Processing, and Graphics*, Lecture Notes in Electrical Engineering 1218,
https://doi.org/10.1007/978-981-97-5212-6_1

and fertiliser consumption can be decreased and irrigation and other management practices can be chosen more wisely.

NIR image stitching combines multiple NIR images to create a seamless image. Large FoV, high-resolution images of fields or other locations are frequently created in agricultural operations and research. This large FoV NIR image creation can be utilised for efficient and precision farming. It can also be used for various purposes in agriculture, such as crop health monitoring, soil quality assessment, nutrient deficiency identification and tracking plant growth.

NIR images have low-contrast, low-resolution and no colour information, making it challenging to extract valuable vital points or features from the image. Thus, NIR image is first converted to an RGB image. Traditional image feature extractors, like Scale-Invariant Feature Transform (SIFT) [1], Speeded Up Robust Features (SURF) [2] and Oriented FAST and Rotated BRIEF (ORB) [3], have been optimised for standard Red–Green–Blue (RGB) images.

This paper proposes using CycleGAN for NIR to RGB translation to benefit from RGB traits for better feature extraction. A combination of features extracted from both RGB and NIR traits is being used by us for efficient NIR image stitching, aiming at the creation of large FoV NIR images.

The rest of the paper follows: Sect. 2 discusses related work, Sect. 3 explains the methodology and Sects. 4 and 5 discuss the result and conclusion, respectively.

2 Related Work

NIR to RGB image conversion has been accomplished using deep learning techniques. To determine how NIR and RGB images relate to one another, these techniques employ neural networks. This makes it possible to display NIR images in a way that is more comprehensible to humans.

Hanhoon Park presents a technique that boosts the medium detail image after decomposing the near-infrared (NIR) image into fine detail, medium detail and base images using weighted least squares filters (WLSF). The luminance detail image of an RGB image is then swapped out for the combined NIR detail image, which is made up of fine and boosted medium detail images [4].

Patricia L. Suarez et al. (2017) have employed a Generative Adversarial Network (GAN) architecture model to concentrate on colourising near-infrared (NIR) images. There are two stages to the suggested architecture. It begins by learning to colourise the supplied input, producing an RGB image [5].

Isola et al. [6] have suggested employing conditional adversarial networks as a general-purpose solution to image-to-image translation issues. These networks learn a loss function to train this mapping in addition to learning the mapping from the input image to the output image. The authors discussed the issue of translating a picture from one domain into another domain, or 'image-to-image translation'.

3 Methodology

The methodology outlined in this paper describes an approach for generating RGB images from NIR images, extracting the features from both NIR images and synthetically generated RGB images and concatenating the feature extracted from both NIR images and synthetically generated RGB images into a single image to increase the number of feature points which will be useful for feature matching and large FoV NIR image creation. An overview of this process is depicted in Fig. 1, which illustrates the overall flow of NIR image stitching.

3.1 NIR to RGB Translation Using CycleGAN

The Cycle Generative Adversarial Network (CycleGAN) [7] is a powerful technique for image-to-image translation. In our methodology, we used CycleGAN, as shown in Fig. 2 to transform NIR images into their RGB counterparts.

CycleGAN comprises two main components: Generator networks and Discriminator networks. Let's consider two domains X (thermal images) and Y (RGB images). There will be two generator networks, G and F. G transforms images from X to Y ($G : X \rightarrow Y$) and F does the inverse, i.e. it transforms images from Y to X ($F : Y \rightarrow X$). On the other hand, there are two discriminator networks, D_X and D_Y. D_X aims to distinguish between images from domain X and images generated by F, while D_Y tries to distinguish between images from domain Y and images generated by G.

The unique aspect of CycleGAN is its incorporation of cycle consistency loss along with the traditional adversarial loss, which enforces a round-trip translation

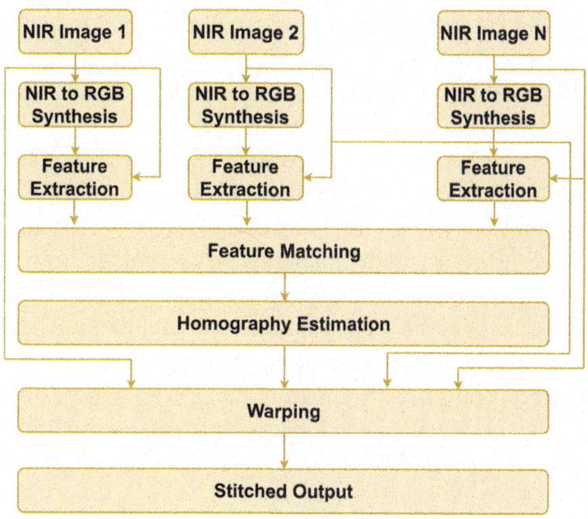

Fig. 1 Proposed flowchart for stitching NIR images to create large FoV

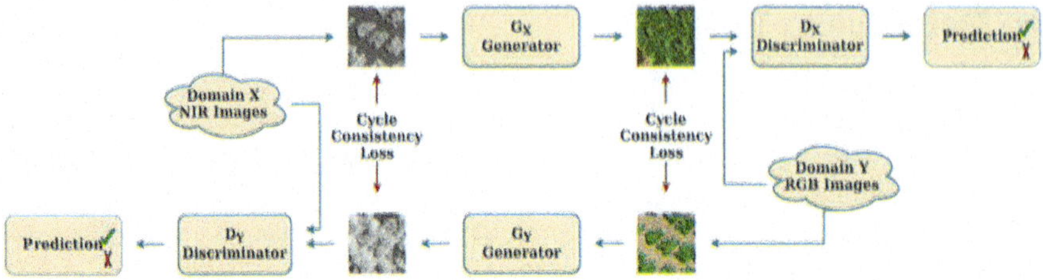

Fig. 2 CycleGAN architecture for NIR to RGB image conversion

between the original and translated images. For instance, an image from domain X is translated to domain Y using generator G and then translated back to domain X using generator F. The difference between the original image and the twice-translated image is minimised in the training process, which is the essence of cycle consistency loss.

The cycle consistency loss ensures that the learned translation does not deviate too much from the original content of the image, thereby preserving the integrity of the source domain while adapting it to the target domain. This balance between content preservation and style adaptation makes CycleGAN a powerful tool for domain adaptation problems.

3.2 Image Stitching

Once the RGB images and their corresponding feature sets are obtained, the next step involves stitching them to create a large FoV image. This process consists of three main stages: feature extraction, homography estimation and warping/stitching of the images.

In the feature extraction stage, we employ feature extractors such as SIFT, SURF and ORB on both synthetic RGB and original NIR images. These algorithms work by detecting distinctive features in images that can be used to align different views of a scene. Post-feature extraction, the process of homography estimation [8] has proceeded. This process involves calculating the perspective transformation, or homography, that best aligns the features between a pair of images. This step is crucial as it enables us to align the images accurately before they are stitched together. Finally, once the homography matrices are estimated, the images are warped or transformed to align correctly. After the images are warped, they are stitched together to create the final large FoV image. It is important to note that the stitching process takes into account the features extracted from both the synthetic RGB images and the original NIR images, thereby ensuring that the final large FoV image maintains the integrity of the original data while benefiting from the additional information provided by the synthetic RGB data.

3.3 Dataset

Dataset used: Aerial view of agriculture field 'Image stitching from drone capture OpenCV' from Kaggle [9] and from 'From RGB to NIR: Predicting of near-infrared reflectance from visible spectrum aerial images of crops [10]'.

4 Results

This section presents the results of our methodology's implementation, demonstrating the effectiveness of the CycleGAN model in generating RGB images from NIR images, the superior performance of RGB-optimised feature extractors on synthetic RGB images and the improved stitching pipeline using amalgamated features.

Our results demonstrate that the CycleGAN model effectively converts NIR images into synthetic RGB images. Figure 3 shows this by contrasting an NIR image with its matching synthetic RGB image generated using CycleGAN. The significant structural similarity between the two demonstrates the model's ability to preserve the integrity of original characteristics.

We discovered that feature extractors trained and optimised for RGB images, such as SIFT, SURF and ORB, perform significantly better on synthetic RGB photos than on actual NIR images. This is seen in Fig. 4, which depicts recognised features on three types of images: synthetic RGB, NIR and NIR images with concatenated features from both synthetic RGB and NIR images. The synthetic RGB image with the combined features clearly shows a greater density and diversity of identified features, confirming our hypothesis. Figure 5a, b, c (first NIR image) and d, e, f (second NIR image) show the feature points extracted from NIR image, synthetic RGB image of corresponding NIR image and combined features from NIR and its

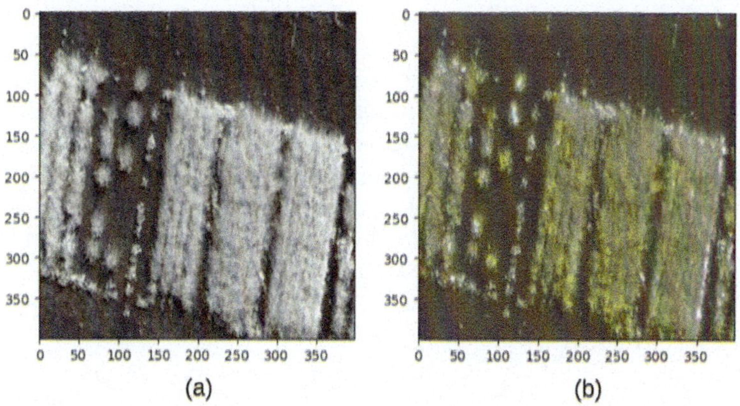

Fig. 3 Result of NIR to RGB image synthesis **a** NIR image and **b** synthetic RGB image

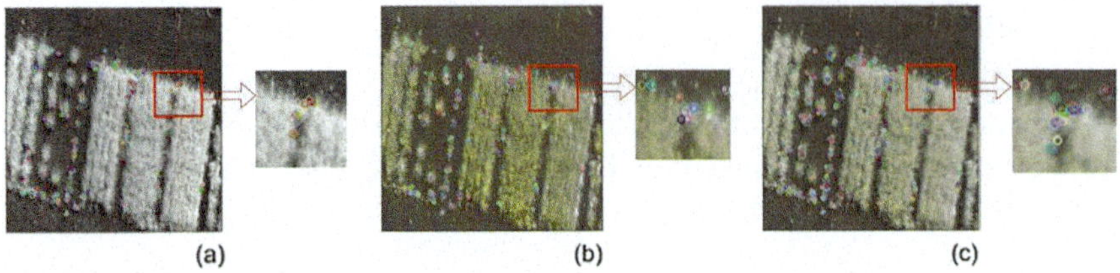

Fig. 4 Features/Keypoints density in **a** NIR image and **b** Synthetic RGB image and **c** Amalgamated feature of NIR and synthetic RGB image

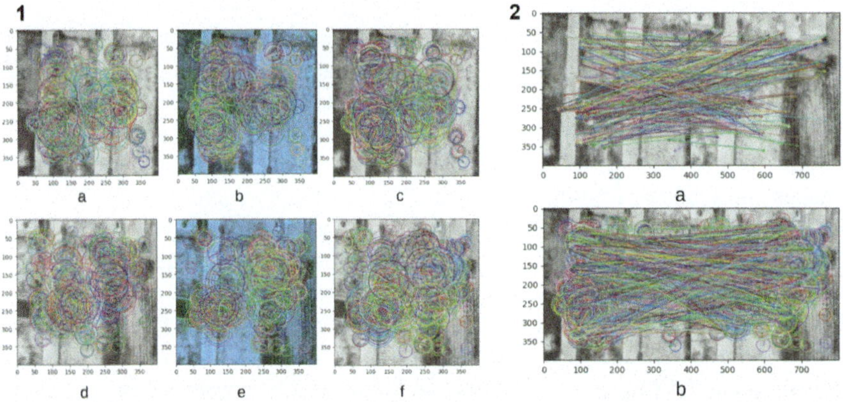

Fig. 5 1: Keypoints in **a** First NIR image **b** Synthetic RGB image of corresponding first NIR image **c** Amalgamated features from first NIR and corresponding synthetic RGB image **d** Second NIR image **e** Synthetic RGB image of corresponding second NIR image **f** Amalgamated features from second NIR and corresponding synthetic RGB image. 2: Keypoints matching in first and second image **a** Features from NIR images only **b** Amalgamated features from NIR and corresponding synthetic RGB image

corresponding synthetic RGB image, respectively. Figure 5 shows the key points matching in the first image and the second image (a) features from NIR image only (b) amalgamated features from NIR and corresponding synthetic RGB image.

Table 1. represents the number of features in the NIR image, the synthetic RGB image of the corresponding NIR image, combined features from NIR and corresponding synthetic RGB image, number of matched features in NIR image (First image + Second image) and Number of matched features in NIR image and corresponding synthetic RGB image(for first image) + NIR image and corresponding synthetic RGB image(for a second image). Table 2. shows the comparison of performance parameters of (a) CycleGAN and (b) pix-to-pix, structural similarity (SSIM), peak signal-to-noise ratio (PSNR) and normalised correlation coefficient (NCC)

Table 1 Number of features in NIR image, synthetic RGB image and amalgamated features from NIR and corresponding synthetic RGB image

Image	Number of features
NIR (First image)	500
Synthetic RGB image of first NIR image	495
NIR (Second image)	500
Synthetic RGB image of second NIR image	491
Amalgamated features from NIR and corresponding synthetic RGB image (First case)	995
Amalgamated features from NIR and corresponding synthetic RGB image (Second case)	991
Number of matched features in NIR images only (First image and Second image)	106
Number of matched features in NIR image and corresponding synthetic RGB image (First case) and NIR image and corresponding synthetic RGB image (Second case)	343

Table 2 Performance parameters of (a) CycleGAN and (b) pix-to-pix, structural similarity (SSIM), peak signal-to-noise ratio (PSNR) and normalised correlation coefficient (NCC)

Ground Truth Image	Generated Image	SSIM	PSNR	NCC
		0.9336861	32.37162	0.9983584
		0.9247694	31.55524	0.9979971
		0.9272308	30.47016	0.9976892

a

Ground Truth Image	Generated Image	SSIM	PSNR	NCC
		0.9599328	29.70617	0.9595281
		0.9741010	31.39933	0.9740803
		0.7252581	29.80797	0.69577295

b

The results of our stitching pipeline further establish the superior performance of amalgamated features extracted from both NIR and corresponding synthetic RGB images. A comparison of the stitching output using features extracted solely from NIR images and those using amalgamated features reveals that the latter provides better performance and more seamless and accurate alignment in image stitching, as shown in Fig. 6.

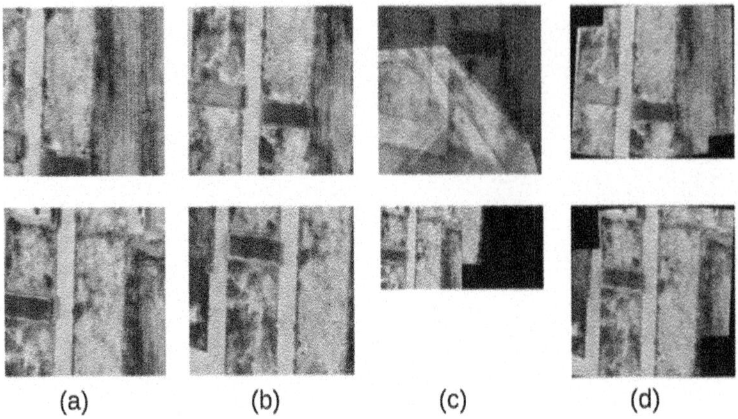

Fig. 6 Stitching results **a** First image **b** Second image **c** Using features of NIR images only and **d** Using Amalgamated features from NIR and corresponding synthetic RGB images

5 Conclusion

This paper proposed generating large Field of View (FoV) NIR picture data synthetically from smaller FoV data. CycleGAN is used to convert NIR images to RGB format utilising CycleGAN for unpaired NIR-RGB data, enabling robust feature extraction from both traits for effective NIR image stitching. The results presented show the efficacy of the proposed pipeline.

References

1. Lowe DG (2004) Distinctive image features from scale-invariant keypoints. Int J Comput Vis 60:91–110
2. Bay H et al (2006) Speeded-up robust features (SURF). Computer vision and image understanding (CVIU). In: Proceedings of the 9th European conference on computer vision. Springer, Austria
3. Tareen SAK, Saleem Z (2018) A comparative analysis of sift, surf, kaze, akaze, orb, and brisk. In: 2018 International conference on computing, mathematics and engineering technologies (iCoMET). IEEE
4. Park H (2020) An RGB-NIR image fusion method for improving feature matching. Int J Eng Technol Innov 10(3):225–234
5. Suárez PL, Sappa AD, Vintimilla BX (2018) Learning to colorize infrared images. In: Trends in cyber-physical multi-agent systems. The PAAMS Collection-15th International Conference, PAAMS 2017 15. Springer International Publishing
6. Isola P et al (2017) Image-to-image translation with conditional adversarial networks. In: Proceedings of the IEEE conference on computer vision and pattern recognition
7. Zhu JY, Park T, Isola P, Efros AA (2017) Unpaired image-to-image translation using cycle-consistent adversarial networks. In: 2017 IEEE international conference on computer vision (ICCV), pp 2242–2251. https://doi.org/10.1109/ICCV.2017.244

8. Hartley R, Zisserman A (2003) Multiple view geometry in computer vision, 2nd edn. Cambridge University Press, New York, NY, USA
9. https://www.kaggle.com/datasets/phsophea101/image-stitching-from-drone-capture-opencv
10. Aslahishahri M et al (2021) From RGB to NIR: predicting of near infrared reflectance from visible spectrum aerial images of crops. In: Proceedings of the IEEE/CVF international conference on computer vision

Deep Root Semantic Segmentation Guided via Super-resolution

Ankit Shukla, Ritika Jha, and Prerana Mukherjee

Abstract Root morphology is a key trait for plants' response, i.e. growth and development under various environmental stresses. Traditionally, the plant biologists relied on manual or semi-automatic methods to accurately compute these root morphological traits. Recently, the high-throughput acquisition of root image data permits automatic extraction of root traits. In this context, root segmentation is a key computer-vision task. Current deep learning-based methods proposed for this task are limited due to the diverse root characteristics such as orientation, size, shape and varying degrees of self-occlusion. To overcome these limitations, we propose a novel framework that utilises high-resolution root features for root segmentation. Specifically, the super-resolution network is employed as a pre-processing module since roots in the investigated images are thin and blurry. These enhanced root images are then subsequently utilised in a root segmentation network. In this paper, we also highlight the effect of different resolution levels on root segmentation task with an ablation study.

Keywords Root phenotyping · Semantic segmentation · Super-resolution · Supervised deep learning

1 Introduction

The morphological analysis of a plant's root traits is crucial in understanding the plants capacity to absorb the nutrition and water for its growth [1]. Therefore, these traits can be utilised as proxy indicators for desirable traits such as yield and stress tolerance (drought, disease, etc.). The application of methodologies to measure these root traits is called root phenotyping [2]. Traditional root phenotyping methods

A. Shukla (✉)
Bennett University, Greater Noida, India
e-mail: anktshkla.1307@gmail.com

R. Jha · P. Mukherjee
Jawaharlal Nehru University, New Delhi, India

S. Chaudhury et al. (eds.), *Computer Vision, Pattern Recognition, Image Processing, and Graphics*, Lecture Notes in Electrical Engineering 1218,
https://doi.org/10.1007/978-981-97-5212-6_2

involve invasive root incisions and manual assessments of root characteristics [3] and hinder temporal root monitoring. Hence, image-based root phenotyping was introduced and has become an efficient alternative to traditional methods. Since soil media hinders the reconstruction of the full root architecture. Recently, a root grown in transparent medium imaging setup was adopted to get over this constraint [4]. In image-based root phenotyping root segmentation from the background is a key computer vision task.

Within the limited literature, the root segmentation task is typically addressed via (a) traditional methods and (b) deep learning-based methods. Traditional method BRAT [5] utilises intensity-based thresholding, while MyRoot [6] relies on ridge filtering and manual threshold selection. Recently, deep learning-based algorithms for semantic segmentation have shown improved performance and have been adopted for root segmentation [7, 8]. Abraham George Smith et al. [9] attempted root segmentation using UNet [10]. Birgit Moller et al. [11] also proposed an efficient UNet-based root segmentation architecture with pre-trained weights and mixed loss function (cross-entropy and dice loss). Although the above approaches [9–11]tried to solve the root segmentation task using deep learning methods, their results fail in the case of diverse root characteristics such as orientation, size, shape, occlusion and less resolution.

One of the prime reasons for the failure of such state-of-the-art models is that the roots in the images are very thin and the image itself is of low resolution, thus making it very difficult for the model to distinguish the root from background. Therefore, there is a demand to improve and optimise UNet-based architectures. To overcome this issue, we propose a novel framework that extracts the super-resolved features of the root structures and utilises these super-resolved images for root segmentation. Specifically, the proposed framework super-resolves the images thus improving the quality of root images. This helps in the segmentation of very thin and blurry roots from complex backgrounds.

The rest of the paper is organised as follows: Sect. 2 presents the methodology, experiments and results analysis are included in Sect. 3. Finally, Sect. 4 concludes the paper.

2 Methodology

Given that the root cross sections in the investigated RGB images are distributed unevenly and it is only about 30–40

For an accurate root segmentation based on the super-resolved image, we employ a combination of UNet architecture and transformer-based models. This hybrid approach permits the investigation of the combined effects of deep learning-based architectures on the root image segmentation task. In this respect, we employ UNet [14], GTUNet [15] and TransUNet [16] for root segmentation. UNet [14] features a U-shaped design consisting of an encoder and a decoder path. It effectively localises and segments objects, particularly small ones, by capturing contextual information and combining it with higher-resolution feature maps. GTUNet, an extension of UNet proposed, addresses the challenge of dense object segmentation, such as pedestrian detection [15]. It incorporates a global-local fusion module that combines global scene context with local details, resulting in an improved performance in dense object segmentation tasks. TransUNet, combines transformer encoders with CNN-based decoders for image segmentation [16]. By leveraging transformers' ability to model long-range dependencies and capture global context, it achieves enhanced feature representation and context understanding. The inclusion of a CNN-based decoder path allows for effective upsampling and feature fusion.

3 Experiment and Result Analysis

In this section, we present the results of our experiments on super-resolving the root images to boost the segmentation performance. We conducted several experiments, we first downsampled the input images by 2x and 4x then a super-resolution method was used to super-resolve the images. After it, super-resolved image is applied to different segmentation network.

A data set consisting of 2614 images of wheat seedling roots [17] was utilised in our experimental study. The training dataset employed in this study is downscaled to image sizes 716x946 and 358x473 through 2x and 4x downsampling, respectively. Multiple segmentation networks were meticulously trained using this dataset, yielding a comprehensive evaluation in terms of both quantitative and qualitative results. In our experiments, we have utilised segmentation metrics, i.e. Precision, Recall, DICE, IoU and F-score [9].

We compare the proposed GTUNet model for super-resolution with three baseline methods: UNet, GTUNet with different threshold values and TransUNet along with different downscale factors. We use precision, recall, dice, IOU and F score as evaluation metrics, to measure the segmentation quality of the root images. We also show some visual examples of the super-resolved and segmented root images.

Table 1 summarises the quantitative results of the three methods with various threshold values and multiple downscale factors on the test set of root images. As can be seen, GTUNet model with a threshold value of 0.5 outperforms other methods in terms of precision, indicating that it can effectively super-resolve and segment the root images. The second best method is GTUNet, which is slightly worse than our GTUNet model. The other methods, UNet, GTUNet with different threshold values and TransUNet with different scale factors, perform significantly worse than GTUNet model, showing that they are not able to handle the low-resolution and noisy root images well.

Figure 2 shows some visual examples of the super-resolved and segmented root images by the four methods. It can be observed that our GTUNet model can produce clear and sharp super-resolved root images, which facilitate the accurate segmentation of the root regions. The other methods, on the other hand, tend to generate less clear and sharp features for root images, which lead to poor segmentation results.

Table 1 Quantitative performance comparison of different super-resolution and segmentation experiments

Experiments	Precision	Recall	Dice	IOU	F score
4x↓ UNet	0.85	0.87	0.86	0.76	0.86
2x ↓ + UNet	0.94	0.65	0.77	0.63	0.77
2x ↓ + G-T-UNet	0.98	0.005	**0.99**	0.005	0.01
2x ↓ + G-T-UNet (Threshold value = 0.0001)	0.83	0.89	**0.99**	0.75	0.86
2x ↓ + G-T-UNet (Threshold value = 0.5)	**0.99**	0.33	**0.99**	0.33	0.50
2x ↓ + G-T-UNet (Threshold value = 0.001)	0.98	0.40	**0.99**	0.40	0.57
4x ↓ + G-T-UNet	0	0.0	**0.99**	0.0	0.0
4x ↓ + G-T-UNet (Threshold value = 0.5)	0.86	0.24	**0.99**	0.23	0.38
4x ↓ + G-T-UNet (Threshold value = 0.0001)	0.86	0.24	**0.99**	0.23	0.38
4x ↓ + TranUNet (Proposed)	0.89	0.75	0.81	0.68	0.81
2x ↓ + TranUNet (Proposed)	0.95	0.65	0.78	0.64	0.78

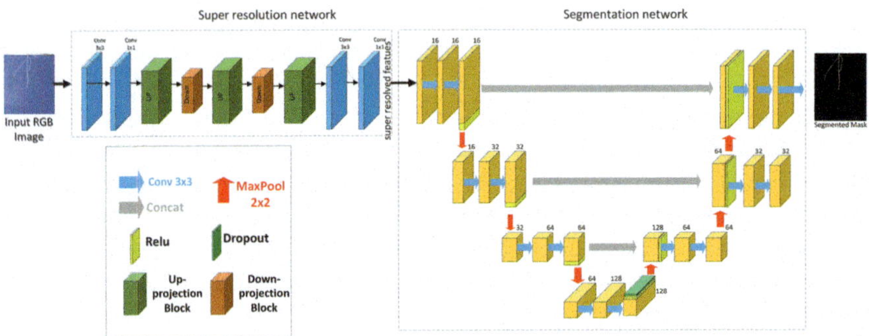

Fig. 1 Architecture of proposed method

For example, in the first row of Fig. 1, UNet and GTUNet with a threshold value of 0.5 fail to capture the thin and curved root structures, while TransUNet with a scale factor of 4x introduces some artefacts in the super-resolved image. In contrast, our GTUNet model can preserve the fine details and contours of the root structures, and segment them correctly.

These results demonstrate that the proposed GTUNet model can effectively leverage the transformer-based super-resolution module to enhance the segmentation performance of root images. This model can handle various challenges in root image analysis, such as low-resolution, noise, occlusion and complex shapes. Our model can also be easily extended to other types of root images, such as from different crops, soils or imaging modalities.

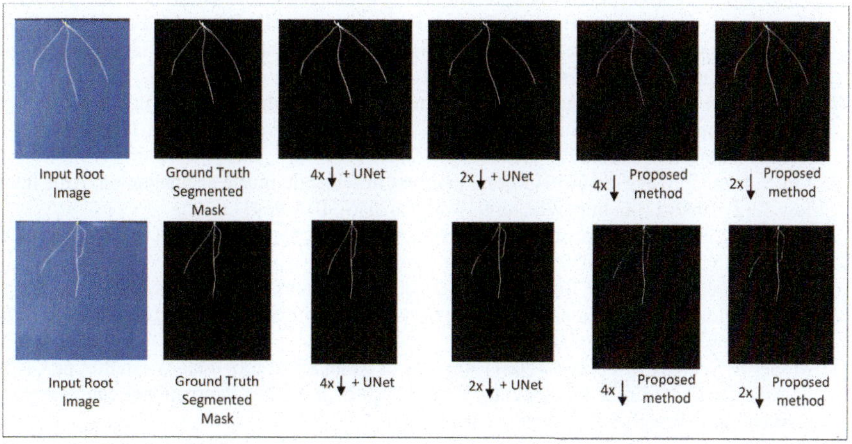

Fig. 2 Qualitative results from various experiments. In the third and fifth columns, input image is downsampled by 4x factor. In the fourth and sixth columns, input image is downsampled by 2x factor

4 Conclusion

We presented a novel super-resolution-based root segmentation framework. The proposed framework successfully segmented the thin roots, their tips and entangled roots. We also presented an ablation study to highlight the importance of resolution levels for robust and resource-efficient segmentation task. Developing a unified end-to-end framework that jointly optimises the super-resolution and segmentation objectives, rather than using separate modules could be a future work for this work. Also use of generative models as super-resolution network to enhance the realism and diversity of the super-resolved root images will be a good research problem.

References

1. Costa C, Schurr U, Loreto F, Menesatti P, Carpentier S (2019) Plant phenotyping research trends, a science mapping approach. Front Plant Sci 9. https://www.frontiersin.org/article/10.3389/fpls.2018.01933
2. Bhugra S, Mukherjee P, Kaushik V, Jha R, Lall B, Chaudhury S (2022) Tarsnet: topology aware root segmentation network for plant phenotyping. In: Proceedings of the thirteenth Indian conference on computer vision, graphics and image processing, pp 1–8
3. Pieruschka R, Schurr U (2019) Plant phenotyping: past, present, and future. Plant Phen 2019:1–6
4. Möller B, Schreck B, Posch S (2021) Analysis of arabidopsis root images–studies on cnns and skeleton-based root topology. In: Proceedings of the IEEE/CVF international conference on computer vision, pp 1294–1302
5. Slovak R, Göschl C, Su X, Shimotani K, Shiina T, Busch W (2014) A scalable open-source pipeline for large-scale root phenotyping of arabidopsis. Plant Cell 26(6):2390–2403

6. González A, Sevillano X, Betegón-Putze I, Blasco-Escámez D, Ferrer M, Caño-Delgado AI (2020) Myroot 2.0: an automatic tool for high throughput and accurate primary root length measurement. Comput Electr Agric 168:105125
7. Shen C, Liu L, Zhu L, Kang J, Wang N, Shao L (2020) High-throughput in situ root image segmentation based on the improved deeplabv3+ method. Front Plant Sci 11. https://www.frontiersin.org/article/10.3389/fpls.2020.576791
8. Liu X, Deng Z, Yang Y (2019) Recent progress in semantic image segmentation. Artif Intell Rev 52(2):1089–1106. https://doi.org/10.1007/s10462-018-9641-3
9. Smith AG, Petersen J, Selvan R, Rasmussen CR (2019) Segmentation of roots in soil with u-net. arXiv:abs/1902.11050
10. Ronneberger O, Fischer P, Brox T (2015) U-net: convolutional networks for biomedical image segmentation. In: International conference on medical image computing and computer-assisted intervention. Springer, pp 234–241
11. Moller B, Schreck B, Posch S (2021) Analysis of Arabidopsis root images - studies on CNNs and skeleton-based root topology. In: Proceedings of the IEEE international conference on computer vision, vol 2021-Octob, pp 1294–1302
12. He K, Gkioxari G, Dollár P, Girshick R (2017) Mask r-cnn. In: IEEE international conference on computer vision (ICCV), pp 2980–2988
13. Haris M, Shakhnarovich G, Ukita N (2019) Deep back-projection networks for single image super-resolution. arXiv:1904.05677
14. Ronneberger O, Fischer P, Brox T (2015) U-net: convolutional networks for biomedical image segmentation. In: Medical image computing and computer-assisted intervention-MICCAI, 18th international conference, Munich, Germany, October 5–9, 2015, Proceedings, Part III 18. Springer, pp 234–241
15. Li Y, Wang S, Wang J, Zeng G, Liu W, Zhang Q, Jin Q, Wang Y (2021) Gt u-net: a u-net like group transformer network for tooth root segmentation. In: Machine learning in medical imaging: 12th international workshop, MLMI (2021) Held in conjunction with MICCAI 2021, Strasbourg, France, September 27, 2021, Proceedings 12. Springer, pp 386–395
16. Chen J, Lu Y, Yu Q, Luo X, Adeli E, Wang Y, Lu L, Yuille AL, Zhou Y (2021) Transunet: transformers make strong encoders for medical image segmentation. arXiv:2102.04306
17. Atkinson JA, Lobet G, Noll M, Meyer PE, Griffiths M, Wells DM (2017) Combining semi-automated image analysis techniques with machine learning algorithms to accelerate large-scale genetic studies. GigaScience 6(10):gix084

RGB to Chlorophyll Fluorescence Image Reconstruction of Maize for Plant Phenotyping

Ankit Shukla, Avinash Upadhyay, Manoj Sharma, and Anil Saini

Abstract The advancement in imaging devices has permitted high-throughput study of plant traits also termed as plant phenotyping. In this context, among the different imaging modalities employed in plant phenotyping, chlorophyll fluorescence imaging provides accurate characterisation of crucial plant traits such as photosynthetic efficiency, water use efficiency and nutrients use efficiency to name a few. However, chlorophyll fluorescence imaging is complex and expensive in contrast to widely adopted visible (RGB) images. This limits the reliable study of the aforementioned plant traits. To relieve this limitation, chlorophyll fluorescence image reconstruction algorithms from widely available visible images are a prime solution. Thus in this paper, we propose a domain translation-based approach using cycle consistency loss for chlorophyll fluorescence image reconstruction from RGB images. The experimental results on the maize dataset demonstrate the efficiency of our approach with respect to this novel application.

Keywords Chlorophyll fluorescence image · GAN · Deep learning · Domain translation · Plant phenotyping · Maize

1 Introduction

The methodologies utilised for computing and analysing plant physiological and morphological plant traits are termed as plant phenotyping [1]. With the emergence of imaging devices, image-based plant phenotyping permits high-throughput and non-invasive study of plant traits such as leaf area, biomass and photosynthetic efficiency to name a few. Among the various imaging modalities, Chlorophyll Fluorescence (ChlF) imaging can be used to measure crucial plant traits such as photosynthetic efficiency photosynthetic stress tolerance [2], water use efficiency and nutrients use

A. Shukla (✉) · A. Upadhyay · M. Sharma
Bennett University, Greater Noida, India
e-mail: ankitshukla.1307@gmail.com

A. Saini
CSIR-CEERI, Pilani, India

S. Chaudhury et al. (eds.), *Computer Vision, Pattern Recognition, Image Processing, and Graphics*, Lecture Notes in Electrical Engineering 1218,
https://doi.org/10.1007/978-981-97-5212-6_3

efficiency [3]. This is because ChlF imaging is primarily based on measuring the amount of light emitted by chlorophyll molecules in a plant leaf. Thus, the amount of emitted light is closely related to photosynthesis efficiency [4]. Despite these advantages, ChlF imaging necessitates the adoption of specific protocols such as dark adaptation of plant illumination with actinic lights, detection of emitted fluorescence with special sensors. Moreover, ChlF imaging devices are often expensive, bulk makes it limited use for on-field applications. Thus, visible (RGB) images have been widely adopted in contrast to ChlF imaging.

This motivates the development of alternative methods to obtain ChlF information with no dependence on complex protocols or imaging equipment. In this context, we propose to reconstruct the ChlF image from its corresponding RGB image. Deep learning-based frameworks [5] have shown promising results in learning the mapping between two images from two domains by exploiting the correlation between two images. Generative Adversarial network (GAN) [6]-based deep learning framework has been widely utilised for the aforementioned domain adaptation task.

Although, few attempts have been made for ChlF image reconstruction from RGB image. For example, Sapoukina et al. [7] proposed data augmentation from RGB to ChlF imaging in order to improve the leaf segmentation in Arabidopsis thaliana. However, this conversion is obtained based on a predefined formulation that is highly dependent on the parameters of RGB and ChlF imaging devices. These parameters are not commonly available for public plant phenotyping datasets and thus not applicable in these scenarios. In another paper, Gong et al. [8] proposed a method to reconstruct the spectral reflectance for RGB spectra of every pixel independently with a neural network. The reconstructed spectral reflectance is then used for chlorophyll estimation of plant leaves. In this paper, we adapt a GAN-based approach with cycle consistency loss [9] to reconstruct ChlF images from RGB images [10]. In contrast to Gong et al. [8], the proposed approach takes into account the spatial contextual information thus reducing noisy reconstruction. We evaluated the proposed method on publicity available maize diversity phenotype dataset [11]. The experimental results demonstrate that our method achieved accurate and robust reconstruction of chlorophyll fluorescence images from RGB images.

The rest of the paper is organised as follows: Sect. 2 elucidates the methodology, experimental analysis is shown in Sect. 3 with Sect. 4 concluding the paper.

2 Methodology

To reconstruct the ChlF image from RGB image, we adopt the domain translation method (shown in Fig. 1). For RGB to ChlF image reconstruction, the proposed cycle GAN consists of two generators and a discriminator. Generator A2B learns the mapping from RGB to ChlF, while Generator B2A learns ChlF to RGB. The discriminator network performs the classification tasks between real and generated images. Apart from adversarial loss [6] for discriminator and MSE loss for generator, cycle consistency loss [9] is employed. The cycle consistency loss imposes a constraint on

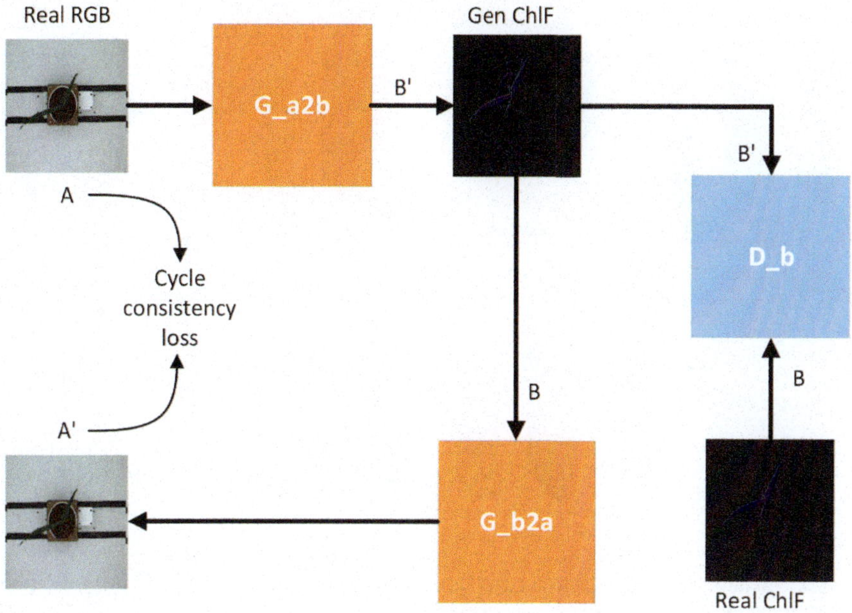

Fig. 1 Block diagram of CycleGAN for RGB to ChlF image reconstruction

generator so that the generated image can be reconstructed back to the original RGB image by an inverse mapping. Cycle consistency loss is defined as

$$L_{cyc}(F, G) = E_{x \sim pdata(x)}[||F(G(x)) - x||_1] + E_{y \sim pdata(y)}[||G(F(y)) - y||_1] \tag{1}$$

where G is the mapping function from domain X to domain Y, F is the mapping function from domain Y to domain X. The cycle consistency loss enforces that $F(G(x) \approx x$ and $G(F(y) \approx y$, constraining the mapping to be inverse of each other [9].

In our proposed method, generator framework consists of three convolution layers followed by four ResBlocks and finally three deconvolution layers are applied as the decoder part Fig. 3. The ResBlock consists of two convolution layers and the input is connected to the output of second convolution layer via skip connection. The discriminator employs five convolution layers connected sequentially (Fig. 2).

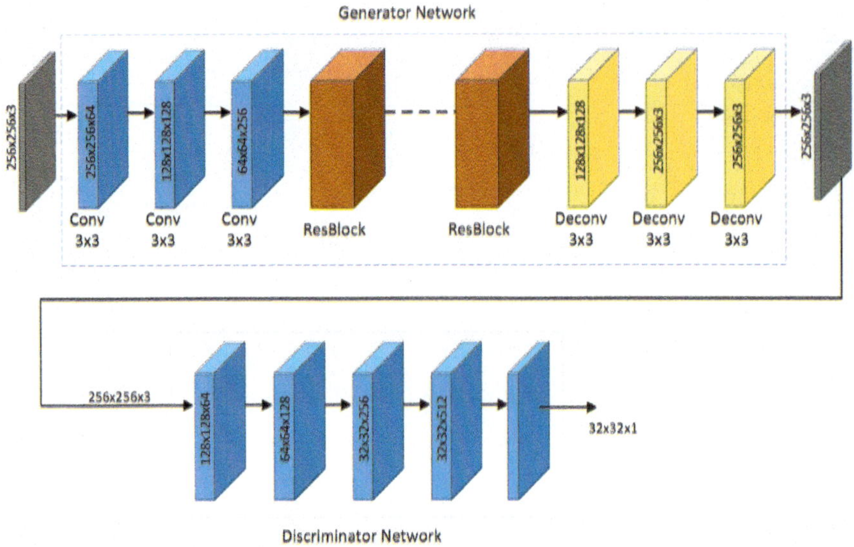

Fig. 2 Architecture of the generator and discriminator in CycleGAN for RGB to ChlF image reconstruction

3 Experiment and Result Analysis

3.1 Dataset Details

We performed our experiment on maize diversity phenotype map dataset [11]. This data set contains images of plants temporally collected over 32 days with four different cameras, i.e. RGB, fluorescence, hyperspectral and thermal. We selected the top view RGB and ChlF images for our experiments.

3.2 Ablation Study

For RGB to ChlF image translation on the maize diversity dataset, we selected 700 images for training and 100 images for testing to train the CycleGAN with adversarial and cycle consistency loss. For the ablation study, we employed two frameworks for the generator. One is UNet-based framework and the other is residual connection-based framework. For all the experiments, we used Adam optimizer with learning rate of 0.001 for both the generator and discriminator, trained for 500 epochs on RTX 2080Ti GPU.

To study about the effectiveness of generator framework, quantitative results of ablation study are provided in Table 1. It is evident that ResNet-based generator

Table 1 Ablation study of different generative networks used. In CycleGAN, we used two different framework as generator network, UNet and ResNet

Methods	PSNR	SSIM	Parameters
Pix2Pix GAN	0.37	0.86	54420617
CycleGAN (UNet)	0.45	0.92	54409600
CycleGAN (ResNet)	0.47	0.94	8411136

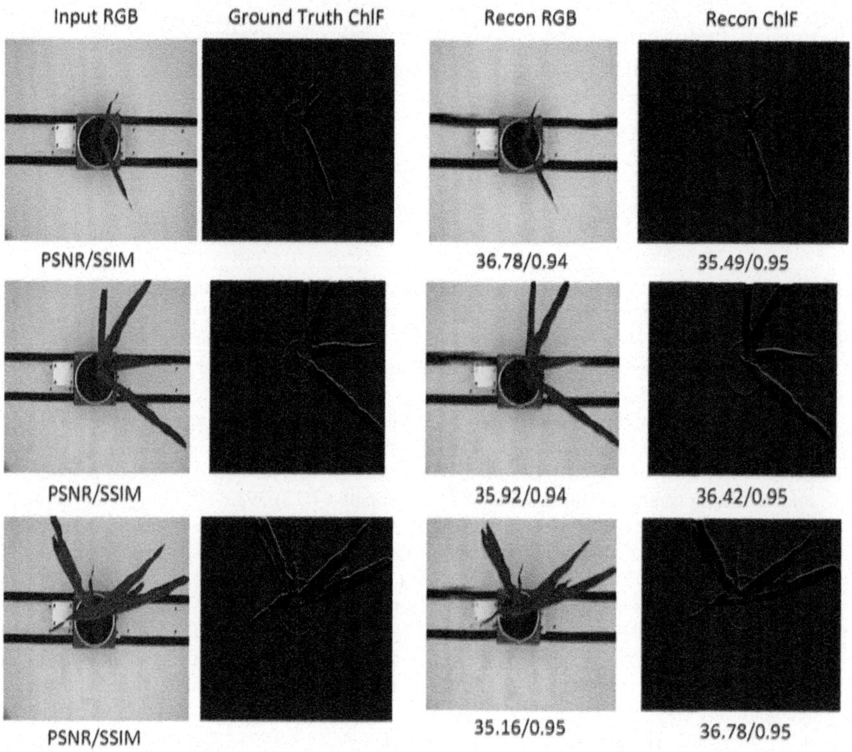

Fig. 3 Sample qualitative results, Recon RGB refers to reconstructed RGB and Recon ChlF denotes reconstructed ChlF image

achieved better results. Thus, we show the corresponding sample qualitative results in Fig. 3.

4 Conclusion

In this paper, we employed domain translation approach (CycleGAN) for chlorophyll fluorescence image reconstruction from widely available RGB images. This study investigates the novel application of the aforementioned approach based on an ablation study. The generated chlorophyll fluorescence image dataset can be further utilised in a non-complex computer vision algorithm such as thresholding, template-based approach for plant and leaf instance segmentation, respectively. This is because chlorophyll fluorescence imaging yields accurate characterisation of plant leaves compared to RGB images, where background moss and green leaves share similar RGB features.

References

1. Li L, Zhang Q, Huang D (2014) A review of imaging techniques for plant phenotyping. Sensors 14(11):20 078–20 111
2. Yao J, Sun D, Cen H, Xu H, Weng H, Yuan F, He Y (2018) Phenotyping of arabidopsis drought stress response using kinetic chlorophyll fluorescence and multicolor fluorescence imaging. Front Plant Sci 9:603
3. Chaerle L, Van Der Straeten D (2000) Imaging techniques and the early detection of plant stress. Trends Plant Sci 5(10):495–501
4. Murchie EH, Lawson T (2013) Chlorophyll fluorescence analysis: a guide to good practice and understanding some new applications. J Exper Botany 64(13):3983–3998
5. Jin KH, McCann MT, Froustey E, Unser M (2017) Deep convolutional neural network for inverse problems in imaging. IEEE Trans Image Process 26(9):4509–4522
6. Goodfellow I, Pouget-Abadie J, Mirza M, Xu B, Warde-Farley D, Ozair S, Courville A, Bengio Y (2014) Generative adversarial nets. Adv Neural Inf Process Syst 27:2672–2680
7. Sapoukhina N, Samiei S, Rasti P, Rousseau D (2019) Data augmentation from rgb to chlorophyll fluorescence imaging application to leaf segmentation of arabidopsis thaliana from top view images. In: Proceedings of the IEEE/CVF conference on computer vision and pattern recognition workshops, pp 0–0
8. Gong L, Zhu C, Luo Y, Fu X (2023) Spectral reflectance reconstruction from red-green-blue (rgb) images for chlorophyll content detection. Appl Spectrosc 77(2):200–209. pMID: 36323648. https://doi.org/10.1177/00037028221139871
9. Zhu J-Y, Park T, Isola P, Efros AA (2017) Unpaired image-to-image translation using cycle-consistent adversarial networks. In: Proceedings of the IEEE international conference on computer vision, pp 2223–2232
10. Shukla A, Upadhyay A, Sharma M, Chinnusamy V, Kumar S (2022) High resolution nir prediction from rgb images: application to plant phenotyping. In: 2022 IEEE international conference on image processing (ICIP). IEEE, pp 4058–4062
11. James Schnable ZL (2017) Maize diversity phenotype map

Novel Unsupervised Disease Segmentation Framework Based on Clustering

Rama Kant Singh, Monika Aggarwal, and Brejesh Lall

Abstract Plant disease is a major limiting factor in yield production. Traditionally, biologists rely on manual screening (localisation) of disease symptoms exhibited on plant leaves. However, this is a highly subjective and error-prone analysis. With the advancement of imaging devices, image-based analysis permits high-throughput disease localisation. In this context, state-of-the-art supervised deep learning-based methods have been presented. However, annotation of disease symptoms is time-consuming and is a current bottleneck. To relieve this limitation, we propose a novel unsupervised framework that utilises Cluster weight as well as Group-local Feature-weight learning using iteration in Fuzzy C-Means (CGFFCM) guided via differentiable clustering algorithm for accurate disease localisation. It is to be noted that the proposed framework does not rely on annotated image data. In this paper, we also performed an exhaustive comparison based on different clustering methods to show the efficacy of the proposed framework.

Keywords Disease phenotyping · Unsupervised segmentation · Differentiable clustering · Fuzzy C-means · CGFFCM

R. K. Singh (✉)
Bharti School, Indian Institute of Technology Delhi, New Delhi, India
e-mail: bsz168461@iitd.ac.in

M. Aggarwal
CARE, Indian Institute of Technology Delhi, New Delhi, India
e-mail: maggarwal@iitd.ac.in

B. Lall
Electrical Engg Dept, Indian Institute of Technology Delhi, New Delhi, India
e-mail: brejesh@iitd.ac.in

S. Chaudhury et al. (eds.), *Computer Vision, Pattern Recognition, Image Processing, and Graphics*, Lecture Notes in Electrical Engineering 1218,
https://doi.org/10.1007/978-981-97-5212-6_4

1 Introduction

Image-based analysis permits high-throughput disease localisation in contrast to traditional manual screening of leaf disease symptoms [1]. In this context, many computer vision-based methods have been proposed for disease localisation (segmentation) [2, 3]. These methods can be broadly categorised into (a) supervised and (b) unsupervised approaches. With respect to supervised methods, state-of-the-art deep learning methods have been proposed for disease region localisation (segmentation) [3]. It is to be noted that the accuracy of these methods is highly dependent on the annotated dataset however, due to the high variance in disease symptoms, the acquisition of disease data and its corresponding annotation is a highly time-consuming task. Thus, the utilisation of limited disease image dataset leads to overfitting [4]. In addition, the supervised deep learning methods lack generalizability [5]. To overcome these aforementioned limitations, unsupervised disease localisation provides a primary solution. With respect to unsupervised disease segmentation methods, initially, thresholding-based segmentation has been presented. Disease region analysis based on different segmentation methods has also been proposed such as K-Mean clustering [6] and Gaussian mixture model [7]. These methods suffer from low accuracy, further using thresholding manual intervention is required and useful specific to that disease only. To overcome the aforementioned limitation, we propose a novel unsupervised framework that relies on Fuzzy C-means (FCM) [8] based on feature weighting and cluster weighting. This algorithm is improved [9] via incorporating local homogeneity for cluster-based segmentation. Disease segmentation is further utilised in a differentiable clustering algorithm [10] for accurately localising the candidate disease regions extracted from the clustering method. We highlight the efficiency of the proposed framework with an exhaustive comparison with current unsupervised methods. The rest of the paper is organised as follows: Sect. 2 contains the methodology, experiments and results analysis are included in Sect. 3. Finally, Sect. 4 concludes the paper.

2 Methodology

The workflow of the proposed framework is shown in Fig. 1. Firstly, we employ Cluster-weight and Group-local Feature-weight learning in Fuzzy C-Means (CGFFCM) [9] clustering method to extract disease candidate regions. The CGFFCM is an automatic cluster weighting technique performed to reduce the sensitivity with respect to the cluster initialisation using group-local feature weighting. The image-based features utilised are related to local homogeneity, including colour and texture features. The author's proposed [9] cluster weighting technique by dynamically considering features and subfeatures to reduce sensitivity to initial centres. The objective function used in CGFFCM clustering method is defined as in Eq. (1).

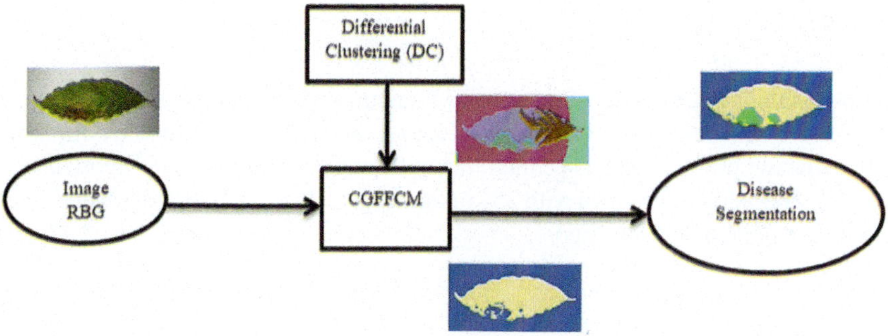

Fig. 1 Flow diagram of proposed method

$$F(\mathbf{M}, \mathbf{C}, \mathbf{R}, s) = \sum_{i=1}^{a*b} \sum_{k=1}^{K} \sum_{f=1}^{Fs} u_{ik}^{\alpha} r_{kf}^{q} s_{k}^{p} d^{2} \left(x_{if} - c_{kf}\right) \tag{1}$$

In Eq. (1), a*b refers to the image size for data samples, Fs represents the number of features for clustering, K represents the number of clusters, $M = [m_{ik}]$ is a K by a*b matrix where m_{ik} represents the membership degree of i_{th} sample's from centre of k_{th} cluster, $C = [c_{kf}]$ is a matrix of size K by Fs, where c_{kf} represents centre of k_{th} cluster and it is defined by u_{ik}. Further, in the same equation, $R = [r_{kf}]$ is a matrix of size K by Fs, where r_{kf} represents the weight of f_{th} feature in k_{th} cluster, $s = [s_k]$ is a K length vector, where s_k represents to k_{th} cluster weight and the distance metric term $d^2(x_{if} - c_{kf})$ represents a non-Euclidean distance. Clustering is performed with the help of these different parameters using a high number of iteration.

To remove the errors due to partial detection of disease regions, differentiable clustering (DC) algorithm [10] has been utilised. In the proposed method [10], label prediction and network parameter learning are alternately iterated to meet these objectives such as pixels of similar features assigned to the same label as well as spatially continuous pixels should be assigned the same label, and the number of unique labels should be large. Similarity loss and spatial continuity loss are reduced and further spatial continuity loss functions to combine regions together having similar features. The loss function (Ls) is combine constraint of feature similarity as well as spatial continuity for assigning same level to similar feature having spatial continuity in Eq. (2), defined as:

$$Ls = \underbrace{L_{\text{feat-sim}} \left(\left\{a_n', b_n\right\}\right)}_{\text{feature-similarity}} + \lambda \underbrace{L_{\text{spat-con}} \left(\left\{a_n'\right\}\right)}_{\text{spatial-continuity}}, \tag{2}$$

In the Eq. (2), a_n' is a normalised response map and b_n is cluster level for each pixel assigned with help of selecting the dimension that has maximum values of a_n'. The λ represent weight balancing between the two constraints. The cluster learnt in an unsupervised approach in DC guides the CGFFCM candidate disease regions to completely capture the disease regions.

3 Result

In this section, we show the qualitative and quantitative comparison of the proposed framework with current unsupervised disease segmentation algorithms. We utilise the coffee dataset presented in [11] containing 500 images belonging to different disease classes. The results are shown with 254 images (size 1024×512) with disease classes, i.e. miner, phoma and cercospora.

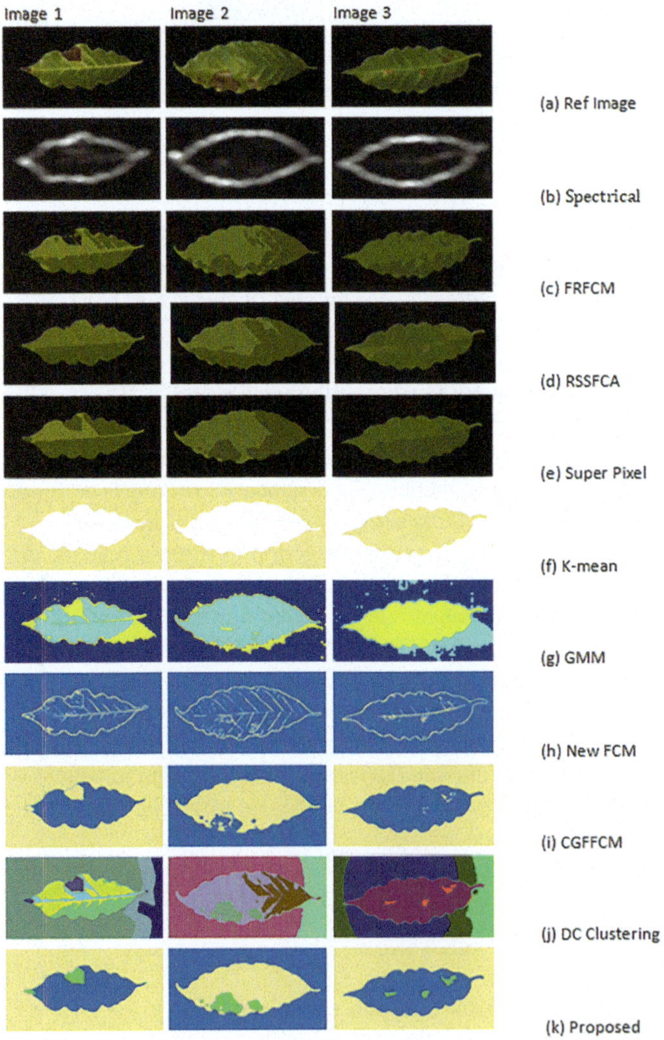

Fig. 2 Comparative analysis with unsupervised state-of-the-art clustering Methods for disease localisation

Analysis with k-mean [6] using features as in [9] generate cluster as in Fig. 2f. The Fuzzy C-mean (FCM) is most widely used for clustering with different fuzzy logic combinations and objective function. For example, Fast and Robust FCM Clustering Algorithm proposed in [12] generate cluster as in Fig. 2c, Robust Self-Sparse FCM proposed in [13], and generate the cluster as in Fig. 2d, Super pixel-based Fast FCM Clustering proposed in [14], and generate cluster as in Fig. 2e. Multi-clustering is proposed in [15] which segments the leaf region into multi-region and clustering boundary generally are edges. A Spectral-based clustering proposed in [16] based on graphs similarity parameter, generates map as in Fig. 2b. The basic Gaussian Mixture Model (GMM) [7] is also widely used for clustering. The results of the GMM model cluster is shown in Fig. 2g. From the image, the disease region reflects but is sensitive to shadow and noise, which introduces significant error in disease prediction and sometimes makes it impossible to predict.

In the proposed framework, modified Fuzzy c-means (FCM) presented in [8] based on features weighting and cluster weighting is utilised. In this method, different features are used for clustering with different feature weighting and cluster membership. The results are shown in Fig. 2h for input Fig. 2a respectively. Subsequently, an improved method is proposed in [9], which incorporates the local homogeneity for cluster-based segmentation (Fig. 2i). It is evident that the performance of the algorithm is still limited by the noise and disease boundary errors. The multi-clustering [10] based on differentiable feature generate clusters as in Fig. 2j. With the help of regions guiding from differentiable clustering [10] into CGFFCM [9], missing disease regions are able to predict as in Fig. 2k. The quantitative results are evaluated with parameters employed for semantic segmentation methods, i.e. (a) Precision, (b) Recall, (c) Jaccard Index and (d) F1-value. Combining both through region guiding is able to increase F1 score and Precision by 4–5% as compared to [9] in Table 1.

Table 1 Disease prediction through clustering method

SN	Clustering method	F1-value	Precision	Recall	Jaccard Index
1	K-mean [6]	0.024	0.064	0.017	0.013
2	Spectral [16]	0.061	0.034	0.463	0.032
3	FRFCM [12]	0.208	0.172	0.542	0.156
4	RSSFCA [13]	0.129	0.294	0.239	0.092
5	SuperPixel [14]	0.525	0.544	0.654	0.467
6	GMM [7]	0.129	0.294	0.239	0.092
7	New FCM [8]	0.173	0.176	0.226	0.097
8	CGFFCM [9]	0.696	0.768	0.688	0.579
9	Proposed	0.736	0.827	0.702	0.636

4 Conclusion

We presented a novel unsupervised framework for disease region segmentation. Our framework permits the segmentation of small regions belonging to varying disease classes with no dependence on annotated dataset. We also highlight the efficacy of the proposed framework with an exhaustive comparison with current unsupervised disease segmentation methods.

References

1. Sandhu GK, Kaur R (2019) Plant disease detection techniques: a review. In: 2019 international conference on automation, computational and technology management (ICACTM), London, UK, pp 34–38. https://doi.org/10.1109/ICACTM.2019.8776827
2. Bashish DA, Braik M, Ahmad SB, Detection and classification of diseases using K-means based segmentation and neural networks based classification. Inf Technol J 10(2):267-275
3. Wang G, Sun Y, Wang JX (2017) Automatic image-based plant disease severity estimation using deep learning. Comput Intell Neurosci 1–8
4. Li H, Li J, Guan X, Liang B, Lai Y, Luo X (2019) Research on overfitting of deep learning. In: 2019 15th international conference on computational intelligence and security (CIS), Macao, China, pp 78–81. https://doi.org/10.1109/CIS.2019.00025
5. Tendle A, Hasan MR (2021) A study of the generalizability of self-supervised representations. Mach Learn Appl 6:100124. ISSN 2666-8270. https://doi.org/10.1016/j.mlwa.2021.100124
6. Anand R, Veni S, Aravinth J (2016) An application of image processing techniques for detection of diseases on brinjal leaves using k-means clustering method. In: 2016 international conference on recent trends in information technology (ICRTIT), Chennai, India, pp 1–6. https://doi.org/10.1109/ICRTIT.2016.7569531
7. Fu Z, Wang L (2012) Color image segmentation using Gaussian mixture model and EM algorithm. In: Wang FL, Lei J, Lau RWH, Zhang J (eds) Multimedia and signal processing. CMSP 2012. Communications in computer and information science, vol 346. Springer, Berlin, Heidelberg. https://doi.org/10.1007/978-3-642-35286-7_9
8. Hashemzadeh M, Oskouei AG, Farajzadeh N (2019) New fuzzy C-means clustering method based on feature-weight and cluster-weight learning. Appl Soft Comput 78:324–345. ISSN 1568-4946. https://doi.org/10.1016/j.asoc.2019.02.038
9. Oskouei AG, Hashemzadeh M (2022) CGFFCM: a color image segmentation method based on cluster-weight and feature-weight learning. Softw Impacts 11:100228. ISSN 2665-9638. https://doi.org/10.1016/j.simpa.2022.100228
10. Kim W, Kanezaki A, Tanaka M (2020) Unsupervised learning of image segmentation based on differentiable feature clustering. IEEE Trans Image Process 29:8055–8068
11. Esgario JGM, Krohling RA, Ventura JA (2020) Deep learning for classification and severity estimation of coffee leaf biotic stress. Comput Electr Agric 169:105162
12. Lei T, Jia X, Zhang Y, He L, Meng H, Nandi AK (2018) Significantly fast and robust fuzzy C-means clustering algorithm based on morphological reconstruction and membership filtering. IEEE Trans Fuzzy Syst 26(5):3027–3041. https://doi.org/10.1109/TFUZZ.2018.2796074
13. Jia X, Lei T, Du X, Liu S, Meng H, Nandi AK (2020) Robust self-sparse fuzzy clustering for image segmentation. IEEE Access 8:146182–146195. https://doi.org/10.1109/ACCESS.2020.3015270
14. Lei T, Jia X, Zhang Y, Liu S, Meng H, Nandi AK (2019) Superpixel-based fast fuzzy C-means clustering for color image segmentation. IEEE Trans Fuzzy Syst 27(9):1753–1766. https://doi.org/10.1109/TFUZZ.2018.2889018

15. Lei T, Liu P, Jia X, Zhang X, Meng H, Nandi AK (2020) Automatic fuzzy clustering framework for image segmentation. IEEE Trans Fuzzy Syst 28(9):2078–2092. https://doi.org/10.1109/TFUZZ.2019.2930030
16. Macgregor P, Sun H (2022) A tighter analysis of spectral clustering, and beyond. In: International conference on machine learning

YOLOv5-MasselNet: In-Field Maize Tassel Detection and Density Estimation Using YOLOv5

Prerana Mukherjee, Kavita Deshpande, Vrishabhdhwaj Maharshi, and Bhavishya Raj

Abstract Conventional object detection machine learning models dedicated to the agriculture industry have improved since the origin of machine learning and computer vision. In this paper, we explore various state-of-the-art models built using different architectures as well as a density estimation model with context awareness for monitoring tassel growth. We explore the performance of pre-existing models like Faster R-CNN, ResNet and YOLOv5 on the Maize Counting Dataset.

1 Introduction

The problem of counting tassels of corn is important in the field of precision agriculture. Although the number of tassels does not determine the final yield, it gives farmers a good estimate of the yield and helps them make economic decisions. In cases where continuous monitoring is done, the tassel count can help determine crop management strategies that are working and those that aren't as well as help identify trouble zones. Counting tassels manually is labour expensive and inaccurate. In recent years, the success of deep learning in object detection tasks has been leveraged to find an automated counting method for tassels.

Traditional computer vision methods face numerous challenges in this problem. To list a few: (i) tassels have very thin petals, (ii) colour characteristics of tassels are not too different from those of leaves, (iii) overlapping of tassels makes its segregation and detection both difficult, (iv) specular reflection spots on leaves often have same colour characteristics as tassels, (v) the shape and colour characteristics of tassels can vary over cultivars, so it is not possible to have uniform segmentation and morphological pre-processing pipeline that might work well for all cultivars simultaneously. As a result, traditional segmentation and detection techniques have

P. Mukherjee (✉) · V. Maharshi · B. Raj
Jawaharlal Nehru University, New Delhi, India
e-mail: prerana@jnu.ac.in

K. Deshpande
Sai University, Chennai, India

S. Chaudhury et al. (eds.), *Computer Vision, Pattern Recognition, Image Processing, and Graphics*, Lecture Notes in Electrical Engineering 1218,
https://doi.org/10.1007/978-981-97-5212-6_5

not been very successful at giving accurate tassel counts. On the other hand, deep learning methods have shown considerable promise in the last few years. In [1], authors have provided a comprehensive review of the current competing detection and crowd counting methods and provided a dataset for maize tassel detection. In [2], authors have demonstrated the efficacy of TasselNet which is the first work in plant phenotyping related to counting problem using computer vision where they count the maize tassels in unconstrained field images using deep convolutional neural network in a regression setting. The maize tassel counting model *TasselNet* [2] and the MTC (maize tassel counting) dataset were introduced in 2017. In [3], the authors extended the TasselNet architecture with contextual knowledge in order to solve the problem of wheat spike counting. They achieved higher accuracy and an order of magnitude faster architecture as compared to TasselNet architecture. In [4], authors introduced SpikeCount method for wheat spikelet counting from in-field images. They leveraged transfer learning over the segmentation and detection tasks. In [5], authors have proposed to identify maize seedlings using deep learning-based regression framework in drone captured imagery. In [6], Global Wheat Challenge 2020 dataset hosted in Kaggle was further expanded. They further accentuated the quality of the data in terms of data size, variability in wheat heads and the reliability of the annotations. In [7], the authors have congregated the local patch extraction framework with a global mask refinement module to segment the wheat spikes for wheat images obtained in a controlled lab facility. In [8], the authors utilized YOLOv4 as the baseline detection model and visualized the feature maps obtained by the Swin Transformer network to localize the maize tassels in remote sensing images. In this paper, we have exhaustively compared the competing detection techniques such as YOLOv5, YOLOv5-Transformer, Faster R-CNN and Retinanet. The Maize Tassel Detection and Counting (MTDC) dataset and collected Maize Tassel dataset, which have been discussed in sections to follow, are used for a fair comparison. We also include a comparison of the above detection-based techniques with CANNet, a density estimation-based technique. In addition to the MTDC dataset, we utilize our own Maize Tassel dataset consisting of 136 annotated images. The images were taken by a drone flown at an average height of 20m over plots containing mixed maize cultivars. The images are of medium to low resolutions (72–96 dpi). The images were manually annotated using Labelling toolbox.[1]

2 Methodology

In this section, we briefly describe the peculiar challenges posed by our Maize Tassel dataset and the methods we have employed for counting. Existing methods for tassel detection can be broadly divided into two categories: detection-based [9–11] and estimation-based [12]. Object detection combines image classification and object

[1] https://github.com/heartexlabs/labelImg.

localization tasks. Estimation-based methods that are generally employed for the problem of crowd counting are based on the idea of density estimation using multiple receptive field-based filters over the entire image and thus compensate the perspective distortion by accounting for the local scale.

2.1 Challenges with the Dataset

With the newly introduced tassel image dataset namely *Maize Tassel (MT) dataset*, we face two new challenges: 1. The images are taken at lower resolution (96 dpi) and 2. The images contain plants of varying cultivars. The colour and shape characteristics of leaves and flowers vary with cultivars. This non-uniformity makes tassel detection with traditional techniques a very challenging task. In most of the prior works [1, 2, 5], images used for training as well as final applications consist of high-resolution images. Moreover, the images contain plants of the same cultivar which means that colour and shape characteristics of leaves and flowers are consistent in those images. As a result, the proposed techniques in such literature do not work as promised for low-resolution images, which are likely to be encountered when the model is to be scaled for larger datasets. This is a problem which we seek to address in our work. We have also been able to meet the second challenge of dealing with mixed cultivars considerably well with our models.

2.2 Tassel Detection Sub-net

The YOLOv5 model relies on the Cross Stage Partial Network (CSPNet) [13] as its backbone, which has been proven to decrease computations and achieve greater accuracy in detecting maize tassels of varying scale, occlusion and view. CSPNet achieves this by incorporating feature maps from both the beginning and end of a network stage, respecting the variability of gradients. The architecture's neck incorporates the Path Aggregation Network (PANet), which enhances instance segmentation while preserving spatial information. PANet's higher accuracy is attributed to its bottom-up path augmentation, adaptive feature pooling and location-sensitive fully connected layers that adjust to different spatial locations. In YOLOv5, PANet is utilized by concatenating adjacent layers and pooling features from all levels, effectively reducing the gap between the bottom and top layers. Transformers [14] have achieved state-of-the-art results in NLP (Natural Language Processing) tasks. In an attempt to improve the efficiency in the task of in-field maize tassel detection, we added the transformer layers to our existing YOLOv5 architecture. It can be observed in the results section that we have achieved improved results as compared to vanilla YOLOv5 variant.

2.3 Context-Aware Tassel Density Sub-net

For density-based counting, we have used the Context-Aware Crowd counting [12] architecture. We first converted the MTDC dataset's bounding box annotations to dot annotations. We were able to determine the existence of maize tassels as a density-map visualization using pre-trained weights of RESNet50 and Context-Aware Crowd counting [12, 15] architecture. This model was created to count and map a set of persons in a photograph (ShanghaiTech dataset). This model was used to create a density map that was specialized in tassel density in an image. For each input image, the model generates four images (1 density map for each quadrant), which are then combined to provide a complete density estimation of the input. Bright dots on the output image indicate the existence of tassels or a collection of tassels, whereas the dark green background of the input image symbolizes the background.

3 Experimental Results and Analysis

3.1 Datasets

We have utilized the following two datasets for our study. The datasets contain aerial images of the fields such that white tassels of the maize plants are visible. It should also be noted that for some tassels there exists overlapping, either by the leaves of the plants or by other tassels. For all experimentation purposes, the datasets were split in an 80:20 ratio for training and validation sets respectively for each dataset. This is intended to provide uniformity to the wide range of experiments that have been conducted.

1. Maize Tassel dataset: It contains RGB images of size ranging from 340×340 to 500×500 along with bounding box notation in PASCAL-VOC format (XML files). The images were taken with a DJI MAVIC drone from an average height of 20 metres with an average GSD of 0.5 centimetres. The resolution of the images is 96 dpi. Data augmentation using rotation, flipping and introduction of black patches has been performed to increase the dataset size.
2. MTDC: Prepared by authors Zou, Hongwei and Lu, Hao and Li, Yanan and Liu, Liang and Cao and Zhiguo, this dataset consists of 361 field images collected from four experimental fields across China. They contain a total of 13, 562 bounding box annotations. The box annotations of all tests and train images are as stored as MATLAB files. For density estimation using crowd counting, we converted the bounding box annotations of the MTDC dataset to dot annotations that denote the centre of the bounding box of each tassel.

3.2 Qualitative and Quantitative Results

As mentioned earlier, we have compared the performance of three detection-based models (Faster R-CNN, RetinaNet and YOLOv5) and one density estimation-based model (CANNet) on the task of tassel detection. We have also compared the performance of YOLOv5 with that of YOLOv5+transformer model on the MTDC dataset.

Each model has been tested on both MTDC and our Maize Tassel dataset. In addition, for the detection-based models, we have performed two sets of experiments: (1) performing training and testing on the same dataset (Tables 1 and 2) and (2) combined training on the two datasets (Table 3) and testing on each dataset separately. This was performed by consecutive training on the datasets by utilizing weights obtained by training one dataset as the pre-trained weights of the other.

For YOLOv5, the learning rate was set to 0.01 while a decay rate of 0.935 was used in the model training. All images were resized to 512 × 512 pixels for the MTDC dataset and 256 × 256 pixels for the MT dataset when experimenting with YOLOv5. In the first set of experiments, the best results were obtained for YOLOv5 trained and tested on the MTDC dataset with a confidence threshold of 0.35 with MSE and MAE approximating 14.26 and 9.88. This result is expected since the quality of images in the MTDC dataset is superior to those in the Maize tassel dataset.

We observe that the best detection results on the Maize Tassel dataset are obtained using the YOLOv5 model when it is trained with a combination of the two datasets—first MTDC and then our Maize Tassel dataset. With this method we obtain an MAE score of 5.03 and an MSE score of 6.71 at 35% confidence level (Table 3). For CANNet, the best results were obtained for a learning rate and decay rate of 0.0001 and 0.0005 with a batch size of 8 (Table 4). We show the detection results in Fig. 2 and density estimation results in Fig. 1.

Table 1 Performance analysis on Maize Tassel dataset

Model	mAP@[0.1:0.95]	MAE	MSE
Faster R-CNN	0.54	3.17	4.130232866
RetinaNet	0.34	4.18	3.029411765
YOLOv5	0.256	12.17	15.77099039

Table 2 Performance analysis on MTDC dataset

Model	mAP@[0.1:0.95]	MAE	MSE
Faster R-CNN	0.40	3.17	4.130232866
RetinaNet	0.34	4.18	3.029411765
YOLOv5	0.41	8.49	11.64
YOLOv5-TR	0.50	6.02	12.02

Table 3 Comparison of YOLOv5 performance when trained on different datasets

	Trained on MTDC dataset		Trained on combined dataset	
	MAE	MSE	MAE	MSE
Testing on MTDC	8.49	11.64	5.93	10.58
Testing on Maize Tassel	12.17	15.77	5.03	6.71

Table 4 Density estimation evaluation on the MTDC and Maize Tassel Datasets

DATASET	CANNet: Density Estimation		
	Cultivar	MAE	RMSE
MTDC	Zhengzhou2011	23.28216028	25.45261222
	Taian2010_2	18.08843029	19.85435399
	Taian2011_2	28.77475317	29.25009578
	Taian2012_2	24.82411492	25.60347185
	Taian2013_2	34.09936047	35.14496251
	Gucheng2014	60.73952628	62.19870507
	Jalaid2015_2	31.84795698	34.94209111
	Jalaid2015_3	26.31910102	30.07603859
	Overall	34.05345618	39.20448793
MAIZE TASSEL	Overall	9.305877433103674	12.857081033946395
MAIZE TASSEL (when the image under test was reshaped to 1000x1000)	Overall	10.306461446425494	11.11784187927184

4 Conclusion

We conclude by observing that YOLOv5 performs the best among all the tested models for tassel detection. In addition, for our low-resolution Maize Tassel dataset, the combined training method—first with high-resolution images followed by low-resolution images—provides the best results for detection using YOLOv5. We observe that the results of YOLOv5 with combined training are significantly improved in comparison with results obtained by training only with the MTDC dataset on both datasets.

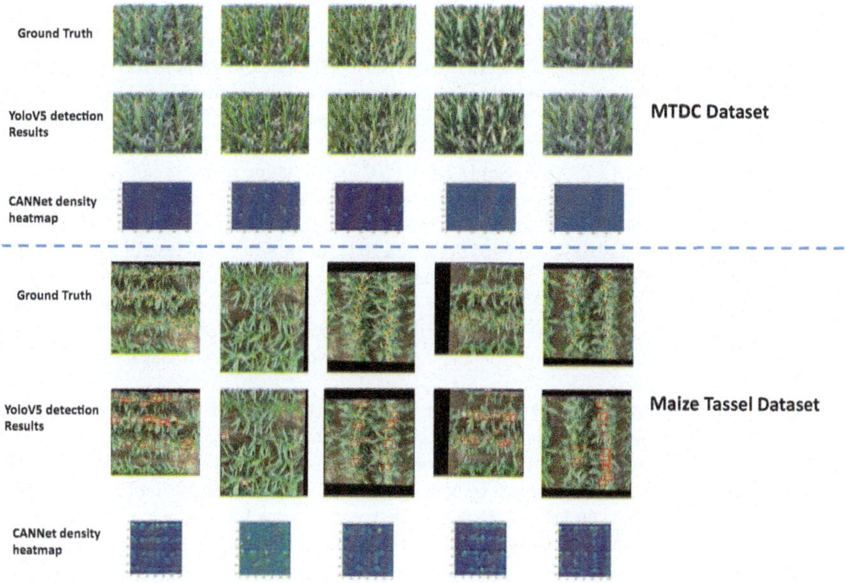

Fig. 1 **a** Ground Truth with tassel dot annotations, **b** Detection results using YOLOv5 and c) Density estimation heatmap using CANNet

Fig. 2 Maize tassel detection results on MTDC and Maize Tassel Datasets

References

1. LH LY e. a. Zou H (2020) Maize tassels detection: a benchmark of the state of the art. Plant Methods 16 16(108):97–111

2. C Z XY.e. a. Lu H (2017) Tasselnet: counting maize tassels in the wild via local counts regression network. Plant Methods 13(79)
3. Xiong H, Cao Z, Lu H, Madec S, Liu L, Shen C (2019) Tasselnetv2: in-field counting of wheat spikes with context-augmented local regression networks. Plant Methods 15(1):1–14
4. Alkhudaydi T, De la Lglesia B (2022) Counting spikelets from infield wheat crop images using fully convolutional networks. Neural Comput Appl 34(20):17 539–17 560
5. Liu S, Yin D, Feng H, Li Z, Xu X, Shi L, Jin X (2022) Estimating maize seedling number with UAV RGB images and advanced image processing methods. Precision Agric 23(5):1604–1632
6. David E, Serouart M, Smith D, Madec S, Velumani K, Liu S, Wang X, Pinto F, Shafiee S, Tahir IS et al (2021) Global wheat head detection 2021: an improved dataset for benchmarking wheat head detection methods. Plant Phenomics
7. Misra T, Arora A, Marwaha S, Chinnusamy V, Rao AR, Jain R, Sahoo RN, Ray M, Kumar S, Raju D et al (2020) Spikesegnet-a deep learning approach utilizing encoder-decoder network with hourglass for spike segmentation and counting in wheat plant from visual imaging. Plant Methods 16(1):1–20
8. Zhang X, Zhu D, Wen R (2023) Swint-yolo: Detection of densely distributed maize tassels in remote sensing images. Comput Electron Agricult 210:107905
9. Ren S, He K, Girshick R, Sun J (2015) Faster r-CNN: Towards real-time object detection with region proposal networks. Advances in neural information processing systems, vol 28
10. Jocher G, Chaurasia A, Stoken A, Borovec J, Kwon Y, Michael K, Fang J, Yifu Z, Wong C, Montes D et al (2022) Ultralytics/yolov5: v7. 0-yolov5 sota realtime instance segmentation. Zenodo
11. Lin T-Y, Goyal P, Girshick R, He K, Dollár P (2017) Focal loss for dense object detection. In: Proceedings of the IEEE international conference on computer vision, pp 2980–2988
12. Liu W, Salzmann M, Fua P (2019) Context-aware crowd counting. In: Proceedings of the IEEE/CVF conference on computer vision and pattern recognition, pp 5099–5108
13. Wang CY, Liao HY, Wu YH, Chen PY, Hsieh JW, Yeh IH (2020) Cspnet: a new backbone that can enhance learning capability of CNN. In: Proceedings of the IEEE/CVF conference on computer vision and pattern recognition workshops, pp 390–391
14. Vaswani A, Shazeer N, Parmar N, Uszkoreit J, Jones L, Gomez AN, Kaiser, Ł, Polosukhin I (2017) Attention is all you need. Advances in neural information processing systems, vol 30
15. Liu W, Lis K, Salzmann M, Fua P (2019) Geometric and physical constraints for drone-based head plane crowd density estimation. In: 2019 IEEE/RSJ international conference on intelligent robots and systems (IROS). IEEE, pp 244–249

MuSiC V1.0: A Software Solution for Automated Mustard Silique Count Using YOLOv5

Chandan Kumar Deb, Madhurima Das, Mahesh Kumar, Sudhir Kumar, Md. Ashraful Haque, Alka Arora, Sudeep Marwaha, Biswabiplab Singh, Dhandapani Raju, and Viswanathan Chinnusamy

Abstract Object detection is a challenging and important field in the domain of computer vision. Automated detection and counting of the number of siliques non-destructively, which is the most important yield component trait in Indian mustard (B. juncea), which is important as well as widely cultivated oilseed in India, is done here. We have used Deep Learning based one-stage object detection model, YOLOv5 in the counting of mustard siliques from the images captured by a DSLR camera (SONY Alpha 7iii, 24.2MP) manually mounted on a tripod. A GUI-based desktop software, MuSiC v1.0 is developed using Tkinter, Python backed by YOLOv5 model developed from annotated training dataset using Roboflow annotator. Approximately 22,800 annotations were used to train the deep learning YOLOv5 model and the whole dataset was partitioned into training, testing and validation in the ratio of 8:1:1. The Confusion matrix, F1 score and mAP showed a moderate result of 66%, 0.51 and 0.38, respectively, with the handcrafted ground truth data. The deployed model in MuSiC v1.0 showed a promising result of approximately good accuracy for silique count. This is the first initiative of creation of a desktop application for mustard silique count non-destructively.

Keywords Silique count · Non-destructive · YOLOv5 · Object detection · Deep learning · Mustard

1 Introduction

Indian mustard (B. juncea (L.) Czern. & Coss) represents the most important and widely cultivated oilseed species (90% of total average) in India. India is the third-largest producer after Canada and China of rapeseed-mustard group of crops with an area of 7.1 mha and a total production of 7.4 million metric tonnes [1]. By 2030,

C. K. Deb (✉) · M. Das · M. Kumar · S. Kumar · Md. A. Haque · A. Arora · S. Marwaha · B. Singh · D. Raju · V. Chinnusamy
ICAR-Indian Agricultural Statistics Research Institute,
New Delhi, Indiae-mail: chandan.deb@icar.gov.in
e-mail: chandan.deb@icar.gov.in

S. Chaudhury et al. (eds.), *Computer Vision, Pattern Recognition, Image Processing, and Graphics*, Lecture Notes in Electrical Engineering 1218,
https://doi.org/10.1007/978-981-97-5212-6_6

vegetable oil demand is expected to increase by 40% and a study of enhanced yield related traits are thus imperative to boost its production and reduce import cost [3].

Object detection can be considered as a combination of classification, localization and segmentation problems. It is the task of correctly classifying an object and also efficient localization of single or multiple objects in an image, taking the help of supervised deep learning algorithms in a sufficiently large labelled training dataset. The deep learning and computer vision concepts, YOLO architectural design and its successors are briefly reviewed by [4, 13]. You-only-look-once (**YOLO**) [7] is a typical Deep Learning-based one-stage object detection algorithm characterized by high detection speed, low background error detection rate and strong versatility. It is recognized as one of the top object identification algorithms in the computer vision research field. The basic architecture of YOLO is adopted from the GooLeNet architecture and implemented and tested on VOC Pascal Dataset 2007 and 2012. Darknet framework is utilized for the training of the model. An immediate successor of YOLOv1 is YOLOv2 which is utilized for detecting objects for around over 9000 categories. Here, ImageNet and COCO datasets were combined which resulted in more than 9418 categories of object instances. YOLOv2 uses Darknet-19 framework of 19 convolutional layers and 5 max pooling layers and built on VGG and Network-in-Network [7]. For overcoming localization error and smaller sized object detection, the YOLOv3 model is built which is trained on the COCO dataset [9]. It is built on Darknet-53 framework that uses 3×3 and 1×1 convolutional filter and powerful architecture with 53 convolutional layers inspired by Feature Pyramid Network (FPN). Alexey Bochkovskiy, Chien-Yao Wang and Hong-Yuan Mark Liao drafted the YOLOv4 model with more accurate and faster performance than the other models. It is inspired by Path Aggregation Network [2]. The latest addition to the YOLO series model is the YOLOv5 which includes in its architecture Focus, BottleneckCSP, SPP and PANet. Here for improving the receptive field Focus is used, for efficient feature extraction Bottleneck CSP is used, for an increment in the non-linear representation capability of the network ssp and PANet for improving the detection precision [11]. Various applications of the YOLO models are documented in the paper by [4–6]. More recent applications of the YOLO series model YOLOv5 include detection of grapevine bunch [10], real-time detection of weed *Solanum* [11], vehicle detection [14] and detection and tracking of abnormal behaviour of fishes [11].

In this study, an automated yield component trait estimation in a non-destructive manner using Deep Learning (DL) model YOLOv5 is used for the development of a desktop application that may help breeders to substitute labour-intensive counting by these models and thus, accelerate mustard yield improvement programme.

2 Mustard Growing Conditions

Plants of Brassica juncea genotypes were grown in plastic pots filled with 13 kg soil. The recommended dose of fertilizer (100–60-40–20 kg/ha N-P-K-S, respectively) for this experiment and three replications were done for each genotype. This experiment was conducted in the climate-controlled greenhouses of Nanaji Deshmukh Plant Phenomics Facility, ICAR-IARI, New Delhi, in the rabi season, 2022–23 with a growing temperature

$$24°C$$

for day time and

$$14°C$$

for night until the complete flowering was achieved and later during maturity temperature was kept around

$$28°C$$

in day time and

$$18°C$$

in night with ambient light coming through 80% transparent polycarbonate sheet. A total 300 number of images of whole mustard plants with standard black backgrounds were used for generating the training image dataset.

2.1 Workflow of Silique Count Software

Image data preprocessing was done using open-source Python packages like OpenCV and Pillow. The preprocessing includes resizing and data annotations. The annotations (Fig. 1.) were done using Roboflow (https://app.roboflow.com/) annotator. Silique count varied in the range of 35 to 145 siliques per plant. The average silique count is 76 which leads to 22,800 annotations. After annotations whole dataset is divided into three parts in Training: Validation: Testing in 8:1:1ratio. The training dataset was used to train the YOLOv5 model. The developed model was saved in .pt format and deployed in the designed desktop application called Mustard Silique Counter (MuSiC v1.0). The flowchart of the workflow for software development is described in Fig. 2.

Fig. 1 Annotations done using Roboflow (https://app.roboflow.com/). Annotations are represented by green rectangles

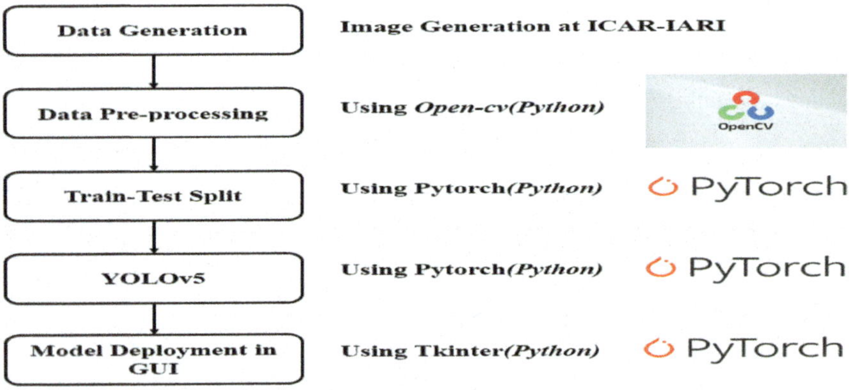

Fig. 2 Whole workflow of the software development process for mustard silique count

3 Model Architecture

3.1 Model Architecture

YOLO (You-Only-Look-Once) is an efficient deep learning network. YOLOv5 is a convolution-deep neural network with CSPDarknet53 backbone feature extractor; the Neck is made of CSP-PAN and the head is made up of YOLOv3.

3.2 Model Performance Metrics

Box loss, Object loss, Precision, Recall, mean average precision (mAP) at Intersection over Union (IoU) threshold of 0.5 and mAP threshold ranges from 0.5 to 0.95 performance metrics were used in our study of silique count.

4 Image Dataset and Programming Details

300 number of images of the whole mustard plant were used for model building, which has an annotation of 22,800 siliques. A rectangle-bounding box was drawn at silique tip for each of the visible siliques in the images using an annotator Roboflow. Images of whole mustard plants were captured with a black background using a DSLR camera (SONY Alpha 7iii, 24.2MP) manually placed on a tripod. The model has been trained using 80% of the images and the remaining images have been used for validation and testing. All the experiments were conducted in NVIDIA DGX GPU Server with Tesla V100 GPUs. The proposed model has been developed using PyTorch, a high level API of Python Framework for Deep Learning. The YOLOv5 repository was replicated from Github (https://github.com/ultralytics/yolov5).

5 Results and Discussion

In this section, we will discuss the result in three different aspects. Firstly, the results derived from deep learning models; secondly, the results showed in developed MuSiC (MuSiC v1.0) software and thirdly, the performance measures between the results in MuSiC (MuSiC v1.0) software and ground truth, i.e. physical count in the lab.

5.1 Model Development

Confusion Matrix The confusion matrix generated from the developed YOLOv5 model has identified the silique with a frequency of 66% of the time correctly and 34% of the time, the model was confused with the background. But it has correctly identified silique against the background (Fig. 3).

Mean Average Precision(mAP) and F1 Score The YOLOv5 model has generated 0.51 F1 Score and 0.383 mAP@0.5 (Fig. 4). The Box loss and Object loss of the model asymptote within 230 epochs (Fig. 5).

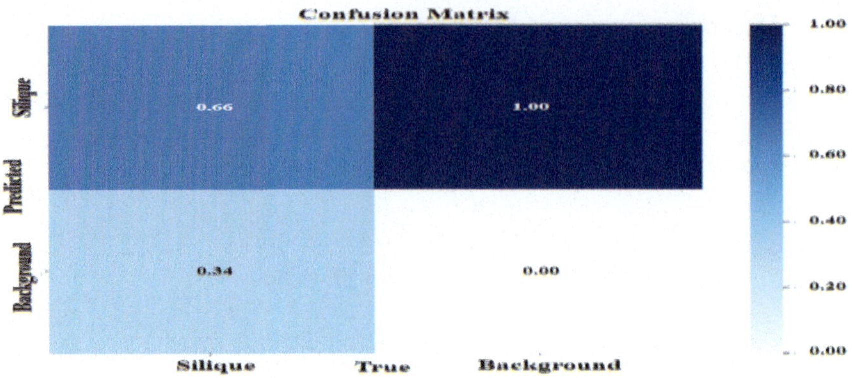

Fig. 3 Representation of the confusion matrix between predicted and true silique

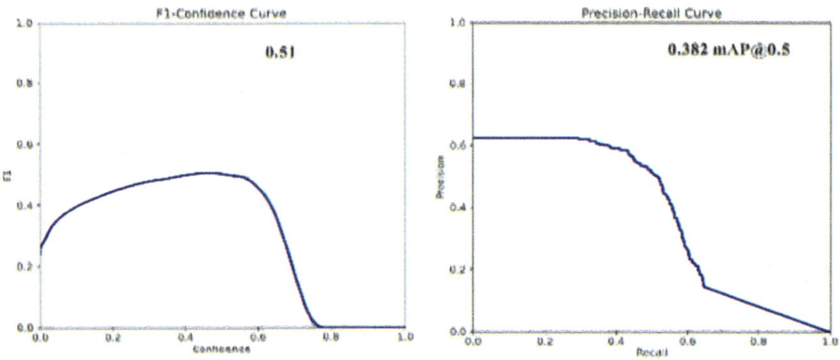

Fig. 4 Graph depicting F1 score and Precision-Recall of developed YOLOv5 model

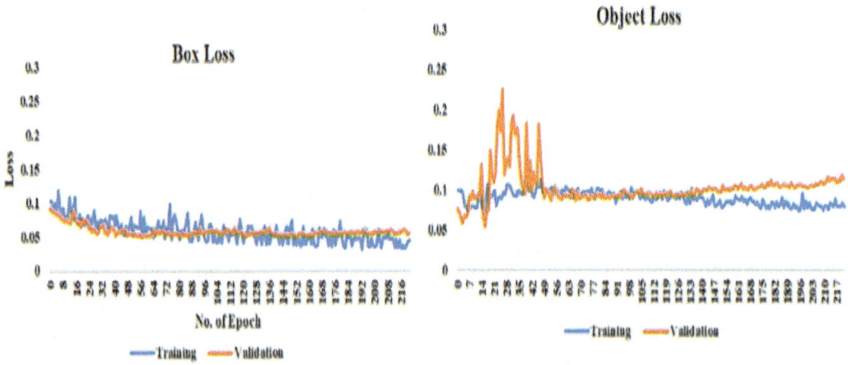

Fig. 5 Graph depicting Box loss and Object loss of developed YOLOv5 model

5.2 MuSiC V1.0 Development

MuSiC v1.0 (Mustard Silique Counter version 1.0) was developed using the Tkinter package of Python. MuSiC v1.0 is a user-friendly GUI-based desktop application. Users need to instal MuSiC v1.0 and then select the mustard images after clicking the button of 'Count Silique' (Fig. 6). Figure 7 depicts the comparison between silique count using MuSiC v1.0 and manual silique count. It shows the counting difference is less than 10.

Our study provided an automatic silique count provision in a non-invasive way in mustard through the developed desktop application MuSiC v1.0, which has the ability to replace the manual cumbersome counting and hence can be added to the toolkit of mustard breeders and in the mustard improvement programme.

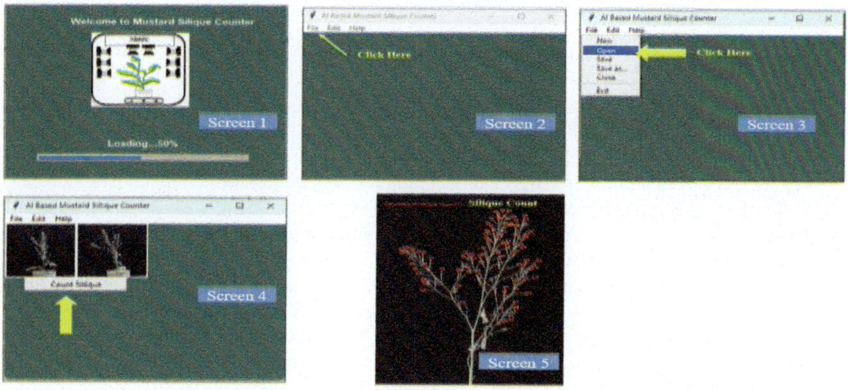

Fig. 6 Steps in the Graphical User Interface (GUI) for mustard silique counter MuSiC v1.0

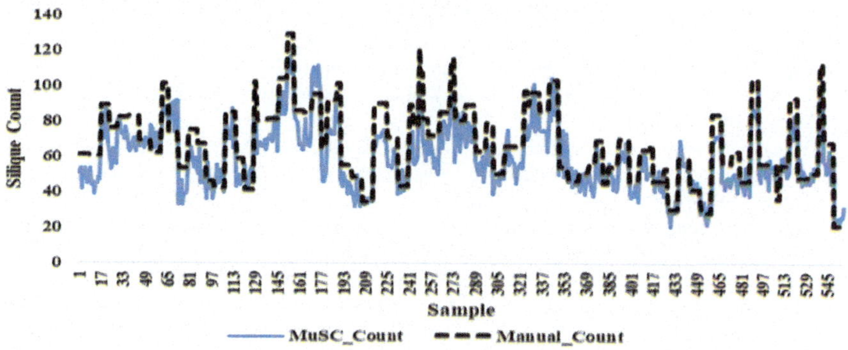

Fig. 7 Comparative depiction between silique count using MuSiC v1.0 and manual counting

6 Conclusion

Our study will open a new avenue in the automated and non-destructive counting task of High Throughput Phenotyping (HTP) of mustard that may help breeders to substitute the labour-intensive counting by these deep learning-based YOLOv5 model and thus, accelerate mustard genetic advancement programme. The developed GUI desktop application MuSiC v1.0 has immense importance to the breeders due to its user friendliness and prompt response if it is available in the public domain. Also, the developed pipeline may be reproducible for other crops undergoing count phenotyping problems.

References

1. Anonymous (2021) Global agricultural information network circular series, WAP 9–21. USDA Foreign Agricultural Service, Washington, DC
2. Bochkovskiy A, Wang CY, Liao HY (2020) YOLOv4: optimal speed and accuracy of object detection. arXiv:2004.10934
3. Delourme R, Laperche A, Bouchet AS, Jubault M, Paillard S, Manzanares-Dauleux MJ, Nesi N (2018) Genes and quantitative trait loci mapping for major agronomic traits in Brassica napus L. The Brassica napus genome, pp 41–85
4. Diwan T, Anirudh G, Tembhurne JV (2023) Object detection using YOLO: challenges, architectural successors, datasets and applications. Multimed. Tools Appl. 82(6):9243–9275
5. Ge Z, Liu S, Wang F, Li Z, Sun J (2021) Yolox: exceeding yolo series in 2021. arXiv:2107.08430
6. Jiang P, Ergu D, Liu F, Cai Y, Ma B (2022) A review of Yolo algorithm developments. Proc Comput Sci 199:1066–1073
7. Redmon J, Divvala S, Girshick R, Farhadi A (2016) You only look once: unified, real-time object detection. In: Proceedings of the IEEE conference on computer vision and pattern recognition, pp 779–788
8. Redmon J, Farhadi A (2017) YOLO9000: better, faster, stronger. In: Proceedings of the IEEE conference on computer vision and pattern recognition, pp 7263–7271
9. Redmon J, Farhadi A (2018) Yolov3: an incremental improvement. arXiv:1804.02767
10. Sozzi M, Cantalamessa S, Cogato A, Kayad A, Marinello F (2022) Automatic bunch detection in white grape varieties using YOLOv3, YOLOv4, and YOLOv5 deep learning algorithms. Agronomy 12(2):319
11. Wang H, Zhang S, Zhao S, Wang Q, Li D, Zhao R (2022) Real-time detection and tracking of fish abnormal behaviour based on improved YOLOV5 and SiamRPN++. Comput Electron Agricult 192:106512
12. Wang Q, Cheng M, Huang S, Cai Z, Zhang J, Yuan H (2022) A deep learning approach incorporating YOLO v5 and attention mechanisms for field re-al-time detection of the invasive weed Solanum rostratum Dunal seedlings. Comput Electron Agricult 199:107194
13. Zaidi SSA, Ansari MS, Aslam A, Kanwal N, Asghar M, Lee B (2022) A survey of modern deep learning-based object detection models. Digital Signal Process 103514
14. Zhang Y, Guo Z, Wu J, Tian Y, Tang H, Guo X (2022) Real-time vehicle detection based on improved YOLO v5. Sustainability 14(19):12274

TaPaSe: Tanjore Paddy Seed Dataset

A. Sasithradevi, M. Vijayalakshmi, SR Varsini, Joshua R Gabriel, S. Mohamed Mansoor Roomi, and P. Prakash

Abstract Rice is a popular staple diet in India, and its demand has recently increased. Thanjavur, located in the Cauvery Delta region, is known as the rice granary of South India. Due to recent technological advancements, digital farming and globalization have significantly impacted the agricultural industry. It is crucial to differentiate between types of rice grains to prevent fraudulent labeling during import and export. To achieve this, a dataset, namely "TaPaSe Dataset", comprising five varieties of rice, including MTU 1010, MTU 1290, Narmadha, Pacha Ponni, and Sonna Masur, which are mainly cultivated in Thanjavur, has been collected. We designed an image acquisition system to capture the aforementioned varieties in real time. The captured paddy rice images are highly challenging in the sense that all the images are captured under illumination and scale variations. We evaluated existing deep learning models to understand their ability to classify paddy seed varieties. The existing pre-trained models attain remarkable recognition rates on the proposed paddy seed varieties dataset.

Keywords Image classification · Deep learning · Pre-trained models

A. Sasithradevi (✉)
Centre for Advanced Data Science, Vellore Institute of Technology, Chennai, India
e-mail: sasithradevi.a@vit.ac.in

M. Vijayalakshmi
School of Electronics Engineering, Vellore Institute of Technology, Chennai, India

S. Varsini · J. R. Gabriel
School of Computer Science and Engineering, Vellore Institute of Technology, Chennai, India

S. M. M. Roomi
Department of Electronics and Communication Engineering, Thiagarajar College of Engineering, Madurai, India

P. Prakash
Department of Electronics Engineering, Madras Institute of Technology, Chennai, India

S. Chaudhury et al. (eds.), *Computer Vision, Pattern Recognition, Image Processing, and Graphics*, Lecture Notes in Electrical Engineering 1218,
https://doi.org/10.1007/978-981-97-5212-6_7

1 Introduction

India is known for its diverse rice seed varieties, each with unique features and properties. Some rice seeds have long and slender grains, while others are short and plump. The color of the grains ranges from white to brown to red. Some seeds are high-yielding, while others resist diseases and pests. Certain varieties are suited for specific growing conditions, such as drought-prone or flood-prone areas. Rice varieties that exhibit excellent cooking quality and exceptional taste are highly preferred. With a rich history of rice cultivation, India has developed numerous indigenous rice seed varieties that have adapted to local conditions and preferences, making them an essential part of the country's food culture. South India has served as the home to a wide range of paddy seed varieties for generations. These seeds are well known for their adaptability to the region's diverse soil and climate conditions. South India has a rich agricultural history of farmers cultivating seed variants ranging from traditional varieties to newer hybridized ones. The legacy of agricultural practices has been treasured and passed down from generation to generation. In addition to rice, South India is known for cultivating other crop varieties such as millet, spices, pulses, and vegetables.

The importance of preserving these seed varieties cannot be overstated. These seeds are an essential part of South India's agricultural heritage and play a crucial role in ensuring food security for the region. However, with the increasing use of hybrid seeds and the encroachment of monoculture, many of these traditional seed varieties are on the brink of extinction. It is, therefore, vital to conserve and promote the use of these seeds to ensure a sustainable future for agriculture in South India. Tamil Nadu, especially the Thanjavur district, is known as "The Rice Bowl of Tamil Nadu" and is home to a diverse range of seed varieties cultivated for centuries. Seeds cultivated here are known for their notable ability to withstand drought conditions. In Thanjavur, seeds are developed through traditional breeding methods by selecting the seed varieties with the best traits, such as drought tolerance, pest and disease resistance, improved flavor, and extended shelf life. This approach has helped farmers in this region to cope with drastic climatic changes and unpredictable weather patterns. These crops have been crucial in ensuring food security for the region's population, particularly during drought and crop failure. Other essential characteristics of these seeds are their nutritional value and unique flavor profiles. Millets and pulses grown in Thanjavur are rich in protein, fiber, and other essential nutrients. The traditional rice varieties of Thanjavur are renowned for their unique flavors and aromas, highly valued by consumers within the region and beyond.

Preserving and promoting these seeds is essential to ensure a sustainable future for agriculture in Thanjavur. MTU 1010 and MTU 1290 are rice varieties developed by International Rice Research Institute, known for their excellent adaptability to diverse agro-climatic conditions, superior taste, texture, and cooking characteristics. Narmadha is a traditional rice variety from Tamil Nadu known for its excellent taste and aroma. Making it a sought-after choice in the market. It is often used for making traditional dishes. Pacha Ponni is a rice variety from Tamil Nadu that is high-yielding and disease-resistant. It is popular among farmers in the region as it exhibits excellent cooking properties, such as fluffiness and non-stickiness, making it a preferred choice for various South Indian culinary delights. Sonna Masur is a popular dal variety grown in Tamil Nadu. This dal variety is preferred by consumers for its versatility in various traditional dishes, making it a staple in many households.

With rapidly growing technology, the agriculture industry is trying to automate harvesting, crop monitoring, quality checking, processing, and packaging. In the first stage, farmers must choose the right variety of crops, especially rice, suitable for the region's agro-climatic conditions. Harvesting low-quality or less desirable rice varieties can lead to adverse depreciation in yield and may cause financial losses. Secondly, importers and exporters must ensure they have received the exact seed type. This not only ensures that their reputation is in check but also helps in maintaining a healthy trade relationship with buyers. Finally, the consumers unknowingly purchasing inferior or lower quality rice can lead to disappointment, compromised taste, and nutritional value. All these have created critical demand for employing deep learning models to automate classifying different paddy seed varieties and segregating best quality seeds from damaged ones.

Several studies have been conducted to explore the use of machine learning, deep learning, computer vision, and image processing techniques for rice seed classification and quality evaluation. It is found that machine vision technology developed to classify 14 Oryza sativa rice varieties yields a good accuracy ranging from 82.71% to 90.61% [1]. Suitable CNN model architectures were built to produce better accuracy than our previous model. As a recent development, a model using convolutional neural networks demonstrated exceptional performance by achieving a flawless classification rate of 100% for seven different varieties of rice seeds [2]. These models can also be incorporated for plant growth prediction. Machine vision models can be employed for varietal classification and germination evaluation using a digital image processing system to obtain better results [3]. Various machine learning techniques were employed to classify paddy rice data and their classification success rates achieved were as follows: LR—93.02%, MLP—92.86%, SVM—92.83%, DT—92.49%, RF—92.39%, NB—91.71%, and K-NN—88.58% [12]. Naïve Bayes algorithm and data mining techniques effectively identify plant diseases, assisting farmers in early diagnosis [8]. PaddySeg algorithm, which uses rapid SURF to extract the features and classify the paddy images based on the extracted features, has outperformed traditional machine learning models [6]. Multivariate analysis offers the advantage of considering multiple features simultaneously, allowing for exploring complex relationships and a more comprehensive understanding of image data. It produces results faster, achieving an accuracy of 83.8–93.9% [7]. We obtain accuracy rates ranging from 80% to 83.33% for paddy seed variety classification by utilizing the transfer learning on state-of-art image classification models [4].

Backpropagation Neural Network (BPNN) achieves a maximum average accuracy of 93.31% in adulteration detection, successfully identifying the presence of substances added to alter the quality of products [5]. Combining spatial and spectral features with a machine vision model can classify rice seed samples and eliminate impure species [9]. It is found that models using image processing techniques and

SVM for classifying rice grain types achieve 92.22% accuracy [10]. A basic CNN model can predict the paddy growth stages with an overall accuracy of 82% [11]. Classification processes were conducted by creating models using Artificial Neural Network (ANN) and Deep Neural Network (DNN) algorithms for the feature dataset and employing the Convolutional Neural Network (CNN) algorithm for the image dataset. Remarkable success rates were achieved in these classifications, with ANN achieving 99.87%, DNN achieving 99.95%, and CNN achieving a perfect 100% accuracy [13]. A non-destructive classification system using hyperspectral imaging and deep CNN will surpass traditional methods in accuracy and performance [14]. Most recently, a hybrid model combining LSTM, CNN, and GAN for paddy disease classification, achieving 97% testing accuracy [15]. For Multi-crops Leaf Disease classification, a simple CNN-based Visual Geometry Group (VGG) model has attained an accuracy of 98.40% of grapes and 95.71% of tomatoes [16]. Studies on traditional and residual CNN for determining the freshness of 6 different types of fruits have shown that residual CNN has obtained a test accuracy score greater than 99% [17]. On a comparative study of the 23 most popular pre-trained ML and DL models for image classification and object detection, fine-tuned InceptionV3 models have produced fascinating results [18]. All these studies prove that transfer learning of CNN models has shown exceptional performance in crop variety classification, especially paddy. CNN model has leveraged the technological influence on traditional agricultural practices, thereby improving the overall efficiency of the industry. These studies collectively demonstrate the potential of machine vision and deep learning techniques in improving rice seed classification, adulteration detection, and disease diagnosis processes.

2 TaPaSe Data Collection Process

2.1 Need for TaPaSe

Preserving paddy seed images is crucial in nurturing agricultural research scientists, as digital farming is fundamental to modern agriculture. The digital documentation of seed images will aid the future research community in analyzing seed quality, facilitating accurate identification across various cultivators, and establishing a comprehensive digital database for organizing and managing seed inventory through categorizing different seed types. Digital documentation ensures transparency throughout the supply chain process by providing a clear and accessible record of every stage, from production to distribution. It enables real-time tracking and authentication, ensuring accountability, reducing fraud, and promoting stakeholder trust while facilitating efficient and secure transactions. It helps the student community learn about each variety's distinct characteristics and growth patterns, aiding their learning process, research endeavors, and agricultural knowledge development.

2.2 *Image Acquisition of Experimental Data and Setup*

Our research team used a 50-megapixel mobile camera to capture images of 5 rice seeds commonly grown in Thanjavur. The images were taken during the afternoon and evening under natural lighting conditions. The rice seed varieties included MTU 1010, MTU 1290, Narmadha, Pacha Ponni, and Sonna Masur. For each type of rice seed, the team collected images of 20 seeds for experimentation. The images were captured by a camera that was mounted at 8 different angles, including 0, 40, 90, 120, 140, and 180°C to ensure a comprehensive view of each seed variety (see Fig. 1). This approach enabled the team to obtain detailed and accurate images of the seeds from multiple angles, aiding in their analysis and identification. The team obtained 800 photos of seeds, with 160 images for each of the 5 varieties of rice seed type. As mentioned above, batches of 20 seeds were taken once at a time from a handful of seeds, and the images were captured from 8 different angles, adding up to 8 images in one iteration. 20 such iterations were performed for different sets of seeds to diversify the images captured.

We augmented the data through horizontal and vertical flips, rotation (± 15), blur(0.75px), noise (3%), and brightness (±25%). The augmentation methods are performed to train the model in classifying test images of paddy types captured in deplorable conditions like low/dim lighting, extensive blurring, or even diminished photo quality. Simulating various real-world scenarios and introducing variations in the training data makes the model more robust and capable of handling diverse images. These data augmentation techniques in image acquisition make the TaPaSe dataset challenging, which can be scaled and deployed in real-time industries. The sample images are shown in Fig. 2. As a consequence of image augmentation, each class size was increased from 180 images in each variety to 480 images. In total, there are 2400 images in the TaPaSe dataset.

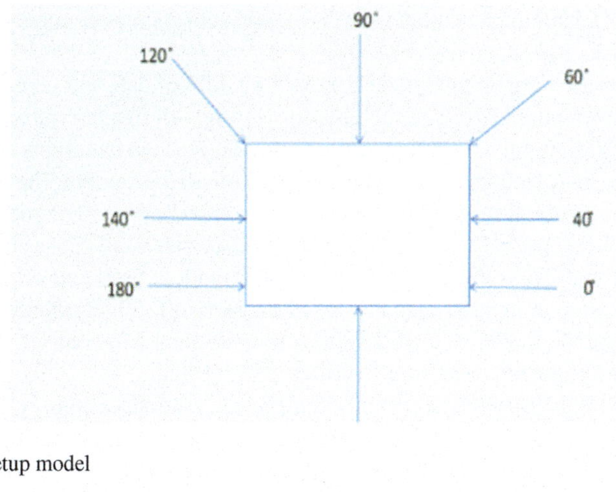

Fig. 1 Setup model

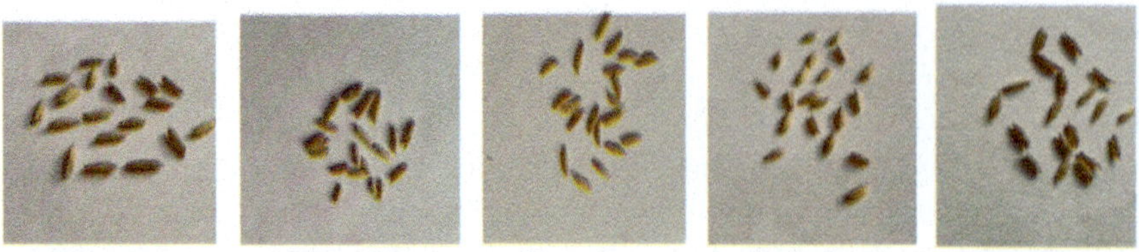

MTU - 1010 MTU - 1290 Narmadha Pacha Ponni Sonna Masur

Fig. 2 Sample images of the TaPaSe dataset

3 Methodology

Convolution neural network is a popular deep learning model for image classification, object detection, and object recognition. CNNs use a complex architecture of interconnected layers to extract features from images and identify patterns. Three significant layers in CNN include convolutional, pooling, and fully connected layers, which are further accompanied by dropouts, batch normalization, and actuation layers. Training results in attaining optimal weights and biases of the neurons and their connections, ensuring the best results for the architecture performance. The major objective of this research is to evaluate the effectiveness of the proposed TaPaSe. As a primary step of this process, pre-trained models trained on large-scale datasets with diverse images are deployed. These models allow efficient evaluation, benchmarking, and performance comparison on the new datasets without starting from scratch. These models are trained using powerful hardware and massive amounts of data, enabling them to learn complex patterns and representations. As our data is novel, pre-trained models are a valuable starting point for assessing the dataset. Transfer learning of pre-trained models enables faster training, improved generalization, and better performance even with limited labeled data. As mentioned above, CNN models have been employed due to their ability to capture spatial relationships, and local patterns, handle translation invariance, and achieve high accuracy in image classification tasks.

The 2400 images were divided in a 9:1 ratio, i.e., 90% of data was considered for training and validation and 10% of the data for testing. All images were resized to 192 X 192 pixels. In order to maintain uniformity and fairness in comparison, same hyperparameter and fully connected layers are taken for all the models. The RMSprop optimizer and categorical cross-entropy loss function were used. The models have been trained for 100 epochs. The learning rate and batch size were kept as the default values of 0.001 and 32, respectively. The five most widely used and efficient pre-trained models were compared, namely Residual Network 50 (ResNet50), Visual Geometry Group 16 (VGG16), VGG19, Inception V3, and EfficientNet. The brief reasoning behind choosing each model is discussed further.

ResNet (Residual Neural Network) introduced residual connections, which allow for the training of very deep neural networks. It consists of convolutional layers with skip connections that bypass some layers, helping to address the vanishing gradient problem. It uses residual connections to enable the flow of information through the network more efficiently. This approach allows for the creation of deeper networks without degrading performance. It has been widely used for various computer vision tasks, such as image classification, object detection, and image segmentation. Its ability to handle deep architectures makes it particularly effective in complex tasks where a high level of accuracy is desired.

GoogleNet, also known as InceptionV1, introduced the concept of the inception module. It consists of multiple parallel convolutional branches with different filter sizes and pooling operations. These branches are then concatenated to form the output of each module. Inception module allows capturing information at multiple scales by using filters of different sizes. It significantly reduces the number of parameters compared to traditional networks, enabling deeper architectures. InceptionV3, an extension of GoogleNet, which introduced several improvements, including factorized 7×7 convolutions, mixed 5×5 and 3×3 convolutions, and aggressive regularization techniques like batch normalization and dropout. These features help in reducing computational complexity and overfitting. It is particularly suitable for tasks requiring high accuracy and efficiency, such as image classification and object detection. Its efficient architecture makes it well-suited for deployment on devices with limited computational resources.

EfficientNet has achieved state-of-the-art performance with fewer parameters and computations. It uses a compound scaling method to balance depth, width, and resolution. It consists of multiple stacked blocks, including depth-wise convolutions and squeeze-and-excitation modules. It employs a compound scaling approach that uniformly scales the network width, depth, and resolution. This strategy ensures optimal resource allocation, achieving better accuracy with fewer parameters. Its ability to achieve excellent performance while resource-efficient makes it a compelling choice for real-world applications.

VGG16 is a deep convolutional neural network comprising 16 layers, including convolutional layers with small 3×3 filters and max pooling layers. It follows a simple, uniform architecture with a ReLU activation function following each convolutional layer. Its simplicity and uniformity make it easy to understand and implement. Using smaller convolutional filters enables more feature extraction, while max pooling helps to downsample and capture essential features. VGG19 is an extension of the VGG16 architecture, which includes additional convolutional layers to deepen the network and capture complex and finer image details. This more profound architecture can improve the model's representation power and performance on specific tasks. This uniform design of both models allows for easy implementation, interpretation, and transferability, making them widely adopted by transfer learning and considered as strong baselines for various computer vision tasks.

4 Results and Discussion

Windows 11 64-bit has been used to perform the suggested model. On a Jupyter Notebook of a laptop with a Full HD (1920×1080) display and an Intel Core i5-8300H processor and 8GB of RAM, the experiment was completed. It made use

Table 1 Accuracy and loss of the pre-trained CNN models on the TaPaSe dataset

Pre-trained models	Accuracy	Loss
ResNet50	46.63	1.31
Inception V3	87.5	0.44
VGG 16	63.0	1.13
EfficientNet	19.0	1.66
VGG 19	63.0	1.12

of an NVIDIA GeForce GTX 1050 graphics processor. The proposed TaPaSe data comprising 2400 images were taken for comparison. Each model was trained for 100 epochs. The augmented data has performed well on each state of art model mentioned. The cumulative observation of the dataset being trained on the models is tabulated in Table 1. The confusion matrix, accuracy and loss plots, and classification report which has precision, recall, and F1-Score for each model are visualized and tabulated below.

Evaluation on ResNet50
See Fig. 3 and Table 2.
Evaluation on Inception V3
See Fig. 4 and Table 3.
Evaluation on EfficientNet
See Fig. 5.

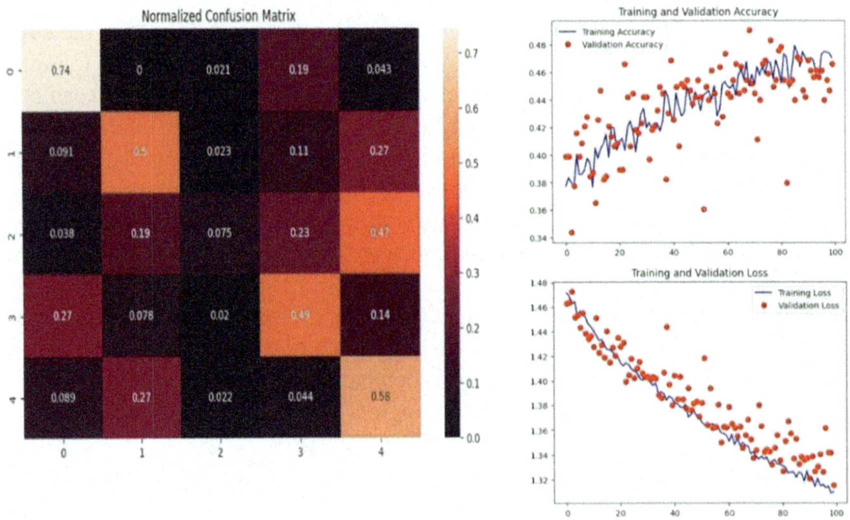

Fig. 3 Confusion matrix for ResNet50 and accuracy plot

Table 2 Classification report for ResNet50 model on the TaPaSe dataset

Types	Precision	Recall	F1-score
Mtu1010	0.59	0.74	0.66
Mtu1290	0.46	0.50	0.48
Narmadha 16	0.50	0.08	0.13
Pacha Ponni	0.47	0.49	0.48
Sonna Masur	0.36	0.58	0.44
Test Accuracy	0.47		

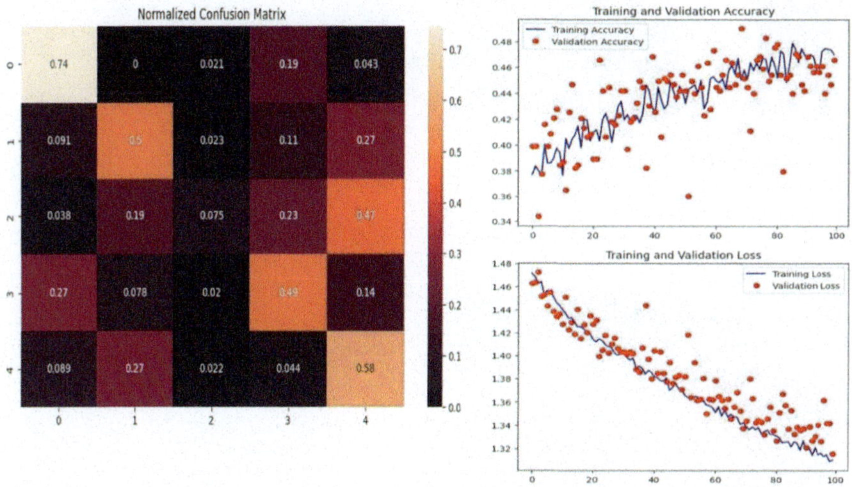

Fig. 4 Confusion matrix for InceptionV3 and accuracy plot

Table 3 Classification report for InceptionV3 model on the TaPaSe dataset

Types	Precision	Recall	F1-score
Mtu1010	0.83	0.83	0.83
Mtu1290	0.66	0.75	0.70
Narmadha 16	0.88	0.81	0.84
Pacha Ponni	0.96	0.94	0.95
Sonna Masur	0.80	0.78	0.79
Test Accuracy	0.82		

Evaluation on VGG16

See Fig. 6 and Table 4.

Evaluation on VGG19

See Fig. 7 and Table 5.

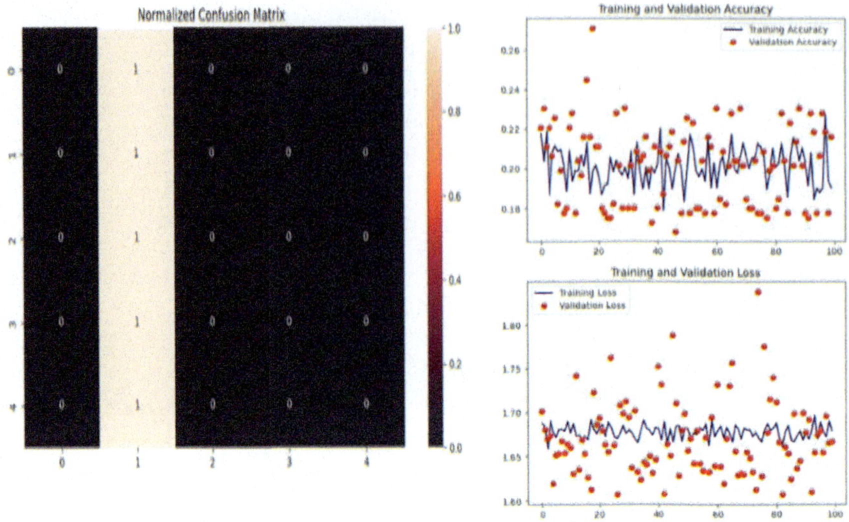

Fig. 5 Confusion matrix for EfficientNet and accuracy plot

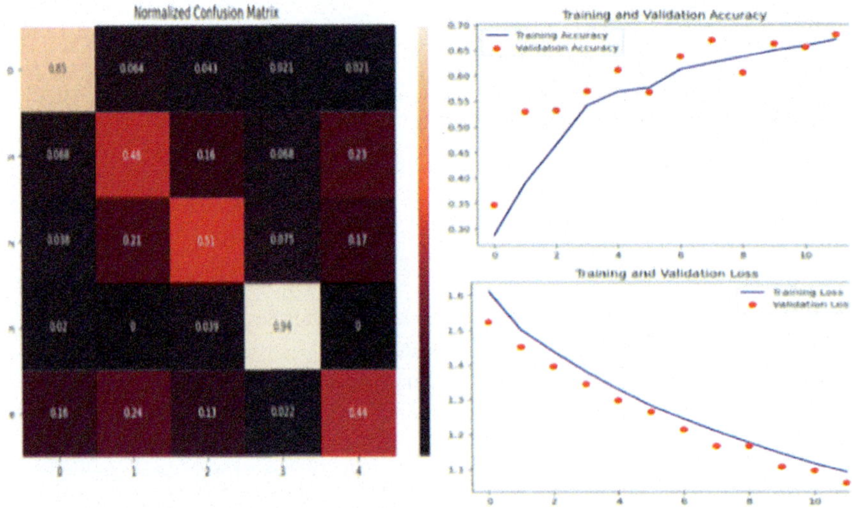

Fig. 6 Confusion matrix for VGG16 and accuracy plot

Table 4 Classification Report for VGG16 model on the TaPaSe dataset

Types	Precision	Recall	F1-Score
Mtu1010	0.75	0.85	0.80
Mtu1290	0.46	0.48	0.47
Narmadha 16	0.61	0.51	0.56
Pacha Ponni	0.84	0.94	0.89
Sonna Masur	0.50	0.44	0.47
Test Accuracy	0.63		

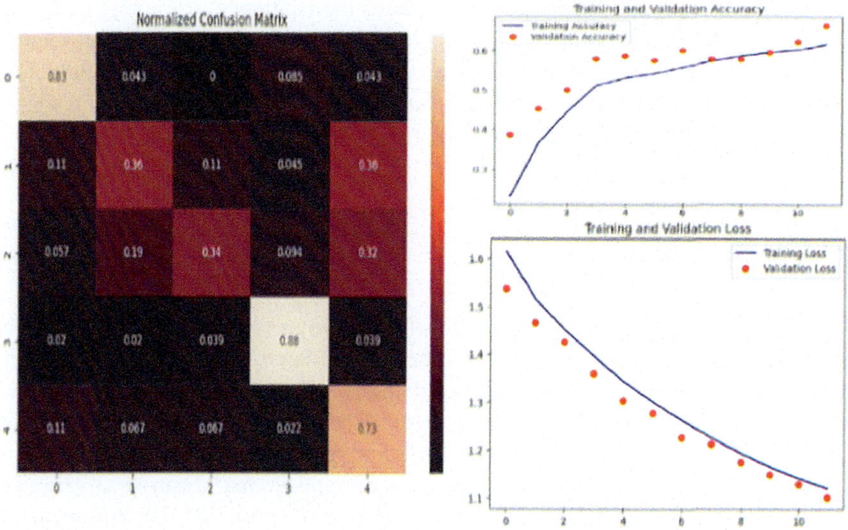

Fig. 7 Confusion matrix for VGG19 and accuracy plot

Table 5 Classification Report for VGG19 model on the TaPaSe dataset

Types	Precision	Recall	F1-score
Mtu1010	0.74	0.83	0.78
Mtu1290	0.50	0.36	0.42
Narmadha 16	0.64	0.34	0.44
Pacha Ponni	0.79	0.88	0.83
Sonna Masur	0.47	0.73	0.57
Test Accuracy	0.63		

In comparing transfer learning approaches using a 20-seeded dataset, several pre-trained models were evaluated, like VGG16, VGG19, EfficientNet, ResNet50, and Inception-V3. The accuracy results were as follows: VGG-16 achieved 63%, VGG19 reached 63%, EfficientNet scored 47%, ResNet50 achieved 47%, and Inception V3 performed remarkably well with an accuracy of 82%. These models possess distinct advantages tailored to specific requirements. A slight downfall in accuracy might be due to a limited number of labeled images. The dataset can be expanded and diversified in future studies to improve its quality. VGG16 and VGG19 are recognized for their straightforward architecture and firm performance in image classification tasks. EfficientNet stands out for its efficient use of computational resources, balancing accuracy and model size. ResNet addresses the challenge of training deep networks through residual connections. GoogleNet's Inception modules reduce parameters while maintaining accuracy, and Inception-V3 further refines the architecture with improved performance. The choice among these models depends on available resources, desired accuracy, and the trade-offs between complexity and efficiency.

5 Conclusion

There is an increasing need for auto-labeling locally produced seeds in the local sector. To increase the precision and efficiency of seed classification systems, it would be necessary to create specialized datasets and models particular to the seed kinds frequently grown in the Thanjavur region. The experiment aimed to evaluate the quality of the manually collected dataset. As a first stage, 20-seeded dataset consisting of Mtu1010, Mtu-1290, Narmadha, Pacha ponni and Sonna Masur seed varieties. For the evaluation purpose, state-of-the-art models ResNet50, VGG-16, EfficientNet, VGG19, and Inception-V3 were taken. Although there was a very minimal difference in the accuracy of these models trained on the proposed TaPaSe dataset, InceptionV3 has outwitted the other models for this particular data. Inferring from the results that the data quality is optimal. As the future develops, this data can be expanded by improving its resolution and training on various recent and complex models with attention mechanisms. This dataset would play a good role in automating seed variety classification, minimizing the wastage of time and resources, and maximizing the productivity of the agriculture sector. Higher resolution images and a more intricate convolutional model with many parameters and activation functions can also enhance this work.

References

1. Kantip, Development of paddy rice seed classification process using machine learning techniques for automatic grading machine. https://doi.org/10.1155/2020/7041310
2. Gilanie G, Nasir N, Bajwa UI, Ullah H (2021) RiceNet: convolutional neural networks based model to classify Pakistani grown rice seeds types. Multimed Syst 27. https://doi.org/10.1007/s00530-021-00760-2
3. Durai S, Mahesh C (2021) Research on varietal classification and germination evaluation system for rice seed using hand-held devices. Acta Agriculturae Scandinavica, Section B - Soil & Plant Sci 71(9):939–955. https://doi.org/10.1080/09064710.2021.1964592
4. Jaithavil D, Triamlumlerd S, Pracha M (2022) Paddy seed variety classification using transfer learning based on deep learning. In: International electrical engineering congress (iEECON). Khon Kaen, Thailand 2022:1–4. https://doi.org/10.1109/iEECON53204.2022.9741677
5. Anami Basavaraj S et al (2019) Automated recognition and classification of adulteration levels from bulk paddy grain samples 6(1):47–60
6. Maheswari S, Devi M (2019) Paddy seed classification and identifying varieties using random assessment classification. Int J Eng Adv Technol 9:2682–2685. https://doi.org/10.35940/ijeat.A9879.129219
7. Ansari Nadia et al (2021) Inspection of paddy seed varietal purity using machine vision and multivariate analysis. J Agricult Food Res 3:100109 March
8. Sahoo P, Annem S (2020) Diagnosis of paddy diseases using data mining technique, pp 13834–13843
9. Fabiyi SD et al (2020) Varietal classification of rice seeds using RGB and hyperspectral images. IEEE Access 8:22493–22505. https://doi.org/10.1109/ACCESS.2020.2969847
10. Shafaf I et al. (2019) Rice grain classification using multi-class support vector machine (SVM). IAES Int J Artif Intell (IJ-AI) 8(3): 215–220 ISSN: 2252-8938. https://doi.org/10.11591/ijai.v8.i3.pp215-220
11. Neforawati Indri et al (2019) J Phys: Conf Ser 1193:012026
12. Cinar I, Koklu M (2019) Classification of rice varieties using artificial intelligence methods. Int J Intell Syst Appl Eng 7:188-194. https://doi.org/10.18201/ijisae.2019355381
13. Koklu Murat et al (2021) Classification of rice varieties with deep learning methods. Comput Electron Agricult 187:106285 August
14. https://doi.org/10.48550/arXiv.1805.11491
15. Lamba S, Baliyan A, Kukreja V (2023) A novel GCL hybrid classification model for paddy diseases. Int J Inf Technol 15(2):1127–1136. https://doi.org/10.1007/s41870-022-01094-6. Epub 2022 Sep 19. PMID: 36159716; PMCID: PMC9484355
16. Paymode AS, Malode VB (2022) Transfer learning for multi-crop leaf disease image classification using convolutional neural network VGG. Artif Intell Agricult 6:23–33. https://doi.org/10.1016/j.aiia.2021.12.002
17. Kazi A, Panda SP (2022) Determining the freshness of fruits in the food industry by image classification using transfer learning. Multimed Tools Appl 81(6):7611–7624. https://doi.org/10.1007/s11042-022-12150-5
18. Jena B, Nayak GK, Saxena S (2021) Convolutional neural network and its pretrained models for image classification and object detection: a survey. Concurren Comput: Pract Exp 34(6). https://doi.org/10.1002/cpe.6767

Processing 3D Point Clouds for High-Throughput Plant Phenotyping

Preety Dagar, Alka Arora, Sudhir Kumar, Sudeep Marwaha, Rajni Jain, Himanshushekhar Chaurasia, and Vishwanathan Chinnusamy

Abstract In recent years, measuring three-dimensional (3D) surface information has gained a great interest in plant phenotyping because it can represent the nature of plant architecture better than conventional 2D images. This paper presents an approach for processing 3D point clouds converted from 2D RGB images in the context of high-throughput plant phenotyping. High-resolution RGB multi-view imagery of a Chickpea plant was collected using a high-end camera. Based on these image sequences, 3D point cloud reconstruction of the canopy was conducted and analyzed. Later sophisticated 3D operations were performed on these images including 3D downsampling and after that clustering was performed on the processed point cloud. The information generated can help in the evaluation of crop traits and provide accurate statistics for the assessment of their growth parameters.

Keywords 3D image processing · 2D to 3D image conversion · Open3D · 3D image processing for plant phenotyping

P. Dagar (✉) · A. Arora · S. Marwaha · R. Jain
Division of Computer Applications, ICAR-IASRI, Library Avenue, New Delhi 110012, Delhi, India
e-mail: preetydagar01@gmail.com

A. Arora
e-mail: alka.arora@icar.gov.in

S. Marwaha
e-mail: sudeep.marwaha@icar.gov.in

R. Jain
e-mail: rajni.jain@icar.gov.in

S. Kumar · V. Chinnusamy
Division of Plant Physiology, ICAR-IARI, IARI Pusa, New Delhi 110012, Delhi, India

H. Chaurasia
ICAR-CIRCOT, Matunga, Mumbai 400019, Maharashtra, India
e-mail: h.chaurasia@icar.gov.in

S. Chaudhury et al. (eds.), *Computer Vision, Pattern Recognition, Image Processing, and Graphics*, Lecture Notes in Electrical Engineering 1218,
https://doi.org/10.1007/978-981-97-5212-6_8

1 Introduction

Plant phenotyping is the process of quantitatively measuring and analyzing the physical and physiological characteristics, or phenotypes, of plants. It plays a crucial role in various fields, including plant breeding, crop improvement, agricultural research, and ecosystem monitoring. By accurately characterizing and understanding plant traits, scientists and breeders can make informed decisions to enhance crop productivity, disease resistance, stress tolerance, and overall plant performance.

The importance of plant phenotyping lies in its ability to provide valuable insights into plant growth, development, and responses to environmental factors. By studying phenotypic traits, researchers can gain a deeper understanding of plant physiology, identify genetic factors that can influence plant performance, and develop strategies for optimizing plant productivity and sustainability.

High-throughput plant phenotyping refers to the development and application of automated, non-destructive, and rapid techniques that enable the efficient characterization of plant traits on a large scale. By increasing the speed and accuracy of data acquisition and analysis, high-throughput methods overcome the limitations of traditional approaches, like time-consuming and labor-intensive, and enable researchers to capture a more complete and detailed understanding of plant phenotypes.

High-throughput plant phenotyping for 2D images has been a valuable approach in plant research and breeding for many years. It involves the analysis of two-dimensional images, such as photographs or scans, to extract phenotypic traits and gain insights into plant characteristics. While 2D plant phenomics has provided important information, the transition to 3D plant phenomics offers several significant advantages and improvements including accuracy and more comprehensive trait analysis.

3D images can be represented in various forms depending on the specific application and requirements including point cloud, mesh, and volumetric representations. Out of all these formats, point clouds are the simplest and are being used regularly. 3D point clouds are sets of data points that represent the three-dimensional coordinates of objects or surfaces in space. Each data point, also known as a "point," consists of its x, y, and z coordinates along with potentially other attributes such as color or intensity. Point clouds are commonly generated by various sensors, including LiDAR (Light Detection and Ranging) scanners, depth cameras, and photogrammetry techniques.

In the context of plant phenotyping, 3D point clouds capture the geometric structure and spatial information of plants. They provide a detailed representation of the plant's surface, including leaves, stems, branches, and flowers, as well as the surrounding environment. Each point in the point cloud corresponds to a specific location on the plant or the background, forming a dense collection of points that collectively represent the plant's three-dimensional shape.

To process 3D images, a lot of Python libraries are present including Open3D [1], Panda3D [2], PyTorch3D [3], Mayavi [4], etc. For the very paper, we used Open3D which is an open-source library for 3D data processing and visualization in Python. It provides a wide range of functionalities for working with 3D data, including point clouds, meshes, and volumetric data. Open3D aims to be a versatile and user-friendly library, allowing researchers and developers to efficiently manipulate, analyze, and visualize 3D data.

In the context of using the advancements of 3D point clouds in the field of plant phenomics, the present study was conducted with the following objectives: (1) capturing multi-view images of chickpea plant using high-end cameras, placed at Limma Tech facility, Nanaji Deshmukh Plant Phenomics Centre situated at ICAR-IARI New Delhi [5]; (2) reconstructing the canopy point cloud of captured images; (3) processing the point cloud and performing clustering operation on it to separate plant canopy from the other information, i.e. noise present in the image.

2 Literature Review

Automated approaches using 3D image processing to measure plant traits can improve the efficiency and accuracy of plant phenotyping, which is critical to understand different aspects like how genetic and environmental factors are linked to plant phenotypes [6–8]. This being said, the plants exhibit architectural complexities due to self-occlusions and leaf crossovers, which create challenges to accurate estimation of phenotype parameters, e.g. leaf length, stem angle, and leaf curvature, using 2D images [9]. To overcome these challenges, attempts have been made by researchers to reconstruct a 3D model of a plant and for accurate estimation of their phenotypes where we can analyze the plant in 360° and with more detail. 3D image processing allows for precise and automated measurement of plant traits that were traditionally challenging to assess in 2D [10, 11]. The results of this processing can be applied in basic plant research and crop plant breeding [12–14]. These results with the adoption of technologies are also expected to relieve the conventional phenotyping bottleneck in conventional 2D approaches [15].

A lot of work has already been done in the field of plant phenomics with 3D point clouds in specific areas/crops. For instance, in their paper Cai et al., 2013 identified temporary wilting of zucchini leaves from the 3D laser-scanned images [16]. Roscher et al., 2016 combined hyperspectral image information with 3D geometry information for the detection of leaf spot disease symptoms on sugar beet plants [17].

Further, Zermas et al., 2018 proposed a pipeline that takes advantage of the technology to create a detailed 3D image of corn plants and segment it into the basic elements like the ground, the plants, the plant stems, and the plant leaves [18]. Elnashef, Filin, and Lati, 2019; Paulus, 2019; and Bekkering, Huang, and Tian, 2020 developed segmentation models for organ level plant phenotyping of wheat using machine learning techniques [19–21]. He, Harrison, and Li, 2017 developed an imaging system, which captured 360° view strawberry fruit. A 3D image of the sample was derived and analyzed with custom-developed software to estimate berry height, length, width, volume, color, and achene number [22].

Gongal, Karkee, and Amatya, 2018 developed an apple fruit size estimation pipeline using a 3D machine vision system. The results were achieved by estimating the major axes of the apples [23]. Mortensen et al., 2018 proposed a novel method for segmenting lettuce in colored 3D Image and estimating its fresh weight. The proposed segmentation method operates by clustering points into leaves. From the segmented lettuce point clouds, the volume, surface area, leaf cover area, and height predictors were extracted and correlated to the fresh weight [24]. Laxman et al., 2018 performed non-invasive quantification of tomato plant biomass through digital imaging using a phenomics platform. They observed highly significant correlations between actual plant fresh mass and digital biomass [25].

Talking about the technique that is used to convert a series of 2D images to 3D point cloud, Structure from Motion(SfM) approach uses a set of 2D images captured by RGB cameras to reconstruct a 3D model from the object of interest [26]. This approach is mostly used on UAV (Unmanned Aerial Vehicle) platforms. As this approach just needs a camera for the image acquisition the hardware setup is very small and lightweight. The method presented by Liu et al., 2017 is based on the Structure from Motion method. They reconstructed an accurate 3D model of the plant using SfM[27]. Zhang et al., 2016 developed a high efficiency Multi-Camera Photography (MCP) system combining Multi-View Stereovision (MVS) with the Structure from Motion (SfM). They measured six variables of nursery paprika plants and investigated the accuracy of 3D models reconstructed from photos taken by four lens types at four different positions [26].

By adopting 3D image processing for plant phenotyping, researchers aimed to overcome the limitations of traditional 2D techniques, gain a deeper understanding of plant morphology, improve measurement precision, and enhance the efficiency of data analysis in large-scale phenotyping studies. These advantages have been identified in previous research, highlighting the potential of 3D imaging techniques to advance plant phenotyping studies which motivated us to take the path of 3D image processing for the field of plant phenotyping.

3 Methodology

The flow of processes as shown in Fig. 1 for the present study is as follows:

1. Data Acquisition: Data was collected in the form of RGB images from Nanaji Deshmukh Plant Phenomics Centre, ICAR-IARI, New Delhi. 72 images of a Chickpea plant were captured at the distance of 5°C. These images were captured through RGB camera (LemnaTec GmbH, Aachen, Germany) having a spatial resolution of 6576 × 4384 pixels at two view angles, i.e. from nadir and from side [5].
2. Data Preprocessing: The collected images were processed using Python libraries. These were first cropped and then resized so that there is no mismatch between the sizes of the images.

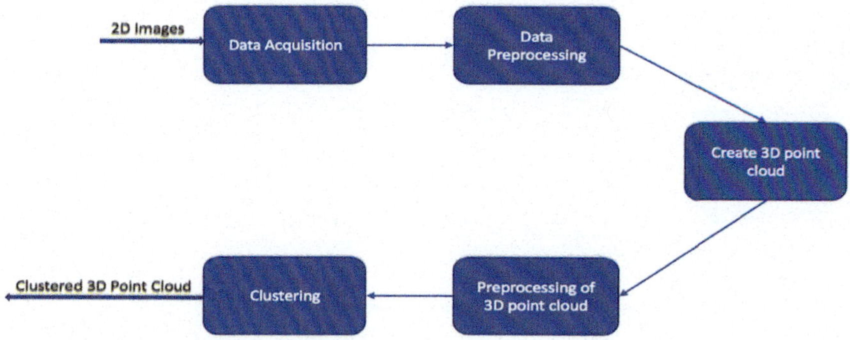

Fig. 1 Schematic for canopy point cloud reconstruction and clustering of 3D images

3. Creating 3D point cloud: The processed images were then used to construct a 3D point cloud. The task was achieved using the software Agisoft Metashape Professional Edition, which is a Structure from Motion (SfM) and photogrammetry tool that allows users to create a 3D object from a series of photos.
4. Preprocessing of 3D point cloud: Open3D library of Python was used to process the generated 3D point cloud. Downsampling method was used to reduce the number of points in a point cloud.
5. Clustering: The point clouds of plant canopy were separated from the rest of the portion in the point cloud that includes pot in the image. Clustering is performed using Open3D library using the cluster-dbscan function. The DBSCAN method of clustering was used in the function to cluster the point cloud.
   DBSCAN (Density-Based Spatial Clustering of Applications with Noise) is a density-based clustering algorithm commonly used in machine learning. It is designed to group together data points that are closely packed in a high-density region while also identifying outliers or noise points.

4 Experimental Details

1. Reconstruction of Chickpea point cloud: The point cloud Fig. 2c was reconstructed from a sequence of 72 images of Chickpea plant. Figure 2a shows the raw images, i.e. the image of Chickpea plant received from the LemnaTec imaging system. Python libraries were used to crop the raw image. The result of which is shown in Fig. 2b.
2. Downsampling the constructed point cloud: We used Open3D library of Python programming language to reduce the number of points in the Chickpea point cloud. The result of which can be seen in Fig. 2d.
3. Performing clustering on processed point cloud: Open3D library was again used to perform clustering on the processed point cloud. After applying the clustering

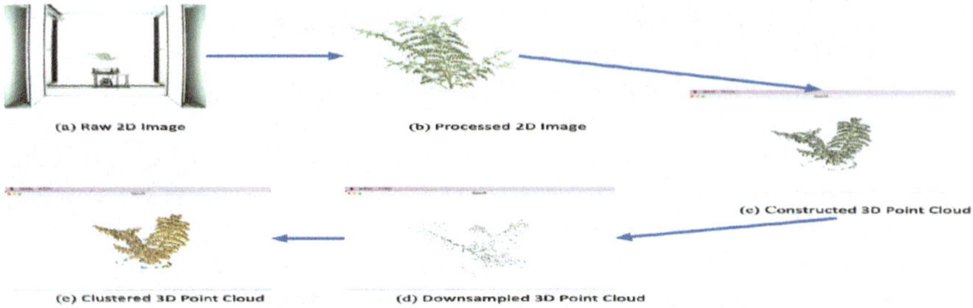

Fig. 2 Schematic for canopy point cloud reconstruction and clustering of 3D images

operation, we get a clustered point cloud shown in Fig. 2(e), which is separating the plant canopy from other information/noise, parts of the plant pot in this case.

5 Conclusion and Future Perspective

In the present study, a high-quality image sequence of a field crop canopy is reconstructed into a 3D point cloud on which a clustering operation was performed. The findings of the present study provide opportunities in the processing of 3D point clouds converted from 2D RGB images in the field of high-throughput plant phenotyping. This procedure allows for the extraction of detailed 3D information from 2D images, enabling a more comprehensive analysis of plant structures and traits. Advancements in point cloud generation combined with automation, deep learning, and robotics can contribute to more efficient and accurate plant phenotyping techniques with significant implications for agriculture and crop management. With that accurate measurements of plant parameters, such as height, leaf area, branching patterns, and overall architecture, can be obtained in a non-destructive and efficient manner.

References

1. Zhou Q-Y, Park J, Koltun V (2018) Open3D: a modern library for 3D data processing
2. Goslin M, Mine MR (2004) The panda3d graphics engine. Computer 37(10):112–114
3. Ravi N, Reizenstein J, Novotny D, Gordon T, Lo W-Y, Johnson J, Gkioxari G (2020) Accelerating 3d deep learning with pytorch3d. arXiv:2007.08501
4. Ramachandran P, Varoquaux G (2011) Mayavi: 3d visualization of scientific data. Comput Sci Eng 13(2):40–51
5. Shivani Nagar RD, Kumar S (2020) Nanaji deshmukh plant phenomics facility: a new dimension in Indian agricultural research. Food Sci Rep 1(3):65
6. Furbank RT, Tester M (2011) Phenomics-technologies to relieve the phenotyping bottleneck. Trends Plant Sci 16(12):635–644

7. Kjaer KH, Ottosen C-O (2015) 3d laser triangulation for plant phenotyping in challenging environments. Sensors 15(6):13533–13547
8. Fiorani F, Schurr U (2013) Future scenarios for plant phenotyping. Annu Rev Plant Biol 64:267–291
9. Das Choudhury S, Samal A, Awada T (2019) Leveraging image analysis for high-throughput plant phenotyping. Front Plant Sci 10:508
10. Finkel E (2009) With 'phenomics,'plant scientists hope to shift breeding into overdrive
11. Berry JC, Fahlgren N, Pokorny AA, Bart RS, Veley KM (2018) An automated, high-throughput method for standardizing image color profiles to improve image-based plant phenotyping. PeerJ 6:5727
12. Japes B, Mack J, Rist F, Herzog K, Töpfer R, Steinhage V (2018) Multi-view semantic labeling of 3d point clouds for automated plant phenotyping. arXiv:1805.03994
13. Magomadov V (2019) Deep learning and its role in smart agriculture. J Phys: Conf Ser 1399:044109. IOP Publishing
14. Kamilaris A, Prenafeta-Boldú FX (2018) Deep learning in agriculture: a survey. Comput Electron Agric 147:70–90
15. Furbank RT, Tester M (2011) Phenomics-technologies to relieve the phenotyping bottleneck. Trends Plant Sci 16(12):635–644
16. Cai X, Sun Y, Zhao Y, Damerow L, Lammers PS, Sun W, Lin J, Zheng L, Tang Y (2013) Smart detection of leaf wilting by 3d image processing and 2d fourier transform. Comput Electron Agric 90:68–75
17. Roscher R, Behmann J, Mahlein A-K, Dupuis J, Kuhlmann H, Plümer L (2016) Detection of disease symptoms on hyperspectral 3d plant models. ISPRS Ann Photogrammetry, Remote Sensing and Spatial Inf Sci 3:89–96
18. Zermas D, Morellas V, Mulla D, Papanikolopoulos N (2018) Extracting phenotypic characteristics of corn crops through the use of reconstructed 3d models. In: 2018 IEEE/RSJ international conference on intelligent robots and systems (IROS). IEEE, pp 8247–8254
19. Bekkering CS, Huang J, Tian L (2020) Image-based, organ-level plant phenotyping for wheat improvement. Agronomy 10(9):1287
20. Elnashef B, Filin S, Lati RN (2019) Tensor-based classification and segmentation of three-dimensional point clouds for organ-level plant phenotyping and growth analysis. Comput Electron Agric 156:51–61
21. Paulus S (2019) Measuring crops in 3d: using geometry for plant phenotyping. Plant Methods 15(1):1–13
22. He JQ, Harrison RJ, Li B (2017) A novel 3d imaging system for strawberry phenotyping. Plant Methods 13(1):1–8
23. Gongal A, Karkee M, Amatya S (2018) Apple fruit size estimation using a 3d machine vision system. Inf Process Agric 5(4):498–503
24. Mortensen AK, Bender A, Whelan B, Barbour MM, Sukkarieh S, Karstoft H, Gislum R (2018) Segmentation of lettuce in coloured 3d point clouds for fresh weight estimation. Comput Electron Agric 154:373–381
25. Laxman R, Hemamalini P, Bhatt R, Sadashiva A (2018) Non-invasive quantification of tomato (solanum lycopersicum l.) plant biomass through digital imaging using phenomics platform. Indian J Plant Physiol 23:369–375
26. Zhang Y, Teng P, Shimizu Y, Hosoi F, Omasa K (2016) Estimating 3d leaf and stem shape of nursery paprika plants by a novel multi-camera photography system. Sensors 16(6):874

A Deep Learning-Driven Contactless Finger Recognition System

Aman Attris, Nagasai Bharat, Vijay Anand, and Vivek Kanhangad

Abstract Fingerprint is one of the most widely explored biometric traits. Specifically, contact-based fingerprint recognition systems reign supreme due to their effectiveness, portability, and research advancements in this field. However, these are issues such as hygiene concerns, sensor degradation due to constant physical contact, and latent fingerprint threats. In this paper, we present the details of a fingerprint recognition system that captures finger photos without contact. The captured finger photos are then processed to obtain global and local (minutiae-based) features. Specifically, a Siamese convolutional neural network is designed to extract global features from a given finger photo. Finally, the matching scores computed using the global and local features are fused to generate the final matching score between the probe and the reference fingerprint templates. We have developed the proposed system using the Nvidia Jetson Nano development kit. The developed system performs contactless fingerprint recognition in real time with minimum latency and acceptable matching accuracy. The performance of the proposed system is evaluated on an in-house IITI contactless fingerprint dataset (IITI-CFD) containing 105 train and 100 test subjects. The proposed system achieves an equal error rate of 2.19% on IITI-CFD.

Keywords Contactless fingerprint · Fingerprint recognition · Siamese CNN

1 Introduction

Faced with the challenges of identity theft from password and PIN-based authentication systems, alternative technological solutions have been explored. One of these technologies, biometrics, has quickly proved itself as the most suitable means of

---

A. Attris · N. Bharat · V. Anand (✉) · V. Kanhangad
Discipline of Electrical Engineering, Indian Institute of Technology Indore, Indore 453552, India
e-mail: vijayanand.phd20@gmail.com

V. Kanhangad
e-mail: kvivek@iiti.ac.in

S. Chaudhury et al. (eds.), *Computer Vision, Pattern Recognition, Image Processing, and Graphics*, Lecture Notes in Electrical Engineering 1218,
https://doi.org/10.1007/978-981-97-5212-6_9

authenticating and identifying individuals in a fast, safe, and reliable way, using unique biometric traits. Among different biometric traits, the fingerprint is perhaps the most widely explored one. Generally, a contact-based AFRS employs an advanced complementary MOSFET (CMOS) image sensor for capturing fingerprint image [22]. Non-linear spatial distortions and low-contrast regions due to improper pressures of the finger on the sensor platen are some of the challenges that are common in contact-based biometric systems [22]. Constant physical contact of different fingers with the sensor in contact-based AFRS often causes hygiene concerns among the users, as it can lead to the spread of contagious diseases. Also, the system might not work as expected due to the accumulation of dust and dirt on the sensor. Furthermore, contact-based sensors have a high maintenance cost as their inappropriate use can lead to faults. There is also a security threat, since the fingerprint acquisition process leaves latent prints of the finger on the sensor surface, which can be lifted.

The aforementioned issues led the researchers to explore contactless fingerprint recognition approaches that employ a camera sensor, which captures fingerprint images in a suitably designed capturing environment. Piuri and Scotti [25] investigated techniques to process the camera images of fingertips such that the processed images are similar to the fingerprint images captured using a dedicated sensor. Labati et al. [18] proposed an approach that corrects perspective deformations and improper fingertip alignments in a CCD camera sensor-based contactless fingerprint recognition system. Researchers have also developed techniques [10–12] to enhance the ridge patterns in fingerprint images captured using a camera sensor. More recently, Lin and Kumar [19] presented a CNN-based framework to match contactless and contact-based fingerprint images. Michael et al. [24] developed a contactless biometric system that relies on features extracted from the visible and infrared images of hand geometry, palm print, palmar knuckle print, palm vein, and finger vein. Kumar [17] explored the possibility of human recognition using contactless finger knuckle images with varying poses. Smartphone-based finger photo authentication has been explored in [6, 20, 21, 26].

A review of the literature indicates that the existing research in contactless fingerprint biometrics has focused only on developing novel approaches for recognition and despite the advances in sensor technology and edge computation power, no attempt has been made to develop a prototype by implementing the algorithms in hardware. This, along with recent advancements in deep learning for biometrics, motivated us to develop a deep learning driven contactless fingerprint recognition system and create a prototype to demonstrate its practical utility. Specifically, the objective of our work is to develop a contactless fingerprint recognition system (CFRS), incorporating both deep learning and standard fingerprint matching algorithm, and implement the system in hardware with minimum latency and high matching accuracy for real-time operations.

2 Proposed System

Our CFRS consists of three major modules, namely, the contactless finger image-capturing module, the CNN-based global feature matching module, and the minutiae feature matching module. The proposed CFRS captures finger images in a contactless manner using Raspberry Pi NoIR camera V2 that has a Sony IMX219 8-megapixel sensor. A schematic diagram of the proposed system is presented in Fig. 1. As can be seen, our approach employs a customized Siamese CNN architecture to process images captured using the camera sensor in the system. Specifically, the Siamese network in our system generates fixed-length embeddings for the input fingerprint images. These embeddings are then used to calculate a similarity score between the probe and the reference finger images. We have also enhanced the captured finger image and performed minutia-based matching using the standard NIST biometric image software (NBIS) [29]. Finally, the scores obtained from both of the modules are fused to obtain the final score.

The development of our system involved the following two stages: developing algorithms and modifying the existing ones to increase the matching accuracy; and implementing it in hardware with minimum latency. Generally, one comes across problems like perspective distortion and deformation [18] when using contactless fingerprint images. Also, the lighting conditions affect greatly the quality, thereby the amount of information in the captured fingerprint image. To circumvent the aforementioned issues with contactless imaging, we have utilized global texture features as well as local features (minutiae information) for extracting as much discriminative information as possible from the input fingerprint image. Therefore, we propose a parallel approach (Fig. 1) that uses deep learning to extract global fingerprint features [30] and state-of-the-art minutiae matching approach that utilizes local features. In the following subsections, we describe each of the modules involved in the proposed CFRS.

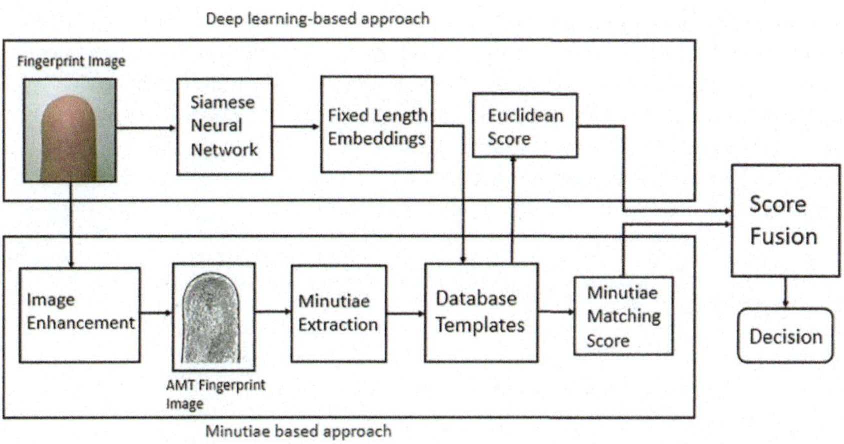

Fig. 1 Schematic diagram of the proposed system

2.1 Minutiae-Based Approach

Ridge-Valley Map Extraction Given a fingerprint image, the first step in minutiae-based approach is to extract its ridge-valley map. In the proposed CFRS, image enhancement part plays a vital role since contactless finger images contain less discriminative information as compared with images acquired using traditional contact-based sensors. We have performed adaptive mean thresholding (AMT) on grayscale finger image to separate it into a foreground containing the pattern of interest and a background based on the difference in pixel intensities of each area [7].

Minutiae Matching To extract minutiae points, we have used the standard NBIS minutiae detector MINDTCT [29]. It automatically detects and records minutiae information in the form of triplet $[x, y, \theta]$, where (x, y) is the position of minutia point and θ represents the orientation. The minutiae information obtained by the MINDTCT algorithm is then used to perform matching. Specifically, the NBIS fingerprint matching algorithm, BOZORTH3, is incorporated for minutiae matching [29]. It calculates similarity scores (S_m) using matched minutiae.

2.2 Deep Learning-Based Approach

The CNNs have been proven to be highly effective for various computer vision tasks, especially image classification [8, 15, 27, 28]. In the proposed approach, to match a given pair of finger images and generate a matching score, a customized Siamese network [23] is employed. While constructing the Siamese architecture, we have taken care to limit the number of parameters utilized in convolution layers and dense layers. This is done to reduce the latency of the system when deployed on the hardware. The number of the convolution layers was limited to 3 having 4, 8, and 8 filters and a batch normalization layer followed each convolution layer. At the end of all the convolution layers, an average pooling is employed so that the number of parameters in the dense layers is reduced. Table 1 presents the architecture of the Siamese CNN used in the proposed CFRS. During training, the objective is to minimize the distance between embeddings of a pair of images belonging to the same class (finger), while maximizing the distance between embeddings of a pair of images belonging to two different fingers. This is achieved using the distance aware contrastive loss function, which is defined as follows [9]:

$$L = (1 - Y)\frac{1}{2}(D_w)^2 + (Y)\frac{1}{2}(max(0, m - D_w))^2 \tag{1}$$

where

$$Y = \begin{cases} 0, & same\ class \\ 1, & different\ class \end{cases} \tag{2}$$

Table 1 The details of the CNN architecture

Layer name	input size	Filter size	No. of filters	Padding	Stride	Output size
Conv1	310 × 240 × 3	3 × 3	4	1	1	310 × 240 × 4
BatchNorm	310 × 240 × 4	–	–	–	–	310 × 240 × 4
Conv2	310 × 240 × 4	3	8	1	1	310 × 240 × 8
BatchNorm	310 × 240 × 8	–	–	–	–	310 × 240 × 8
Conv3	310 × 240 × 8	3	8	1	1	310 × 240 × 8
BatchNorm	310 × 240 × 8	–	–	–	–	310 × 240 × 8
AveragePool	310 × 240 × 8	2	–	–	2	155 × 120 × 8
Flatten	155 × 120 × 8	–	–	–	–	148800 × 1
Dense1	148800 × 1	–	–	–	–	256 × 1
Dense2	256 × 1	–	–	–	–	128 × 1
Dense3	128 × 1	–	–	–	–	16 × 1

D_w represents the Euclidean distance between output vectors or embeddings of size 16 × 1 of the Siamese network and m is the margin value, which ensures that dissimilar pairs beyond this margin do not contribute to the loss.

A schematic diagram of the Siamese network employed in our system is presented in Fig. 2. At the time of verification, a pair of embeddings generated from the probe and reference finger image (stored as a template in the database) are compared using Euclidean distance. The resulting dissimilarity score is then converted to a similarity score (S_d). As described previously, both the minutiae matching module and the deep learning-based module generate their respective scores, which are represented

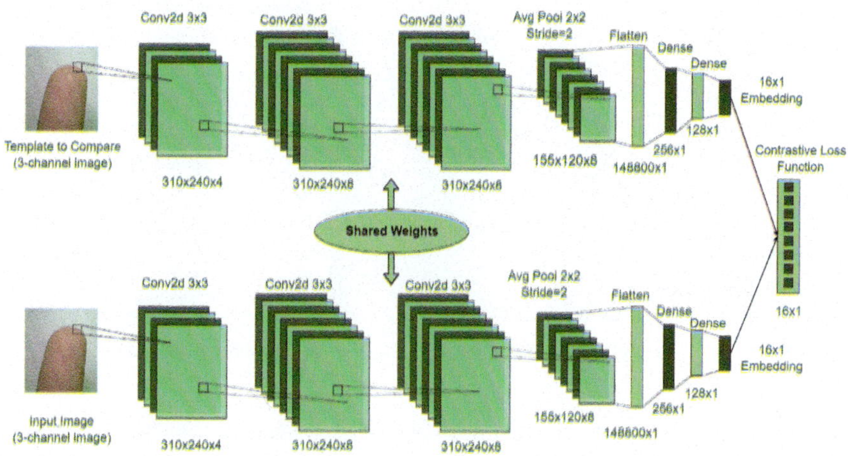

Fig. 2 The architecture of the Siamese network

as S_m and S_d. Prior to their fusion, both the scores are normalized to the range [0, 1] using min-max normalization [14]. Finally, a weighted sum is computed as

$$S_f = w_d S_d + w_m S_m \tag{3}$$

where w_d and w_m represent the weight associated with scores obtained from the deep learning and the minutiae matching-based modules, respectively. These weights w_d and w_m have been set empirically to 0.4 and 0.6.

2.3 Hardware Implementation

Electrical Components and Image-Capturing Environment In our system, we required a sensor which can work in bright as well as dim light. Therefore, we have used Raspberry Pi NoIR Camera V2 [2]. It has a Sony IMX219 8-megapixel sensor, and it does not employ an infrared filter (NoIR). We have used NVIDIA Jetson Nano Developer Kit [1] as a computing system. It is a compact but powerful embedded computer that enabled us to run our matching algorithms. It requires at most 5 Watts of DC power supply. To capture good quality finger images, we have designed a finger image-capturing environment (Fig. 3a) using cardboard. As presented in Fig. 3a, an LED bulb is used to illuminate the capturing environment. The camera sensor is fixed at the top to capture image of the finger placed beneath it. A small square opening is made on the front of the cardboard to present the finger to the sensor. Our system is designed to capture only the fingerprint on distal phalanges, on which we have applied AMT in real time to minimize the latency (Fig. 3b).

(a) CFRS prototype (b) Real-time AMT output

Fig. 3 CFRS prototype showing finger image-capturing setup and the segmented finger image displayed (real time) on the monitor

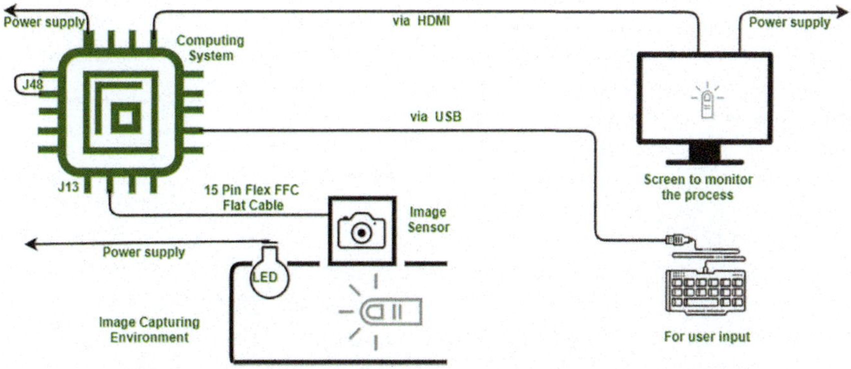

Fig. 4 A schematic diagram showing interconnection of various components of CFRS

System Implementation Methodology Our CFRS is designed to work in the verification mode. In this mode of operation, there are two phases, namely, enrollment and verification. In enrollment phase, our system captures three finger photos of the user's finger in different placements and orientations. The average of the three 16×1 embeddings corresponding to the three finger photos from the deep-learning model, and minutiae data of one of the finger photos are stored separately as templates in the local database and a unique ID is assigned to the user. At the time of verification, the system first captures the finger photo of the user and asks for the unique ID provided during the enrollment phase. Using the captured finger photo, the system generates its 16×1 embedding, and minutiae data and then computes a similarity score through a comparison with the templates of the claimed ID stored in the database. If the similarity score is above the system threshold, the system displays *correct match established* message on the connected monitor.

Hardware Connections A detailed schematic of all the components, along with connections, is presented in Fig. 4. As can be observed, the image sensor is connected to the computing system's camera connector J13 pin. A monitor is connected via HDMI cable along with a keyboard and a mouse via USB cables. The image sensor is attached to the top of the image-capturing environment. This setup requires the users to present fingers facing up inside the image-capturing environment. All the components are powered separately.

3 Experimental Results and Discussion

3.1 Database Preparation

As presented in Fig. 3a, we have developed a contactless image-capturing environment which is used to collect an in-house contactless fingerprint dataset referred to as IITI-CFD. Specifically, we have captured a total of 1640 finger images from 205

Table 2 Details of IITI-CFD

Dataset	Image size (pixels)	Fingers	Images per finger	Total images
Training set	310 × 240	105	8	840
Test set	310 × 240	100	8	800

fingers, each contributing eight impressions. A detailed description of IITI-CFD is presented in Table 2. To train the CNN-based approach, IITI-CFD is divided into train and test sets. Specifically, the training set consists of 840 finger images from 105 fingers and the remaining images from 100 fingers from the test set.

3.2 Performance Measures

To evaluate the performance of the developed system, we have employed the following performance measures namely, equal error rate (EER), FMR100, and FMR1000 [4]. FMR is defined as the percentage of impostor pairs whose similarity score is greater than th, while FNMR is the percentage of genuine pairs whose similarity score is lower than th. Generally, the performance of a system is reported at all operating points (th) by plotting the receiver operating characteristic (ROC) curve or the detection error trade-off (DET) curve. In this work, we have plotted DET curve and used to calculate FMR100 and FMR1000 of the proposed system.

3.3 Experimental Results

The Siamese network has been trained using the finger images in the IITI-CFD training set. Specifically, the model has been trained for 70 epochs using the adaptive moment estimation (ADAM) [16] to optimize the loss function. We have employed ReLU activation function [3] and batch normalization [13] after each convolutional layer in the proposed model. The model has been trained on the Google Co-laboratory (Colab) platform [5] that uses a Tesla K80 which has 2496 CUDA cores as the GPU and a single-core hyper-threaded Xeon Processor with 2.3 GHz of processing speed. Besides, 12 GB GDDR5 VRAM was also provided by Google Colab.

In order to calculate the performance metrics, a set of genuine scores are obtained by comparing a pair of images of the same finger and a set of impostor scores are obtained by comparing a pair of images of two different fingers. For test finger images, the feature embeddings are obtained using the trained Siamese network and Euclidean distance between a set of genuine pairs and a set of imposter pairs is calculated. These scores are then used in computing the EER and plotting the DET curve by varying the decision threshold. For the test dataset containing 800

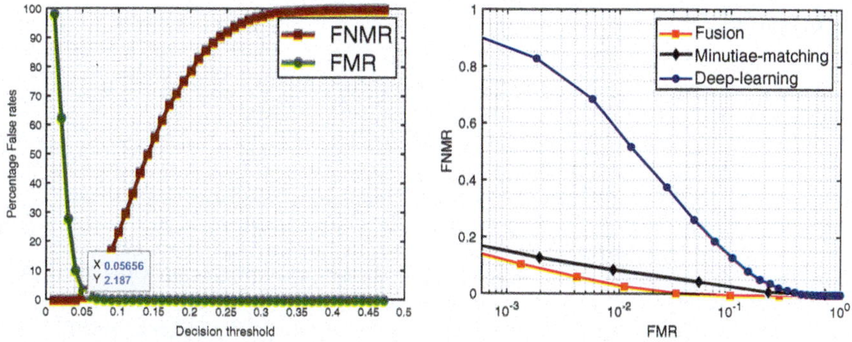

(a) Score fusion based approach (b) DET Curve

Fig. 5 Performance curve

Table 3 Performance comparison

Approach	EER	FMR100	FMR1000
Deep learning	11.39%	0.573	0.872
Minutiae matching	4.09%	0.081	0.150
Score fusion	2.19%	0.037	0.123

images (8 images each from 100 fingers), a total of 2800 genuine pairs and 14850 imposter pairs are formed and Euclidean distance between feature embeddings of each of these pairs is calculated. The same set of genuine and impostor pairs was also used for evaluating the NBIS-based minutiae matching approach. Figure 5a presents the plots of FNMR and FMR by varying threshold values. The intersection of the FNMR and FMR provides the EER of the system. The EERs for the individual modules, i.e., deep learning-based approach, minutiae-based approach, and score fusion are summarized in Table 3. Further, DET curve depicting the error-rate trade-off at all possible operating points is plotted in Fig. 5b. FMR100 and FMR1000 derived from the DET curves of all three approaches are summarized in Table 3 The results presented in Table 3 suggest that the fusion of the deep learning score with the minutiae matching score provides a significant improvement in the final results as compared with the individual approaches. In the developed CFRS, the fused score value is compared with a threshold to generate the final decision of the system. On average, the developed system takes 3 s to complete a verification task. The experimental results presented in this section clearly indicate that minutiae-based matching performs better than global feature-based matching for contactless fingerprint recognition. Their score-level fusion results in a significant improvement in EER, FMR100, and FMR1000. The proposed approach can serve as the baseline for real-time contactless fingerprint recognition systems.

References

1. Nvidia Jetson Nano Development Kit. https://developer.nvidia.com/embedded/jetson-nano-developer-kit, [Online; accessed 23-Jan-2020]
2. Raspberry Pi NoIR V2 Cam. https://www.raspberrypi.org/products/pi-noir-camera-v2, [Online; accessed 23-Jan-2020]
3. Agarap AF (2018) Deep learning using rectified linear units (relu). arXiv:1803.08375
4. Cappelli R, Ferrara M, Maltoni D, Turroni F (2011) Fingerprint verification competition at ijcb2011. In: 2011 international joint conference on biometrics (IJCB), pp 1–6
5. Carneiro T, Da NóBrega RVM, Nepomuceno T, Bian G, De Albuquerque VHC, Filho PPR (2018) Performance analysis of google colaboratory as a tool for accelerating deep learning applications. IEEE Access 6:61677–61685. https://doi.org/10.1109/ACCESS.2018.2874767
6. Chopra S, Malhotra A, Vatsa M, Singh R (2018) Unconstrained fingerphoto database. In: 2018 IEEE/CVF conference on computer vision and pattern recognition workshops (CVPRW), pp 630–6308
7. Davies E (2012) Computer and machine vision: theory, algorithms and practicalities, 4th edn. Academic Press
8. Guo T, Dong J, Li H, Gao Y (2017) Simple convolutional neural network on image classification. In: 2017 IEEE 2nd international conference on big data analysis (ICBDA), pp 721–724. https://doi.org/10.1109/ICBDA.2017.8078730
9. Hadsell R, Chopra S, LeCun Y (2006) Dimensionality reduction by learning an invariant mapping. In: Proceedings of the 2006 IEEE computer society conference on computer vision and pattern recognition CVPR '06, vol 2. IEEE Computer Society, USA, pp 1735–1742. https://doi.org/10.1109/CVPR.2006.100
10. Hiew B, Teoh AB, Ngo DC (2006) Preprocessing of fingerprint images captured with a digital camera. In: 2006 9th international conference on control, automation, robotics and vision, pp 1–6. https://doi.org/10.1109/ICARCV.2006.345189
11. Hiew BY, Teoh ABJ, Ngo DCL (2006) Automatic digital camera based fingerprint image preprocessing. In: International conference on computer graphics, imaging and visualisation (CGIV'06), pp 182–189.https://doi.org/10.1109/CGIV.2006.27
12. Hiew BY, Teoh ABJ, Pang YH (2007) Digital camera based fingerprint recognition. In: 2007 IEEE international conference on telecommunications and Malaysia international conference on communications, pp 676–681. https://doi.org/10.1109/ICTMICC.2007.4448572
13. Ioffe S, Szegedy C (2015) Batch normalization: accelerating deep network training by reducing internal covariate shift. CoRR arXiv:1502.03167
14. Jain A, Nandakumar K, Ross A (Dec2005) Score normalization in multimodal biometric systems. Pattern Recognit 38(12):2270–2285. https://doi.org/10.1016/j.patcog.2005.01.012
15. Jmour N, Zayen S, Abdelkrim A (2018) Convolutional neural networks for image classification. In: 2018 international conference on advanced systems and electric technologies (IC_ASET), pp 397–402
16. Kingma DP, Adam JB (2014) A method for stochastic optimization. arXiv:1412.6980
17. Kumar A (2019) Toward pose invariant and completely contactless finger knuckle recognition. IEEE Trans Biom Behav Identity Sci 1(3):201–209. https://doi.org/10.1109/TBIOM.2019.2928868
18. Labati RD, Genovese A, Piuri V, Scotti F (2013) Contactless fingerprint recognition: a neural approach for perspective and rotation effects reduction. In: 2013 IEEE symposium on computational intelligence in biometrics and identity management (CIBIM), pp 22–30. https://doi.org/10.1109/CIBIM.2013.6607909
19. Lin C, Kumar A (2019) A cnn-based framework for comparison of contactless to contact-based fingerprints. IEEE Trans Inf Forensics Secur 14(3):662–676. https://doi.org/10.1109/TIFS.2018.2854765
20. Malhotra A, Chopra S, Vatsa M, Singh R (2019) User authentication via finger-selfies. Springer International Publishing, Cham, pp 21–47

21. Malhotra A, Sankaran A, Vatsa M, Singh R (2020) On matching finger-selfies using deep scattering networks. IEEE Trans Biom Behav Identity Sci 2(4):350–362
22. Maltoni D, Maio D, Jain A, Prabhakar S (2009) Handbook of fingerprint recognition, 2nd edn. Springer Science & Business Media
23. Melekhov I, Kannala J, Rahtu E (2016) Siamese network features for image matching. In: 2016 23rd international conference on pattern recognition (ICPR), pp 378–383. https://doi.org/10.1109/ICPR.2016.7899663
24. Michael GKO, Connie T, Teoh ABJ (2012) A contactless biometric system using multiple hand features. J Vis Commun Image Represent 23(7):1068–1084
25. Piuri V, Scotti F (2008) Fingerprint biometrics via low-cost sensors and webcams. In: 2008 IEEE second international conference on biometrics: theory, applications and systems, pp 1–6. https://doi.org/10.1109/BTAS.2008.4699379
26. Sankaran A, Malhotra A, Mittal A, Vatsa M, Singh R (2015) On smartphone camera based fingerphoto authentication. In: 2015 IEEE 7th international conference on biometrics theory, applications and systems (BTAS), pp 1–7. https://doi.org/10.1109/BTAS.2015.7358782
27. Sharma N, Jain V, Mishra A (2018) An analysis of convolutional neural networks for image classification. Procedia Comput Sci 132:377–384. https://doi.org/10.1016/j.procs.2018.05.198, http://www.sciencedirect.com/science/article/pii/S1877050918309335. International conference on computational intelligence and data science
28. Sultana F, Sufian A, Dutta P (2018) Advancements in image classification using convolutional neural network. In: 2018 fourth international conference on research in computational intelligence and communication networks (ICRCICN), pp 122–129
29. Watson CI, Garris MD, Tabassi E, Wilson CL, Mccabe RM, Janet S, Ko K (2007) User's guide to NIST biometric image software (NBIS)
30. Zhang F, Xin S, Feng J (2019) Combining global and minutia deep features for partial high-resolution fingerprint matching. Pattern Recognit Lett 119:139–147. https://doi.org/10.1016/j.patrec.2017.09.014

Deep Features for Contactless Fingerprint Presentation Attack Detection: Can They Be Generalized?

Hailin Li and Raghavendra Ramachandra

Abstract The rapid evolution of high-end smartphones with advanced high-resolution cameras has resulted in contactless capture of fingerprint biometrics that are more reliable and suitable for verification. Similar to other biometric systems, contactless fingerprint verification systems are vulnerable to presentation attacks. In this paper, we present a comparative study on the generalizability of seven different pre-trained Convolutional Neural Networks (CNNs) and a Vision Transformer (ViT) to reliably detect presentation attacks. Extensive experiments were carried out on publicly available smartphone-based presentation attack datasets using four different Presentation Attack Instruments (PAI). The detection performance of the eighth deep feature technique was evaluated using the leave-one-out protocol to benchmark the generalization performance for unseen PAI. The obtained results indicated the best generalization performance with the ResNet50 CNN.

Keywords Biometrics · Fingerprint · Attacks · Spoofing · Smartphone

1 Introduction

Contactless fingerprint verification is widely accepted and deployed in various access control applications. The outbreak of COVID-19 further accelerated the demand for contactless capture devices for the inflection-free and reliable person verification. The contactless fingerprint can be captured using dedicated sensors, in which fingerprint images are captured in a contactless fashion and processed further to perform verification. A contactless fingerprint can also be captured using a smartphone, either using a frontal or back camera. The back camera from the smartphone is prominently used to capture fingerprints by considering the high image quality, usability,

H. Li · R. Ramachandra (✉)
Norwegian University of Science and Technology (NTNU), Gjøvik, Norway
e-mail: raghavendra.ramachandra@ntnu.no

H. Li
e-mail: hailin.li@ntnu.no

S. Chaudhury et al. (eds.), *Computer Vision, Pattern Recognition, Image Processing, and Graphics*, Lecture Notes in Electrical Engineering 1218,
https://doi.org/10.1007/978-981-97-5212-6_10

and good resolution that are useful for extracting minutiae features. The contactless fingerprint captured using smartphones is also referred to as a fingerphoto because the captured fingerprint images are postprocessed using build image processing tools before they are used for biometric authentication. Fingerphoto recognition has been studied extensively and has achieved promising results [12].

The popularity of smartphone-based fingerprint verification systems has increased their deployment and attracted the attention of attackers. This resulted in the vulnerability of contactless fingerprint or fingerphoto-based biometric systems for different types of Presentation Attack Instruments (PAI), such as 2D and 3D print artifacts, replay attacks, and generating replicas of the fingerprint using different materials. The vulnerability of contactless fingerprint systems has encouraged researchers to develop Presentation Attack Detection (PAD) techniques to improve system reliability. Table 1 summarizes the existing techniques for contactless fingerprint PAD, which can be broadly classified as hand-crafted features (e.g., micro-texture, gradients, and light reflection) and deep features, based on which the pre-trained CNNs are used for feature extraction. Despite several existing PAD techniques, the generalization of these techniques for unseen PAI has not been well exploited, particularly with deep features. Readers can refer to a comprehensive survey on the fingerprint PAD [8] for a more detailed description of the existing PAD. Owing to the small size of Presentation Attack (PA) datasets, the use of a pre-trained CNN as a feature extraction method is widely employed in the literature. Therefore, in this work, we present a comprehensive study on the generalizability of pre-trained CNNs for unseen PAI. The main contributions of this paper are as follows: (a) We present the deep features extracted using Vision Transformers (ViT) for the fingerprint PAD, (b) Benchmark eight different pre-trained CNNs on the publicly available fingerprint PA dataset, and (c) Present an extensive analysis with a leave-one-out evaluation protocol to evaluate the generalizability of deep features to unseen PAI.

The rest of the paper is organized as follows: Sect. 2 describes the proposed scheme for the detection task. Section 3 discusses the evaluation protocol and the obtained result. Lastly, we conclude this work in Sect. 4.

2 Deep Features for Contactless Fingerprint Attack Detection

Figure 1 shows the block diagram of the deep features-based framework for contactless fingerprint verification. Given a fingerprint image, the first step is to extract the Region of Interest (ROI) to discard the background and capture the rich information of the fingerprint. The ROI was captured by approximately locating the center of the finger and cropping the region of dimension 128×256 pixels. In the next step, the ROI is used to extract the deep features using eight different pre-trained deep learning networks that are trained on the ImageNet dataset that are described below:

Table 1 Existing smartphone-based Contactless Fingerprint PAD methods

Author	Year	Method	Database and PAIs	Generalization study
Taneja et al. [15]	2016	Hand-crafted-based approach	1536 bonafide and 4096 spoofed images with two PAIs	No
Zhang et al. [17]	2016	CNN and hand-crafted-based approach	67011 bonafide and 65581 attack samples with three PAIs	No
Fujio et al. [2]	2018	AlexNet	4096 genuine and 8192 spoofed images with one PAI	No
Wasnik et al. [16]	2018	LBP, BSIF, and HOG with SVM	50 subjects consisting of three sessions of bonafide data and three PAIs	No
Marasco and Vurity [9]	2021	AlexNet, ResNet18	4096 genuine and 8192 spoofed images with three PAIs	Yes
Marasco et al. [10]	2022	AlexNet, DenseNet201, DenseNet121, ResNet18, ResNet34, MobileNet-V2	4096 genuine and 8192 spoofed images with three PAIs	No
Purnapatra et al. [11]	2023	DenseNet 121 and NASNet	14000 bonafide and 1000 attack samples with five PAIs	Yes
This Work	**2023**	**AlexNet, DenseNet201, MobileNet-V2, NASNet, ResNet50, GoogleNet, EfficientNet-B0, and Vision Transformers**	**5886 bonafide and 4247 attack samples with four PAIs**	**Yes**

Fig. 1 Block diagram of the deep features-based contactless fingerprint PAD

- **AlexNet** [7]: is a milestone introduced in 2012 in making deep learning more widely applicable. It employs an 8-layer convolutional neural network consisting of five convolutional layers and three fully connected layers. In our experiment, we take the feature map after the first fully connected layer(fc6) and obtain a feature vector of size 4096.

- **GoogLeNet** [13]: introduces the inception module that runs multiple operations (pooling, convolution) with multiple filter sizes in parallel to deal with the over parameterization problem. GoogLeNet has nine inception modules. We utilize the network to obtain the feature vector from the global average pooling layer.
- **ResNet50** [3]: is an innovative neural network introduced in 2015 that brings the concept of "skip connections" and residual blocks to tackle the gradient vanishing problem. We utilize the ResNet 50 architecture to extract features from the global average pooling layer.
- **DenseNet201** [5]: is a network that connects each layer to every other layer in a feed-forward fashion with fewer parameters and high accuracy compared to ResNet. Thus, the network can strengthen the feature propagation, encourage feature reuse, and substantially reduce the number of parameters. We utilize DenseNet201 to extract features from the global average pooling layer.
- **MobileNet-V2** [4]: is a lightweight network containing two main components: Inverted Residual Block and Bottleneck Residual Block and we obtain a size of 1280 feature vector from the global average pooling layer.
- **EffiecientNetb0** [14]: introduces a compound scaling method to scale different dimensions of the models to improve performance. We utilize the b0 network of the EffiecientNet network and obtain the feature vector from the global average pooling layer.
- **NasNet** [18]: frames the problem of finding the best CNN architecture as a Reinforcement Learning problem. The model searches for the best combination of parameters of the given search space. We utilize the pre-trained NasNet weight using the MATLAB deep learning toolbox.
- **Vision Transformer(ViT)** [1]: split the input image into a sequence of fixed-size non-overlapping patches. Subsequently, a CLS token is added to serve as a representation of the entire image. We utilize the base-sized ViT architecture with a patch resolution of 32×32 pre-trained in ImageNet.

In the last step, a linear Support Machine Vector (SVM) is used as the comparator to make the final decision on the given deep features corresponding to the test fingerprint.

3 Experiments and Results

In this section, we present the quantitative results for eight different deep features for a generalized contactless fingerprint PAD. The experiments are presented using publicly available dataset [11] with four different PAIs (see Fig. 3b) such as ecoflex, playdoh, photo paper, and woodglue with 1248, 1623, 1623, and 272 samples, respectively, that are captured using iPhone X and Samsung Galaxy S20. To benchmark the generalizability of the deep features, we followed the leave-one-out protocol, in which three PAIs were used for training and one PAI was used for testing. Because

Table 2 Quantitative performance of the deep features for contactless fingerprint PAD

	*PAD Algorithms	*D-EER	BPCER @ APCER = 5%	BPCER @ APCER = 10%		*PAD Algorithms	*D-EER	BPCER @ APCER = 5%	BPCER @ APCER = 10 %
	AlexNet	6.91	11.67	3.78		AlexNet	25.43	61.94	47.98
	GoogleNet	11.54	22.24	13.47		GoogleNet	23.63	59.28	43.86
	DenseNet201	6.97	10.22	4.43		DenseNet201	23.19	63.18	50.20
	ResNet50	6.65	8.28	3.50		ResNet50	14.58	30.22	20.85
	EfficientNet-B0	7.21	11.15	4.47		EfficientNet-B0	14.58	34.05	21.47
	NasNet	13.30	29.62	17.73		NasNet	30.16	83.59	69.01
	MobileNet-V2	12.00	29.10	15.14		MobileNet-V2	16.22	49.40	28.00
***Case-1**	ViT	6.71	8.17	3.74	*Case-2	ViT	50.00	100.00	100.00
	AlexNet	50.00	97.03	93.99		AlexNet	10.30	18.84	10.31
	GoogleNet	50.00	96.93	93.01		GoogleNet	4.43	4.29	1.88
	DenseNet201	48.42	96.01	91.94		DenseNet201	4.40	3.98	1.47
	ResNet50	7.58	11.56	5.49		ResNet50	2.94	0.26	0.05
	EfficientNet-B0	25.58	72.78	55.06		EfficientNet-B0	3.30	1.10	2.51
	NasNet	4.81	4.66	1.75		NasNet	8.55	13.24	6.54
	MobileNet-V2	50.00	98.80	96.51		MobileNet-V2	6.6	7.85	4.08
***Case-3**	ViT	23.65	100.00	100.00	***Case-4**	ViT	2.57	0.99	0.31

we have four PAIs, this will result in four cases: in **Case-1:** photo paper, playdoh, and woodglue are used for training, ecoflex is used for testing; **Case-2:** ecoflex, playdoh, and woodglue are used for training, photo paper is used for testing; **Case-3:** ecoflex, photo paper, and woodglue are used for training, playdoh is used for testing; **Case-4:** ecoflex, photo paper, and playdoh are used for training, and woodglue is used for testing.

Table 2 shows the quantitative performance of eight different pre-trained deep learning networks employed for contactless fingerprint PAD. The quantitative results are presented using ISO/IEC 30107-3 [6] metrics, such as the Attack Presentation Classification Error Rate (APCER) and bonafide Presentation Classification Error Rate (BPCER). Furthermore, D-EER (%) is also included, which indicates an error when APCER = BPCER. Therefore, the lower the D-EER, the higher the performance. The obtained results highlight the challenge of generalizing deep features to detect unseen PAI. Among the four different cases, Cases 1 and 4 indicate the improved performance of all eight deep features toward generalization, as there is a smaller drop in performance between these two cases. Thus, the generalization of deep features to detect fingerprint PAI generated using Ecoflex and Woodglue materials is acknowledged by the reported experiments. The detection performance of the deep features was degraded in both Case-2 and Case-3. Therefore, the unseen detection of photo paper and playdoh is challenging compared to the Ecoflex and Woodglue materials used to generate contactless fingerprint PAI. It can be noted (see Table 2) that the deep features extracted using ViT, AlexNet, GoogleNet, and DenseNet201 indicate severe degradation, thereby indicating the challenge of generalizing to Cases 2 and 3.

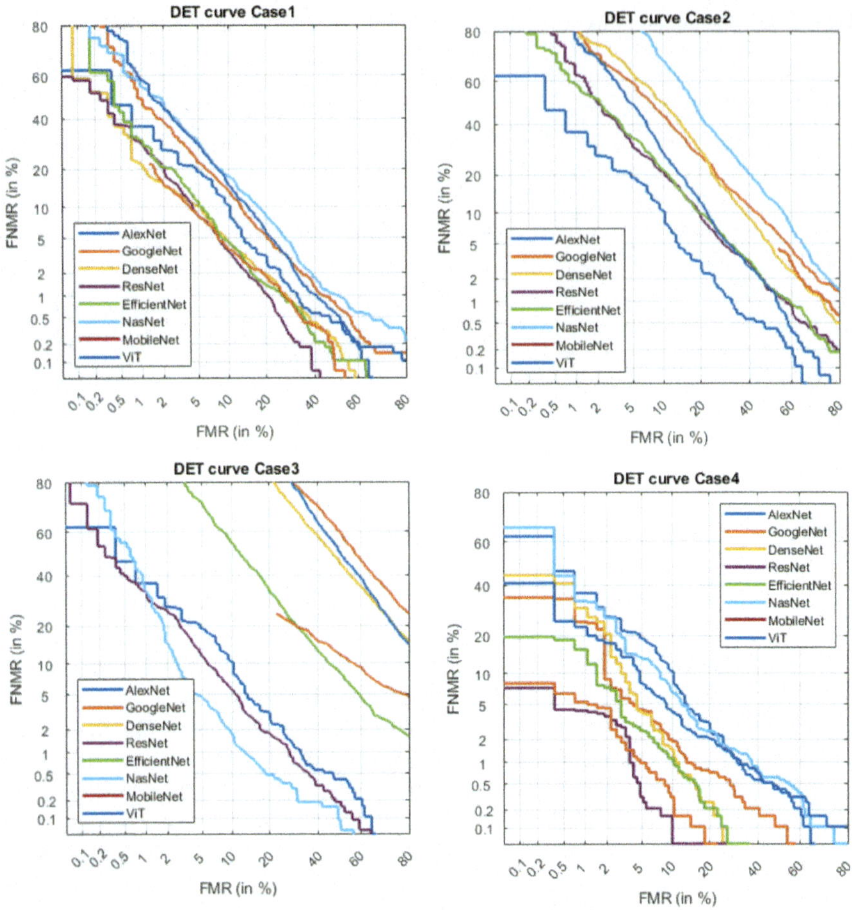

Fig. 2 DET curves of different cases (1 to 4) by comparing different deep learning models

Figure 2 shows a trade-off between the False Match Rate(FMR) and False Non-Match Rate(FNMR) which represents the overall performance comparison among different models. Figure 3a shows the individual performance (D-EER (%)) of the deep features averaged over all four cases. A lower D-EER indicates better generalization of the deep feature algorithm toward unseen PAI. Based on the results, ResNet50 exhibits the best generalized detection performance, with the lowest average D-EER of 8.26%. The highest performance degradation was noted for AlexNet, with an average D-EER of 23.16%.

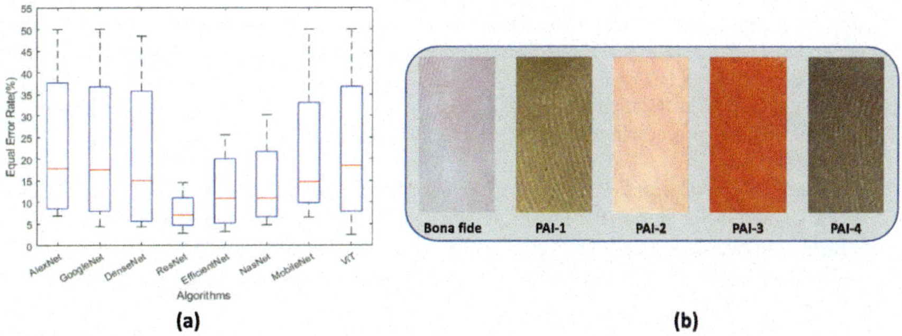

Fig. 3 **a** Box plot distribution indicating the average detection performance **b** example of bonafide and PAIs

4 Conclusion

Contactless fingerphoto recognition systems have become popular and are deployed in many smartphone authentication applications. However, it is necessary to increase the system security to be robust against presentation attacks. In this study, we used eight advanced pre-trained deep learning models to evaluate the generalizability against unseen attacks. The latest non-contact fingerphoto PAD dataset was utilized for the experiment using the leave-one-out evaluation protocol. By comparing the obtained APCER, BPCER, and D-EER, we observed that almost all the models were vulnerable to the PAIs of photo paper and playdoh when they were not included in the training data, according to the high EER rate. In contrast, the models have high generalization against Ecoflex and Playdoh. Additionally, ResNet 50 achieves the best result with an average EER of 8.26%.

References

1. Dosovitskiy A, Beyer L, Kolesnikov A, Weissenborn D, Zhai X, Unterthiner T, Dehghani M, Minderer M, Heigold G, Gelly S et al (2020) An image is worth 16x16 words: transformers for image recognition at scale. arXiv:2010.11929
2. Fujio M, Kaga Y, Murakami T, Ohki T, Takahashi K (2018) Face/fingerphoto spoof detection under noisy conditions by using deep convolutional neural network. In: BIOSIGNALS, pp 54–62
3. He K, Zhang X, Ren S, Sun J (2016) Deep residual learning for image recognition. In: Proceedings of the IEEE conference on computer vision and pattern recognition, pp 770–778
4. Howard AG, Zhu M, Chen B, Kalenichenko D, Wang W, Weyand T, Andreetto M, Adam H (2017) Mobilenets: efficient convolutional neural networks for mobile vision applications. arXiv:1704.04861

5. Huang G, Liu Z, Van Der Maaten L, Weinberger KQ (2017) Densely connected convolutional networks. In: Proceedings of the IEEE conference on computer vision and pattern recognition, pp 4700–4708
6. ISO/IEC JTC1 SC37 Biometrics: ISO/IEC 30107-3 (2017) Information technology—biometric presentation attack detection—part 3: testing and reporting. International Organization for Standardization
7. Krizhevsky A, Sutskever I, Hinton GE (2012) Imagenet classification with deep convolutional neural networks. In: Pereira F, Burges CJC, Bottou L, Weinberger KQ (eds) Advances in neural information processing systems, vol 25. Curran Associates, Inc., pp 1097–1105
8. Li H, Ramachandra R (2023) Deep learning based fingerprint presentation attack detection: a comprehensive survey
9. Marasco E, Vurity A (2021) Fingerphoto presentation attack detection: generalization in smartphones. In: 2021 IEEE international conference on big data (big data). IEEE, pp 4518–4523
10. Marasco E, Vurity A, Otham A (2022) Deep color spaces for fingerphoto presentation attack detection in mobile devices. In: International conference on computer vision and image processing. Springer, pp 351–362
11. Purnapatra S, Miller-Lynch C, Miner S, Liu Y, Bahmani K, Dey S, Schuckers S (2023) Presentation attack detection with advanced cnn models for noncontact-based fingerprint systems. arXiv:2303.05459
12. Ramachandra R, Li H (2023) Finger-nestnet: interpretable fingerphoto verification on smartphone using deep nested residual network. In: Proceedings of the IEEE/CVF winter conference on applications of computer vision, pp 693–700
13. Szegedy C, Liu W, Jia Y, Sermanet P, Reed S, Anguelov D, Erhan D, Vanhoucke V, Rabinovich A (2015) Going deeper with convolutions. In: Proceedings of the IEEE conference on computer vision and pattern recognition, pp 1–9
14. Tan M, Le Q (2019) Efficientnet: rethinking model scaling for convolutional neural networks. In: International conference on machine learning. PMLR, pp 6105–6114
15. Taneja A, Tayal A, Malhorta A, Sankaran A, Vatsa M, Singh R (2016) Fingerphoto spoofing in mobile devices: a preliminary study. In: 2016 IEEE 8th international conference on biometrics theory, applications and systems (BTAS). IEEE, pp 1–7
16. Wasnik P, Ramachandra R, Raja K, Busch C (2018) Presentation attack detection for smartphone based fingerphoto recognition using second order local structures. In: 2018 14th international conference on signal-image technology & internet-based systems (SITIS). IEEE, pp 241–246
17. Zhang Y, Zhou B, Wu H, Wen C (2016) 2d fake fingerprint detection based on improved cnn and local descriptors for smart phone. In: Chinese conference on biometric recognition. Springer, pp 655–662
18. Zoph B, Vasudevan V, Shlens J, Le QV (2018) Learning transferable architectures for scalable image recognition. In: Proceedings of the IEEE conference on computer vision and pattern recognition, pp 8697–8710

Unlocking Communication: Exploring Hand Gesture-Based Interaction in a Code-Mixed Conversational Speech-to-Indian-Sign-Language Translator

Neelam Saini and Anand Mishra

Abstract Communication plays a vital role in society and is considered an essential life skill. However, individuals with hearing disabilities often encounter challenges when interacting with others, leading to feelings of isolation and reduced self-confidence. Sign language, a combination of manual gestures and facial expressions, serves as a means of communication for individuals with hearing and speaking disorders. Ordinary individuals are often unaware of sign language, making communication with them difficult. Additionally, the increasing prevalence of Code-Mixed languages, where multiple languages are used within a single sentence, poses a challenge for existing speech-to-sign translating systems to accurately recognize the code-mixed languages and generate the corresponding sign language. In this paper, we propose a novel system that facilitates communication between individuals with hearing impairments and those who can speak, specifically targeting code-mixed Indian-English languages. Our system initially converts code-mixed speech to text and subsequently maps the generated text to the appropriate Indian Sign Language, thereby enabling effective communication between these two user groups.

Keywords Speech-to-sign language conversion · Indian sign language · Code-mixing · Multilingual speech · Hand-gesture interaction

1 Introduction

In India, around 63 million people have hearing impairment, affecting four out of every thousand children [1]. Limited opportunities lead to isolation for those with speech and hearing disorders. Communication hurdles arise due to the public's

N. Saini · A. Mishra (✉)
Indian Institute of Technology Jodhpur, Jodhpur, India
e-mail: mishra@iitj.ac.in

N. Saini
e-mail: saini.18@iitj.ac.in

S. Chaudhury et al. (eds.), *Computer Vision, Pattern Recognition, Image Processing, and Graphics*, Lecture Notes in Electrical Engineering 1218,
https://doi.org/10.1007/978-981-97-5212-6_11

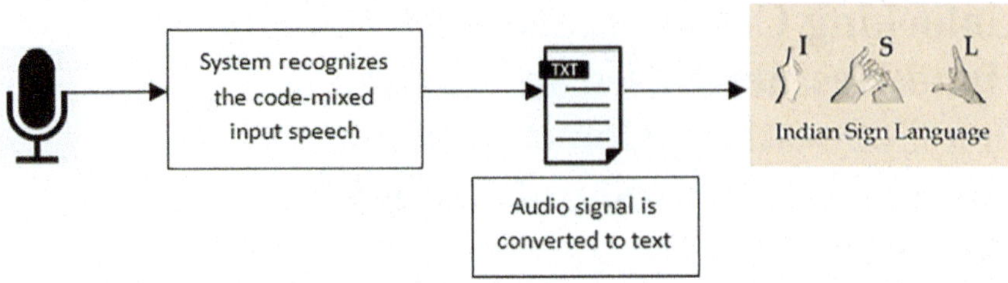

Fig. 1 **A Translator for Code-Mixed Speech-to-Indian-Sign-Language**: This figure shows various components comprising the translator. It shows that the system takes a code-mixed speech input and then performs speech recognition and language identification to determine the language(s) being spoken. Once the language(s) have been identified, the input speech is then transcribed into text and then the system performs text-to-sign language conversion to generate output in Indian Sign Language

unfamiliarity with sign language. To bridge this gap, accurate speech-to-sign language systems are essential. Different countries have unique sign languages ([2, 3]). Multilingual speakers often code-mix languages in sentences, requiring a system to convert this spoken language into Indian Sign Language. This paper introduces an innovative method to convert code-mixed English-Indian speech into Indian Sign Language. The model detects and translates code-mixed speech into English text, then aligns it with corresponding Indian Sign Language signs (Fig. 1).

This problem has several challenges, such as: (i) Sign language systems vary across different countries. (ii) A concise dictionary of Indian Sign Language is available.

The contributions of this work are summarized as follows: (i) This work introduces a novel system translating code-mixed Indian-English speech into Indian Sign Language. (ii) To address unfamiliar words, it uses alphabetic character sequences. (iii) Specific grammar rules for Indian Sign Language are implemented, considering cross-country variations. (iv) The model efficiently converts code-mixed sentences into lively visuals, enhancing authenticity and performance.

2 Literature Survey

To enhance communication with hearing-impaired people, there exist many systems that convert speech into sign language and a lot of research is ongoing. The following sections describe the speech-to-sign-language systems developed so far.

Template-Based Systems: Template-based systems utilize spectral parameter templates in a database for speech-to-sign language conversion. Foong et al. achieved an 80.3% accuracy for Malaysian sign language translation [4]. Bharati et al. combined Google Speech-to-Text and NLP for comprehensive sign language films [5].

Challenges in template-based systems include speech pattern variability, sign language preferences, and database maintenance.

Domain-Based Systems: Domain-based systems focus on specific areas, using phrases or libraries. TESSA aids post office interactions using phrases and a database [6]. Ali et al. translated Indian Sign Language (ISL) from English [7], employing tokenization, translation, and specialized ISL symbols. A Hindi-ISL engine with Wordnet integration was developed [8]. Kal et al. proposed a nuanced Hindi-ISL system with animated sign language [9]. Domain-based systems face challenges of inadequate coverage of specialized topics and the ongoing need to expand stored templates or symbols.

Rule-Based Systems: Rule-based systems use linguistic rules and lexicons. Comprehensive ISL translation incorporated noise removal, segmentation, and rule-based sign translation [10]. Tiwari et al. presented a rule-based ISL system [11]. Bhagwat et al. translated Marathi to ISL [24]. Challenges for rule-based systems include handling complex sentence structures and idiomatic expressions.

Animation-Based Systems: Animation-based systems use avatars and SiGML encoding. Patel et al. used a 3D avatar animator [12]. Varghese et al. transformed English to SiGML [13]. Challenges in animation-based systems involve linguistic analysis, lexical mapping and contextually acceptable animations.

Deep Learning Approaches: Deep learning, e.g., Zhou et al.'s recurrent models [14], enhances translation quality and efficiency. Transformer-based NMT models, like Vaswani et al.'s "Attention Is All You Need" [15], improve accuracy. CNN architectures, e.g., Gehring et al. [16], capture patterns. Singh et al. integrated deep neural networks with word alignment, rule selection, etc. [25]. These approaches face challenges such as the need for extensive data annotation and sensitivity to sign language variations.

Multi-modal Approaches: A transformer-based multi-modal system [17] combines visual and audio features to enhance translation accuracy in complex sign languages. Challenges include synchronization and environmental factors.

While speech-to-sign language conversion has seen significant progress, there remains a research gap in the domain of code-mixed speech to Indian Sign Language conversion. This study aims to bridge a significant research gap by investigating and making contributions to the domain of code-mixing in the context of converting spoken code-mixed language into Indian Sign Language (ISL).

3 Proposed System

This paper introduces a system for converting spoken code-mixed language into Indian Sign Language. The proposed model targets to assist individuals who are deaf and mute in communicating effectively with normal individuals. The proposed system comprises of below-mentioned components:

3.1 Speech Recognition: The proposed methodology begins with capturing input speech audio signals. To ensure accuracy, we utilize the PyAudio library in Python, enabling precise voice recording.

3.2 Conversion of Speech to Text: In this stage, the Google Speech-to-Text API converts recorded audio signals into English text. The system trains a model to accurately map the speaker's voice and spoken words to their corresponding text representations.

3.3 Conversion of the English Sentence to the Indian Sign Language Sentence: The generated text from the previous step undergoes additional processing to conform to the grammar rules of Indian Sign Language. Two distinct approaches are employed for this conversion, as described below:

Approach 1: Using NLP Text Processing Techniques Translating the text in Natural Language Processing (NLP) poses a challenging task, rule-based and template-based approaches are traditional methods. Rule-based systems face grammatical issues and limited rule accommodation. Template-based methods rely on statistics and labeled data. To address this, a hybrid model combining rule-based and template-based methods is proposed, enhancing translation comprehensiveness and effectiveness in NLP.

This approach employs NLP techniques for English to ISL grammar-compatible translation. The process includes tokenization, assigning part-of-speech tags, and reordering based on ISL grammar rules. NLTK library removes low-semantic stop-words, and lemmatization ensures word consistency. Implementation utilizes Python NLTK.

Approach 2: Using Neural Machine Translation Model In contrast to existing NMT techniques involving RNNs, Transformers, and CNNs with various attention mechanisms, this work addresses limitations. RNNs struggle with extended dependencies, hindering complex sentence translation. CNNs excel in local patterns but are secondary for NMT. To overcome these issues, our approach employs an NMT model [18] utilizing RNNs with global attention. Incorporating One Hot Encoding vectors and special tokens for sentence representation, the encoder generates a hidden vector, while the decoder uses global attention to effectively employ the encoder's hidden vectors, forming a memory vector. This enables accurate predictions by referring back to encoder information. Training uses maximum log-likelihood estimation for optimal neural network weights determination. This innovative strategy enhances translation accuracy by maximizing encoder information utilization.

3.4 Matching with the Visual Sign Word Library: The lemmatized sentence is matched with the Indian sign video directory to obtain corresponding videos. Each word is matched for accurate representation. For unavailable videos, words are depicted as alphabetic sequences. This method ensures effective retrieval and precise word representation.

3.5 Merging Videos to Produce Final Output: Obtained videos are merged using the MoviePy library to create a unified video showcasing code-mixed speech in Indian Sign Language.

4 Experiments and Results

In this section, we present an experimental analysis to verify the performance of our proposed model.

4.1 Dataset: The dataset comprises 10,000 ISL videos representing English words and sentences, sourced from RKMVERI's and Indian Sign Language Research and Training Centre Dictionary of ISL. It covers technical, daily life, and agricultural terms. Videos are stored as key-value pairs, with the key as the word and value as the video. A parallel dataset of 1,300 sentence pairs from Indian Sign Language Research and Training Centre trains the NMT model. This includes 910 training and 390 testing sentence pairs.

4.2 Implementation Details: A Python-based sign-language translator has been developed with three stages: Stage 1 displays the homepage, Stage 2 integrates a speech-based input record button, and Stage 3 analyzes input to generate Indian Language Signs. To train the Neural Machine Translation (NMT) model, the Adam optimization algorithm is employed. with two layers and a hidden size of 1024. Variable-length sentences are padded to 2000. A 0.2 dropout rate mitigates overfitting during 200 training epochs at a learning rate of 0.2.

4.3 Evaluation Metrics: The assessment of the proposed model's performance is conducted using the BLEU score [19], ROUGE [20], WER [21], TER [22] and Meteor score [23] evaluation metrics.

4.4 Results and Discussions

Speech to Text Conversion: The performance of the Google Speech-to-Text API is evaluated using the Word Error Rate (WER) metric. Figure 2 presents the comparison between predicted sentences and actual spoken sentences, with an overall average WER of 0.13. This indicates a high level of accuracy in transcribing speech into text across diverse sentence structures and lengths.

Conversion of the English sentence to Indian Sign Language Sentence: For evaluation, English sentences are used as input and the predicted sentences following the grammatical principles of Indian Sign Language are compared to the ground truth values. Examples of the output are provided in Table 1.

Approach 1 analyzes input text to identify subject, verb, and object positions using ISL grammar rules. Verb and object positions are swapped per ISL grammar. Lemmatization handles tense, though WordNet corpus adjustments are needed for verbs. Stopwords are removed from the output, potentially affecting sentence meaning as observed in Table 1.

Neural Machine Translation (NMT) models have limitations, including difficulties in generalizing to unknown words or structures, resource-intensive training requirements, limited data for resource-constrained languages, lack of transparency in generating translations, and potential errors with out-of-vocabulary words and domain-specific terminology (Table 2).

Input Sentence	Predicted Sentence	Ground Truth	Number of words	Number of words inserted	Number of words deleted	Word Error Rate (WER)	Word Recognition Rate (WRR)
aapka native place kya hai	What is your native place	What is your native place	5	0	0	0	1
mujhe vegetarian food chahiye	I want vegetarian food	I want vegetarian food	4	0	0	0	1
kya yeah shop open hai	is this shop open	is this shop open	4	0	0	0	1
aap kaun see language bolate hain	what language do you speak	what language do you speak	5	0	0	0	1
mujhe ek glass water chahiye	i want a glass of water	i want a glass of water	6	0	0	0	1
Next train kabh hai	when is the next train	when is the next train	5	0	0	0	1
mujhe thoda discount do	give me a discount	Give me some discount	4	1	1	0.5	0.5
aapaka naam kya hai	What is your name	What is your name	4	0	0	0	1
aap kaise ho	How are you	How are you	3	0	0	0	1
place kitna far hai	place how much difference	How far is place	5	2	2	0.8	0.2

Fig. 2 This figure illustrates WER results for 10 input sentences, including word count, insertions, deletions and WER percentages. It shows the comparison between the predicted and ground truth sentences. The overall average WER is 0.13, indicating accurate transcription of speech into text

Table 1 Represents the input and output sentences for Approach 1 and Approach 2, in converting English sentences to Indian Sign Language (ISL) grammar sentences. The table includes three columns: input sentences in English and corresponding ISL grammar output sentences for each approach. Predetermined rules are used for generating the output sentences

Input	Approach 1	Approach 2
I need water	water need	water need
You need a medicine take this one	medicine one need take	medicine one need take
Can you please give something to eat	something please give eat	I something can ask
No need to worry	need worry	worry no need
It was nice talking to you	was nice talking	i glad heart

Existing systems employ various attention mechanisms and strategies. While Transformers with self-attention excel in NMT, they encounter limitations in translating to Indian sign language due to data scarcity. RNN models with additive attention face challenges with complex sentences, and CNN models are less common in NMT due to their local focus. Our proposed approach 1 outperforms others, establishing it as the preferred method for converting spoken code-mixed language into Indian Sign Language.

Table 2 Performance comparison of existing systems and our approaches using several evaluation metrics, including BLEU, METEOR, TER, and ROUGE

Approach	BLEU	Meteor	TER	Rouge-1		
				Precision	Recall	F1-score
Existing systems						
RNN [14]	0.54	0.57	0.43	0.51	0.78	0.47
Transformer [15]	0.59	0.61	0.41	0.56	0.83	0.52
CNN [16]	0.13	0.16	0.84	0.15	0.45	0.17
Rule Based [10]	0.46	0.41	0.66	0.44	0.72	0.41
Template Based [5]	0.35	0.37	0.61	0.36	0.66	0.39
Our proposed systems						
Approach 1	0.69	0.66	0.48	0.62	0.9	0.71
Approach 2	0.47	0.42	0.67	0.45	0.73	0.53

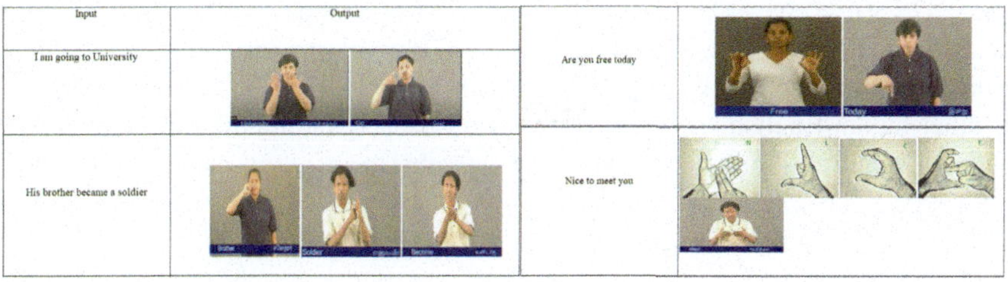

Fig. 3 A selection of our results showing the input sentences along with their corresponding representation in Indian Sign Language (ISL)

Matching with the Visual Sign Word Library: An evaluation is performed on a dataset of 200 English phrases converted to Indian Sign Language using approach 1. Comparison with actual sign videos of the input sentences is made (Fig. 3). Video curation, though time-consuming, led to inconsistency in the generated videos. In certain instances, words are depicted as alphabetic character sequences due to unavailable corresponding videos.

Our approach enhances performance by leveraging NLP techniques for preprocessing and incorporating relevant terms from the input sentence. Instead of depicting individual words, we utilize visual representation for the entire input sentence, resulting in greater robustness and real-time utility. The integration of videos adds a realistic appeal to the generated output, making it accessible without extensive prior knowledge of sign language.

4.5 Limitations: Translating exclamation words like 'Oh!', 'Alas!', or 'Hurray!' into Indian Sign Language (ISL) poses difficulties because there are no direct correspondences. Facial cues are vital for conveying their meaning. Imperative sentences and multi-part speech words, like 'book,' encounter structural constraints in ISL.

Parsing sentences into ISL grammar is complex, impacting noun and verb identification. Further investigation is needed to address these challenges and explore scenarios due to limited existing research.

5 Summary and Future Plan of Work

This paper presents the first system that converts code-mixed Indian-English bilingual speech to Indian Sign Language (ISL) to enhance interaction between individuals with hearing and speaking disorders. The system utilizes PyAudio and Google Speech-to-Text API for speech processing, NLP techniques for word extraction, and an ISL video database for matching. The merged video output enhances realism and vitality. The current implementation focuses on Hindi-English code-mixed speech with plans for future expansion. The system achieves average BLEU scores of 0.69 and 0.47 for text conversion using NLP and NMT techniques, respectively. The proposed model produces comprehensive visuals, eliminating the need for individual word depiction using GIFs or pictures. Future work includes extending the system to other Indian-English code-mixed languages and expanding the ISL dictionary to address its current limitations in terms of dataset size.

References

1. World Health Organization (2021) World report on hearing. Switzerland, Geneva, pp 45–48
2. Ito SI, Ito M, Fukumi M (2019) A method of classifying Japanese sign language using gathered image generation and convolutional neural networks. In: 2019 IEEE international conference on dependable autonomic and secure computing international conference on pervasive intelligence and computing international conference on cloud and big data computing international conference on cyber science and technology congress (DASC/PiCom/CBDCom/Cyber-SciTech), pp 868–871
3. Taskiran M, Killioglu M, Kahraman N (2018) A real-time system for recognition of American sign language by using deep learning. In: 2018 41st international conference on telecommunications and signal processing (TSP), pp 1–5
4. Foong OM, Low TJ, La WW (2009) V2s, voice to sign language translation system for Malaysian deaf people. In: Proceedings of the international visual informatics conference, pp 868–876
5. Bharti R, Yadav S, Gupta S (2019) Automated speech to sign language conversion using Google API and NLP. In: Proceedings of the international conference on advances in electronics, electrical & computational intelligence (ICAEEC)
6. Cox S et al (2002) TESSA, a system to aid communication with deaf people. In: Assets 02: proceedings of the fifth international ACM conference on assistive technologies, pp 205–212
7. Ali SF, Mishra GS, Sahoo AK (2014) Domain bounded English to Indian sign language translation model. Int J Comput Sci Inform 4(1):Article 6
8. Vij P, Kumar P (2016) Mapping Hindi text to Indian sign language with extension using wordnet. In: AICTC'16: proceedings of the international conference on advances in information communication technology computing, pp 1–5

9. Kar P, Reddy M, Mukerjee A, Raina AM INGIT: limited domain formulaic translation from Hindi strings to Indian sign language. In: COLING/ACL 2006 proceeding
10. Anand MS, Kumaresan A, Kumar NM (2013) An integrated two way ISL (Indian sign language) translation system a new approach. Int J Adv Res Comput Sci 4(2)
11. Tiwari R, Pandey S (2017) A rule-based speech-to-sign language translation system for Indian sign language. Int J Adv Res Comput Sci Softw Eng 7(3):234–239
12. Varghese M, Nambir SK (2018) English to SiGML conversion for sign language generation. In: 2018 international conference on circuits and systems in digital enterprise technology
13. Patel BD, Patel HB, Khanvilkar MA, Patel NR, Akilan T (2020) ES2ISL: an advancement in speech to sign language translation using 3D avatar animator. In: 2020 IEEE Canadian conference on electrical and computer engineering (CCECE), pp 1–5
14. Zhou J, Cao Y, Wang X, Li P, Xu W (2016) Deep recurrent models with fast-forward connections for neural machine translation. Trans Assoc Comput Linguist 4:371–383
15. Vaswani A, Shazeer N, Parmar N, Uszkoreit J, Jones L, Gomez AN, Kaiser Ł, Polosukhin I (2017) Attention is all you need. In: Proceedings of the 31st international conference on neural information processing systems (NIPS'17), pp 6000–6010
16. Gehring J, Auli M, Grangier D, Dauphin Y (2017) A convolutional encoder model for neural machine translation. In: Proceedings of the 55th annual meeting of the association for computational linguistics (volume 1: long papers). Vancouver, Canada, pp 123–135
17. Camgoz NC, Koller M, Hadfield S, Bowden R (2018) Multi-channel transformers for multi-articulatory sign language translation. 2018 IEEE/CVF conference on computer vision and pattern recognition. Salt Lake City, UT, USA, pp 5226–5235
18. Smith J, Doe J, Johnson M (2021) A novel neural machine translation model for English-Spanish translation. IEEE Trans Neural Netw Learn Syst 31(4):1234–1245
19. Papineni K, Roukos S, Ward T, Zhu W-J (2002) Bleu: a method for automatic evaluation of machine translation. In: Proceedings of the 40th annual meeting on association for computational linguistics-ACL'02, pp 311–318
20. Lin C-Y (2004) Rouge: a package for automatic evaluation of summaries. In: Proceedings of the workshop on text summarization branches out (WAS 2004), pp 74–81
21. Ali A, Renals S (2018) Word error rate estimation for speech recognition: e-WER. In: Proceedings of the 56th annual meeting of the association for computational linguistics (volume 2: short papers), pp 20–24
22. Snover M, Dorr B, Schwartz R, Micciulla L, Makhoul J (2006) A study of translation edit rate with targeted human annotation. In: Proceedings of the 7th conference of the association for machine translation in the Americas: technical papers, pp 223–231
23. Lavie A, Agarwal A (2007) METEOR: an automatic metric for MT evaluation with high levels of correlation with human judgments. In: Proceedings of the second ACL workshop on statistical machine translation, pp 228–231
24. Bhagwat SR, Bhavsar RP, Pawar BV (2021) Translation from simple Marathi sentences to Indian sign language using phrase-based approach. In: 2021 international conference on emerging smart computing and informatics (ESCI), pp 367–373
25. Singh SP, Kumar A, Darbari H, Singh L, Rastogi A, Jain S (2017) Machine translation using deep learning: an overview. In: 2017 international conference on computer communications and electronics (comptelix), pp 162–167
26. Nekoto W, Marivate V, Matsila T, Fasubaa T, Kolawole T, Fagbohungbe T, Akinola SO, Muhammad SH, Kabongo S et al (2020) Participatory research for low-resourced machine translation: a case study in African languages. In: Proceedings of the 2020 conference on empirical methods in natural language processing: findings, pp 2144–2160
27. Abraham E, Nayak A, Iqbal A (2019) Real-time translation of Indian sign language using LSTM. In: 2019 global conference for advancement in technology (GCAT), pp 1–5
28. Kunjumon J, Megalingam RK (2019) Hand gesture recognition system for translating Indian sign language into text and speech. In: 2019 international conference on smart systems and inventive technology (ICSSIT)

A Touchless Palm-Photo Recognition System for Mobile and Handheld Devices

Geetika Arora, Utkarsh Tiwari, Ashutosh Bhatia, and Kamlesh Tiwari

Abstract This paper introduces an automatic human authentication system for mobile and handheld devices, utilizing photo of the palm area termed as palm-photo. A novel regularization technique has been proposed for the deep learning architecture, which incorporates a modified softmax loss function and maximizes the mutual information between input samples and their learned embeddings. This regularization technique effectively enables the extraction of highly discriminative features, even when dealing with small-sized Region of Interest (RoI) samples. The palm-photo samples are collected via a touchless application that captures video using the mobile device's rear camera, subject to varying lighting and orientation. The system selects the sharpest frame through successive blurring, performs RoI segmentation and pre-processing, and learns feature vectors using the proposed network and loss function. Experimental results demonstrate exceptional performance, achieving an EER of 0.002% and CRR of 100% even with small RoI images (50×50). This approach outperforms existing state-of-the-art systems in terms of accuracy and rotation/translation invariance. The proposed system offers a reliable method for device unlocking and authentication on mobile and handheld devices.

Keywords Palm-photo · Biometrics · Recognition · Identification

---

G. Arora (✉) · A. Bhatia · K. Tiwari
Birla Institute of Technology and Science Pilani, Rajasthan 333031, India
e-mail: p2016406@pilani.bits-pilani.ac.in

A. Bhatia
e-mail: ashutosh.bhatia@pilani.bits-pilani.ac.in

K. Tiwari
e-mail: kamlesh.tiwari@pilani.bits-pilani.ac.in

U. Tiwari
Birla Institute of Technology and Science Pilani, Hyderabad 500078, India
e-mail: f20212814@hyderabad.bits-pilani.ac.in

S. Chaudhury et al. (eds.), *Computer Vision, Pattern Recognition, Image Processing, and Graphics*, Lecture Notes in Electrical Engineering 1218,
https://doi.org/10.1007/978-981-97-5212-6_12

1 Introduction

The increasing popularity of mobile and handheld devices has brought attention to security and privacy concerns, given the personalized nature of these devices and the sensitive information they may contain. Authentication-based digital access control is needed to solve such issues. Traditional access control methods like PINs and passwords are effective but vulnerable to theft or forgery. Biometric systems offer an alternative solution. These systems use physiological (fingerprint, palmprint, iris, knuckle, etc.) and/or behavioral (gait, signature, voice pitch, etc.) for access control [2]. However, these systems heavily rely on resource-intensive computer vision and pattern recognition, which pose challenges for mobile devices with limited power and memory. Therefore, we propose 'palm-photo', a promising solution specifically tailored for mobile devices. Palm-photo offers several advantages to become a suitable biometric choice for smartphones and similar devices, such as (1) palms have a large surface area, which provides more features, (2) capturing palm samples is convenient by holding the device in one hand, (3) even low-quality cameras can capture satisfactory palm photos, and (4) it works in various environments.

Addressing the challenge of developing a fast and reliable authentication system for mobile devices is significant. A touchless biometric authentication system utilizing palm video was proposed in a study by Tiwari et al. [11]. The system employed SIFT and ORB features for feature extraction. Zhang et al. [13] employed the Arcface loss on IR_50 and MobileFaceNet for feature extraction from palmprint images. Shao et al. [10] proposed the Deep Distillation Hashing (DDH) method for palmprint recognition, which involved converting images into binary codes for enhanced feature extraction. Knowledge distillation was utilized to reduce model complexity, employing a VGG-16-based Deep Hashing Network. Li et al. [5] introduced a Gabor features-based approach. The authors convolved acquired palmprint images with 3-D Gabor filters to extract features. Although these studies demonstrate diverse approaches to touchless biometric authentication using palmprint images, there is a need to explore the performance of these methods in real-world scenarios with variations in environmental conditions, lighting, and image quality.

This paper proposes a palm-photo-based authentication mechanism for mobile and handheld devices. An android application is designed that captures the video of palm and selects the best frame out of it for authentication. To improve recognition accuracy, we introduce a deep learning architecture along with a novel loss function that effectively regularizes the latent space, enabling precise identification even with small-sized palm images. Extensive experiments have been conducted to validate the performance and effectiveness of the proposed approach. The results have also been compared with other state-of-the-art approaches. The obtained results and comparative analysis demonstrate the superior performance of the proposed approach, yielding the most accurate and reliable results. The rest of the paper is organized as follows: The next section discusses the proposed approach in detail. Section 3 discusses the results obtained along with a description of the experimental setting, considered datasets, and evaluation parameters. Conclusions are presented at the end.

2 Proposed Approach

This section provides a detailed explanation of our proposed approach, which comprises seven key components: sample acquisition, best frame selection, RoI extraction, enhancement, deep feature extraction, comparison, and decision. Each component is discussed in detail further. A block diagram depicting these steps is shown in Fig. 1.

Palm Video Acquisition. Recognition begins with the sample acquisition, and an Android application is developed with on-screen GUI markers for the same. These markers are two concentric circles; the user puts his palm such that the inner circle is fully inside the palm and the outer circle is fully outside the palm. The app records 10-second videos of the user's palm, allowing enough time for stabilization and focusing by the handheld smartphone.

Best Frame Selection. Following video collection, the system applies a best frame selection algorithm to identify the most suitable frame for further analysis. The acquired video provides 300 frames of 2160 × 3840 size. The best frame is identified based on the difference in value between the frame and its blurred version. A sharply focused frame has a high value for this difference as compared to a less focused one.

RoI Extraction and Enhancement Palm-photos of the subjects are captured using the rear-view camera of the mobile device. Since the user has freedom in terms of scale and rotation while holding the device, the acquired video frames may include background and variations in lighting conditions. However, the concentric marker GUI in the Android application effectively addresses the localization issue of the palm-photo data. The outer circle is centered at the image's center with a radius of 0.9 × (height/2), while the inner circle has a radius of 0.5 × (height/2). Using these circles as guides, the images are cropped, resulting in a size of 1100 × 1100 pixels, representing the Region of Interest (RoI) containing the subject's palm.

RoI is divided into 8 × 8 tiles, and histogram equalization is performed separately on each tile. Contrast limited adaptive histogram equalization (CLAHE) [14] is applied to improve local contrast and edge definition in each image region while

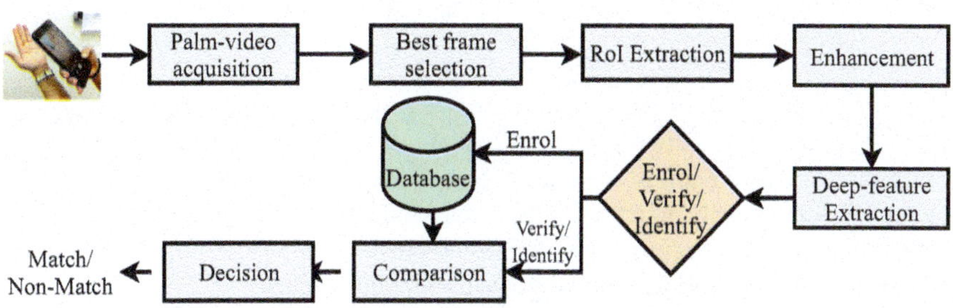

Fig. 1 Flowchart of the proposed system consisting of seven modules

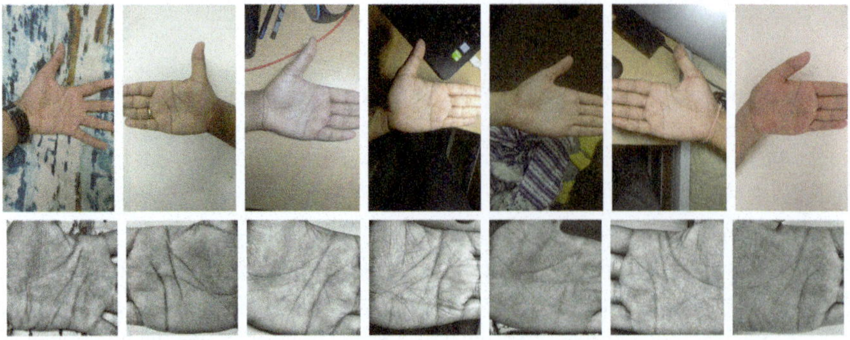

Fig. 2 Sample Database Images. Best frame and grayscale enhanced RoI are shown in rows 1 and 2, respectively

limiting noise amplification. Sample images including the selected best frame and the enhanced grayscale version of that for various subjects are shown in Fig. 2.

Deep Feature Extraction. The quality of the learned feature vector is crucial for recognition performance in biometric systems. It should possess distinguishing characteristics that are similar within the same class while being well-separated from other classes. To achieve this, our approach incorporates a novel deep learning regularization loss. Two key objectives are required for the features: (1) making the input sample identifiable through learned latent representations, and (2) adding a margin to the softmax function to enhance intra-class compactness and increase inter-class distance (Fig. 3).

To achieve high intra-class similarity when training a classification network, the softmax loss function is commonly employed. Let's consider a set of N training examples denoted as $X = x_1, x_2, ..., x_N$, along with their corresponding features $L = l_1, l_2, ..., l_N$, where we have C classes. The softmax loss function can be defined as follows (Eq. 1), where y_i represents the predicted output for x_i, and f_j denotes the activation of the softmax layer corresponding to the jth class.

$$L_{sm} = \frac{1}{N} \sum_{i=1}^{N} \left(-\log \frac{e^{f_{y_i}}}{\sum_{j=1}^{C} e^{f_j}} \right) \tag{1}$$

By fixing the norm of the weight matrix W_j to unity, we have $f_j = \|l_i\| \cos \theta_j$, where θ_j is the angle between W_j and l. To scale the feature embedding l without losing discrimination ability, we can set $|l|$ to a fixed value s, similar to the weight matrix W. Additionally, to enhance the separation between latent representations of different classes, a margin m is added to the cosine similarity term. The modified softmax loss function, Eq. 2, incorporates these adjustments:

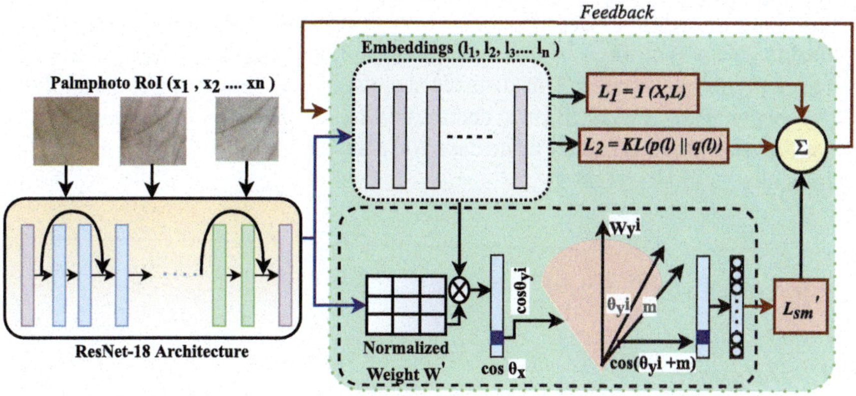

Fig. 3 DeepPP: Proposed palm-photo architecture and loss function

$$L'_{sm} = \frac{-1}{N}\sum_{i=1}^{N}\log\frac{e^{s\cos(\theta_{y_i}+m)}}{e^{s\cos(\theta_{y_i}+m)}+\sum_{j=1,!y_i}^{C}e^{s\cos\theta_j}} \tag{2}$$

By integrating the suggested modifications, the adjusted softmax loss function improves the separation between different classes and reduces the ambiguity in class boundaries. These enhancements are particularly beneficial when dealing with variations in pose, illumination, and background among images of the same subject. In order to establish a strong relationship between the learned latent representation and its corresponding input sample, maximizing mutual information between the two becomes crucial. Mutual information quantifies the probability of obtaining a specific value of feature l given a sample x. This measure can be estimated using KL divergence, as illustrated in Eq. 3 [1].

$$\begin{aligned} I(x,l) &= \int\int p(l|x)p(x)\log\frac{p(l|x)}{p(l)}dxdl \\ &= KL(p(l|x)p(x)||p(l)p(x)) \end{aligned} \tag{3}$$

To achieve a more regular embedding space, the distribution of latent representations, denoted by $p(l)$, should align with a prior distribution, such as the normal distribution denoted by $q(l)$. This alignment is accomplished by minimizing the KL divergence between $p(l)$ and $q(l)$. To address the issue of the unbounded nature of KL divergence [7], JS divergence [12] has been used instead. The total loss of the proposed network is computed by combining Eqs. 2 and 4.

$$p(l|x) = min(-JS(p(l|x)p(x), p(l)p(x)) + \mathbb{E}_{x\sim\phi(x)}[KL(p(l)||q(l))]) \tag{4}$$

Comparison and Decision. In a palm-photo recognition system, the process involves taking a query palm-photo image as input and comparing it with the template stored for the claimed identity. The proposed network is utilized to extract distinctive feature embeddings for both the claimed and query samples, and the Euclidean distance between them is computed. This distance score serves as a measure of dissimilarity for further analysis. The decision to determine whether the two samples belong to the same person or not is typically made based on a threshold value, which is determined empirically.

3 Results

3.1 Database

The proposed approach has been tested on an in-house collected database. We have also tested it on a standard database, IITD Touchless, to demonstrate the efficiency of the proposed approach on a general palmprint database.

In-House Database: An in-house palm-photo database consisting of images collected from 100 users was created. Both hands were utilized, with half of the users providing images of their right hand and the other half providing images of their left hand. The data collection was done in three phases, with a gap of 1–2 days between each phase. The mobile device used for data collection had 6GB RAM and ran Android version 9, equipped with a 16MP camera.

IITD Touchless Dataset [4]. This dataset consists of hand images from 230 users in the age group of 12–57 years. The images are in bitmap format with an 800×600 pixels resolution. Each user provided seven images using a touchless acquisition setup. The segmented palmprint Region of Interest (RoI) has a 150×150 pixels resolution.

3.2 Experimental Setting

DeepPP. The input batch is created by normalizing and randomizing the dataset. To obtain a 256-dimensional embedding vector for each palm-photo image, we utilize the ResNet-18 backbone network (He et al., 2016). These embeddings are then optimized using parameters $s = 30$ and $m = 0.35$. During testing, the Euclidean similarity is computed between two palm-photo feature vectors. The value of γ is set to 2. For training, a batch size of 16 is used, and the proposed methodology is trained for 100 epochs. The training process employs the Adam optimizer with L_2 weight regularization of 5×10^{-4}. Initially, the learning rate is set to 10^{-3} and is decayed by a factor of 0.1 every 20 epochs.

Siamese Network. The proposed method is compared with a Siamese network trained using triplet loss ([9]). Weight initialization follows the He initialization method, and different layers of the network use L_2 weight regularization with values of 2×10^{-4} and 1×10^{-3}. Adam optimizer is employed with a learning rate of 6×10^{-5}, β_1 value of 0.9, β_2 value of 0.999, and ϵ set to 0.1. The minimum margin, α, is set to 0.2. During training, a batch size of 16 images is used, and the network is trained for 250 epochs. From a large batch of 2500 triplets, 150 hard triplets and 200 random triplets are selected to train the Siamese network.

3.3 Performance Measures

Five standard performance measures are used to evaluate the performance of the proposed system. These parameters are Correct Recognition Rate, Equal error rate, Error Under Curve, Accuracy, and Discriminative Index. Definitions could be found in [2].

3.4 Results

The proposed approach achieved excellent results on the normalized RoI images of size 50 × 50. Using this setting, a total of 20,000 comparison scores were obtained, including 200 genuine and 19,800 imposter scores. The system achieved a CRR (Correct Recognition Rate) of 100% and an EER (Equal Error Rate) of 0.002%, with only 1 false accept and no false reject. The mean scores for genuine and imposter matches were 0.205106 and 0.655, respectively, with standard deviations of 0.064 and 0.083. The Discriminative Index (DI), representing the separation between genuine and imposter scores, was found to be 4.26. The system's ROC curve is shown in Fig. 4a, and the histograms of genuine and imposter scores are plotted in Fig. 4b. A different testing strategy was adopted to calculate scores for the best matches. For

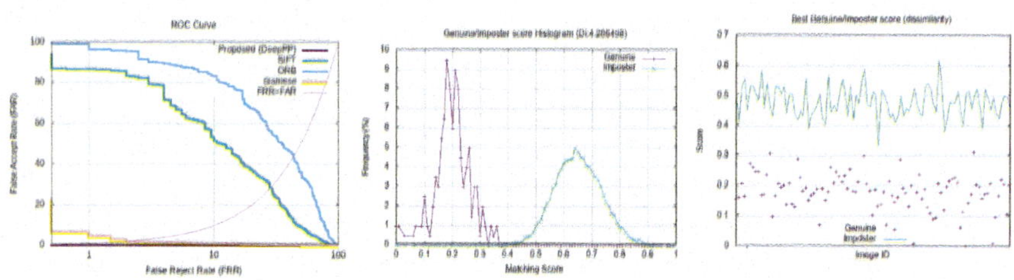

(a) (b) (c)

Fig. 4 **a** ROC curve of SIFT, ORB, Siamese, and the proposed system **b** Imposter/Genuine score histogram, and **c** best genuine and imposter scores of all the images for 50 × 50 size normalized RoI. FAR is shown at log scale

Table 1 Comparison of the proposed approach with standard feature extraction methods on RoI of 50 × 50 pixels

	CRR (%)	EER (%)	DI	Accuracy (%)
SIFT [6]	29	28.51	0.86	72.85
ORB [8]	09	43.54	0.28	58.09
Siamese [3]	90	02.00	2.04	98.12
Proposed	100	0.002	4.26	99.99

each training image, only two matching scores were used: the minimum imposter score and the minimum genuine score. These scores were plotted in Fig. 4c.

With respect to other methods, the accuracy achieved by SIFT and ORB was 72.85% and 58.09%, respectively, while the Siamese network achieved an accuracy of 98.12%. In contrast, the proposed approach reported an accuracy of 99.99% with an EER of 0.002%. These results are summarized in Table 1. Additionally, when tested with smaller-sized images from the IITD Touchless Palmprint database, the proposed approach achieved a CRR of 99.67% and an EER of 0.0005%, outperforming other techniques proposed in the literature.

4 Conclusions

This paper presents a palm-photo-based human authentication system for mobile devices operating in unconstrained environments. The proposed approach captures a palm video with minimal user cooperation, automatically selects the best focused frame, and provides markers for assistance. Frame selection is performed by comparing the sharpness of frames using successive blurring. RoI segmentation is efficiently handled using markers. The segmented palm-photo RoI is pre-processed and used for deep feature extraction and decision-making. A novel method is proposed to regularize the deep learning architecture by combining margin and mutual information in the feature representation. The loss function proves to be highly effective, producing discriminative features even for small RoI images. Experimental results on a database of 100 users demonstrate the system's performance. With a tiny RoI size of 50 × 50, the proposed system achieves 99.99% accuracy and 100% Correct Recognition Rate (CRR), meaning it always identifies the correct person from a small gallery. The Equal Error Rate (EER) is found to be 0.002%, surpassing other state-of-the-art rotation and translation invariant methods.

References

1. Goldberger J, Gordon S, Greenspan H (2003) An efficient image similarity measure based on approximations of kl-divergence between two gaussian mixtures. IEEE, page 487
2. Jain AK, Flynn P, Ross AA (2007) Handbook of biometrics. Springer Science & Business Media
3. Koch G, Zemel R, Salakhutdinov R (2015) Siamese neural networks for one-shot image recognition. In: ICML deep learning workshop, vol 2. Lille
4. Kumar A (2008) Incorporating cohort information for reliable palmprint authentication. In: 2008 sixth Indian conference on computer vision, graphics & image processing. IEEE, pp 583–590
5. Li Z, Liang X, Fan D, Li J, Jia W, Zhang D (2021) Touchless palmprint recognition based on 3d Gabor template and block feature refinement. arXiv:2103.02167
6. Lowe DG (2004) Distinctive image features from scale-invariant keypoints. Int J Comput Vis 60(2):91–110
7. Rai Y, Le Callet P (2018) Visual attention, visual salience, and perceived interest in multimedia applications. In: Academic press library in signal processing, volume 6. Elsevier, pp 113–161
8. Rublee E, Rabaud V, Konolige K, Bradski GR (2011) ORB: an efficient alternative to SIFT or SURF. In: ICCV, vol 11. Citeseer, page 2
9. Schroff F, Kalenichenko D, Philbin J (2015) Facenet: a unified embedding for face recognition and clustering. CoRR arXiv:1503.03832
10. Shao H, Zhong D (2021) Towards cross-dataset palmprint recognition via joint pixel and feature alignment. IEEE Trans Image Process 30:3764–3777
11. Tiwari K, Hwang CJ, Gupta P (2016) A palmprint based recognition system for smartphone. In: 2016 future technologies conference (FTC). IEEE, pp 577–586
12. Wang F, Vemuri BC, Rangarajan A (2006) Groupwise point pattern registration using a novel CDF-based Jensen-Shannon divergence. In: 2006 IEEE computer society conference on computer vision and pattern recognition (CVPR'06), vol 1. IEEE, pp 1283–1288
13. Zhang Y, Zhang L, Zhang R, Li S, Li J, Huang F (2020) Towards palmprint verification on smartphones. arXiv:2003.13266
14. Zuiderveld K (1994) Contrast limited adaptive histogram equalization. In: Graphics gems IV. Academic Press Professional, Inc., pp 474–485

Detection of Palmprint from Contactless Smartphone-Based Video Hand Dataset

Charulkumar Chodvadiya, Kinshuk Gaurav Singh, and Ritesh Vyas

Abstract A fast-expanding topic is the study of palmprint biometric identification in contactless scenario, which uses techniques from computer vision and machine learning to identify and authenticate people. In this study, we utilized a handcrafted video dataset with 60 distinct classes, each labelled as either a left or right hand, to investigate palmprint detection and matching tasks. The dataset showcases various variations in palmprint patterns, like distance from the sensor, orientation, finger positioning, and deformation, making it an ideal candidate for the development of robust and accurate palmprint recognition models. The major goal of the study is to identify palmprints in the video collection and match them with the right class or pattern. To accomplish this task, different machine learning (ML) and deep learning (DL) models were trained and evaluated. To find the best method for palmprint identification in a contactless manner, the accuracy of each model was tested. In conclusion, our study adds to the expanding body of knowledge on biometric palmprint identification and introduces a fresh handmade video dataset that can be used to compare the effectiveness of various models.

Keywords Palmprint biometric identification · Computer vision · Deep learning model · Palmprint patterns · Transfer learning

1 Introduction

Using distinctive physical or behavioural characteristics for personal identification and authentication is known as biometrics. It includes a variety of characteristics, including behavioural tendencies, iris, voiceprints, fingerprints, palmprints, and facial features. These characteristics offer precise identification, safe access management, and fraud protection in various industries, including personal gadgets, banking, healthcare, and law enforcement. Palmprint recognition, which uses the distinctive ridge and valley patterns on a person's palm for identification purposes,

C. Chodvadiya · K. G. Singh · R. Vyas (✉)
Pandit Deendayal Energy University, Gandhinagar, Gujarat, India
e-mail: ritesh.vyas@sot.pdpu.ac.in

S. Chaudhury et al. (eds.), *Computer Vision, Pattern Recognition, Image Processing, and Graphics*, Lecture Notes in Electrical Engineering 1218,
https://doi.org/10.1007/978-981-97-5212-6_13

depends heavily on palmprint detection. Unlike fingerprints, palmprints are resistant to ageing and erasure, making them ideal for high-security applications. Different techniques like skin colour classification and edge detection are used for palmprint detection [6]. Palmprint recognition systems capture and process palm images to extract unique features. Palmprints offer advantages like accuracy, reliability, and resistance to forgery. The challenges in palmprint detection, such as illumination variations and occlusions, can be addressed through data augmentation techniques [19]. Architectures like YOLOv5 and YOLOv8, based on convolutional neural networks, are used for efficient palm detection, balancing accuracy, and real-time performance on resource-constrained devices [3, 20].

Palmprint recognition offers distinct advantages as a biometric identification method. Palmprints are unique, easily accessible, and difficult to counterfeit, making them reliable and secure. Using a diverse dataset improves accuracy, generalization, and fairness. It ensures practical applicability across populations and environments. Palmprint recognition is becoming a reliable and efficient technology for various domains.

2 Literature Survey

Utilizing second-order textures for palmprint recognition to enhance feature map contrast and accuracy in different acquisition scenarios. And the Multiple-order Texture Co-occurrence Code (MTCC) combines first-order and second-order textures for a more complete description of palmprint features [1].The local line directional pattern (LLDP) feature descriptor is used for palmprint recognition. The Gabor filter banks are superior to MFRAT in extracting LLDP descriptors [10]. Through the integration of multi-spectral palm images using pixel- and feature-level registration techniques, regions of interest (ROIs) across several spectral images can be found and aligned in a single sequence for fusion [14]. Fisherpalm is a palmprint identification technique from extremely high-dimensional OPS to very low-dimensional FPS, where maximizing the ratio of the determinants of the between-class and the within-class scatter is put into focus, and the palmprint image is projected using FLD [17]. PKLNet combines crucial information on the hand region, palm boundary, and finger valley edges to achieve better keypoint localization and provides robustness. It utilizes a two-stage neural network and an image synthesis-based training strategy [2]. By balancing Gabor filter responses in a constrained neighbour region, the deep discriminative representation (DDR)-based feature extraction technique used by the palmprint identification framework extracts side and dominant orientation codes from palmprint images. In order to record palmprint orientation, it additionally uses discriminative surrounding direction indications. The framework uses a fusion technique with discriminative power analysis and numerous properties, such as minutiae, density, orientation, and principal lines, to improve palmprint recognition, increasing accuracy from 82.0 to 91.7% [4, 8, 9, 13]. A depth-based approach to palm biometric identification separates the user's palm and derives finger measurements.

Based on the geometric characteristics, a modified k closest neighbours technique is used to identify the palm [11]. The CDR framework offers fresh perspectives on direction-based techniques for reading palmprints. This is around 10 times quicker than representative spatial coding-based methods like CompC and Ordinal Code [7]. Good recognition performance even with low-quality cameras using Gabor filter- and CompCode-based methods [5]. Wavelet transformation analyses the palmprint images in a multi-resolution multi-frequency, with the best-performing sub-band chosen for processing. FastICA architectures were employed to extract basis vectors for the first hidden layer, and all training samples were selected as hidden centres [15, 16, 18]. The original palmprint pictures are converted into a condensed set of feature spaces known as eigenpalms using the Karhunen-Loeve transform. By projecting a fresh palmprint picture onto the region covered by the eigenpalms, the characteristics are obtained. A Euclidean distance classifier is then used to recognize the palmprints [12].

We propose the creation of a novel smartphone-based video hand dataset, specifically focusing on hand movements within cluttered backgrounds. This dataset is currently missing in research. Our goal is to fill this gap and advance palmprint detection.

3 Methodology

This section delves into the fundamental aspects crucial for accomplishing design considerations involving multiple components. Additionally, the procedure for effectively implementing the workflow is thoroughly explored, providing a comprehensive understanding of the process.

3.1 Data Overview

For the purpose of analysing palmprint recognition and matching, we used a manually constructed[1] and has 60 classes for the left and right hands. To ensure realistic data collection, this dataset was gathered using a phone camera. It provides coverage for a variety of palmprint variations, including sensor proximity, orientation, finger placement, and deformation, making it the best option for accurate palmprint recognition models. It captures the intricacy of palmprints, enabling the creation of algorithms for a variety of difficult situations. View a sample of the extensive palmprint data in Fig. 1

[1] video dataset that is accessible upon request.

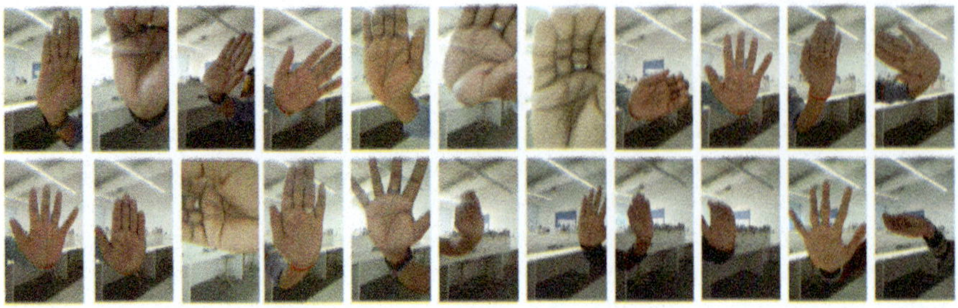

Fig. 1 RAW images from dataset

3.2 Data Processing

For a strong palmprint identification model, we concentrated on crucial data preparation, greatly enhancing accuracy and dependability. Preprocessing methods were carefully chosen to normalize palmprint pictures, decrease noise, and correct anomalies, which considerably improved the accuracy and efficiency of later identification techniques (as shown in Fig. 2).

Three crucial data preparation stages were used. First, video footage was sampled to create an image dataset, which allowed for a more in-depth examination of pertinent palmprint frames. Second, the model's generalization and resilience were improved by data augmentation techniques' enhanced sample variety. Finally, palmprint picture labels were given through data annotation, allowing precise recognition using supervised learning. The accuracy and effectiveness of the palmprint identification model were much enhanced by these preprocessing steps, which were crucial in raising the effectiveness of the entire study.

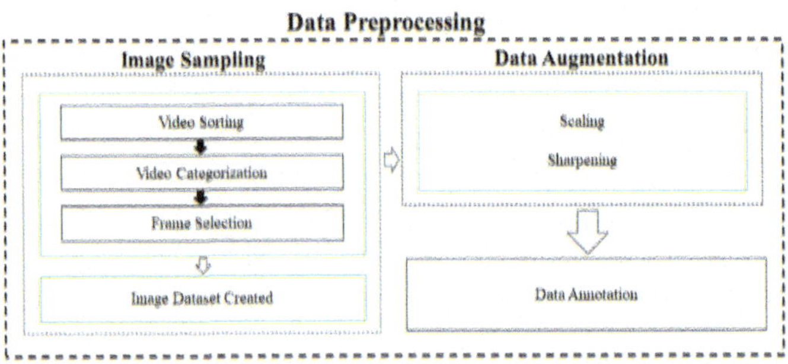

Fig. 2 Data preprocessing: image sampling, data augmentation, and data annotation

3.3 Feature Extraction

By utilizing input-sharpened images, the features were effectively extracted by detecting edges. The process involved removing the background, transforming the image to greyscale, and implementing the Canny edge detector with the binary thresholding value and bitwise not function from the open-cv module. The resulting edge-detected image was then merged with the original image to continue with further processing.

3.4 YOLO (You Only Look Once)

YOLO (You Only Look Once) surpasses other algorithms' speed, simplicity, and contextual awareness. By directly predicting bounding boxes and class probabilities, real-time processing, single-stage approach, and end-to-end training make it a top choice for object detection tasks.

State-of-the-art real-time object detection architectures include YOLOv5 and YOLOv8. For thorough object recognition, YOLOv5 uses a deep convolutional neural network with a CSPDarknet53-based backbone that can handle various filter sizes and depths. Additionally, a feature pyramid network (FPN) is used to improve the recognition of tiny and big objects. However, YOLOv8 has a strong backbone, head, and neck modules that extract high-level information and enhance predictions. It improves object identification for a range of sizes and ratios while doing exceptionally well in bounding boxes, class probabilities, and objectness scores. When it comes to real-time object identification tasks, these architectures are leading the way [3, 20].

Upon completing the data preprocessing step, a detailed analysis was conducted. Figure 3 showcases the results of examining approximately 50 images for each of the 60 classes. The scatter graphs within Fig. 3 provide valuable information regarding

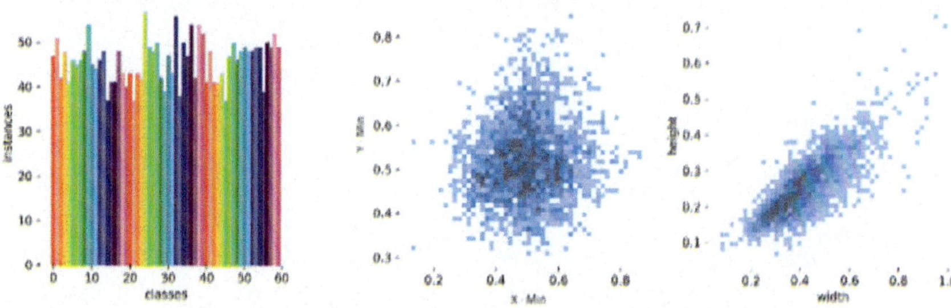

Fig. 3 Graphs depicting statistical information about the ground truth annotations **a** instances per class, **b** scatter plot of xmin-ymin coordinates of ground truth bounding boxes, and **c** scatter plot of width and height of ground truth bounding boxes

Table 1 Training hyperparameters

Hyperparameters	YOLOv5s	YOLOv5m	YOLOv5l	YOLOv8s	YOLOv8m
Initial learning Rate	0.01	0.01	0.01	0.01	0.01
Optimizer	SGD	SGD	SGD	SGD	SGD
Momentum	0.937	0.937	0.937	0.942	0.937
Weight decay	0.0005	0.0005	0.0005	0.001	0.001
Warmup epochs	3.0	3.0	3.0	3.2	3.0

the bounding box areas. The x and y coordinates in the graph represent the xmin and ymin values. The height and width of the bounding box are indicated by the width and height axes, respectively.

3.5 Model Training

A genetic algorithm-based hyperparameter optimization process was used to train the five models. Table 1 provides a summary of the training hyperparameters used. Additionally, using these parameters, each model was trained for 25 epochs with a batch size of 16 and an image size of 768×432.

4 Result and Discussion

4.1 Models Evaluation Measures

The implemented model's performance is evaluated with three main metrics: Mean Intersection over Union (MIoU), Average Precision (AP), and Mean Average Precision (mAP).

4.2 Performance of the Models

Table 2 presents the performance metrics of various models tested with our dataset. The YOLOv8(s/m) model architecture has the quality of positively predicted classes comparatively. And in identifying the actual correct classes the YOLOv5l model architecture is well-performing. Figure 4 shows the F1 confidence curve for all

Table 2 Performance comparison models

Model	Precision	Recall	mAP@ 0.5	mAP@ 0.5:0.95
YOLOv5s	0.898	0.899	0.949	0.654
YOLOv5m	0.965	0.973	0.981	0.703
YOLOv5l	0.969	0.978	0.982	0.706
YOLOv8s	0.974	0.972	0.985	0.743
YOLOv8m	0.974	0.976	0.985	0.734

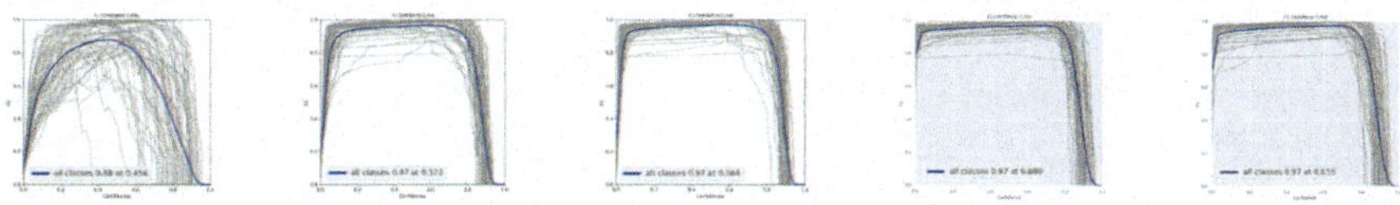

(a) Yolov5s (b) Yolov5m (c) Yolov5l (d) Yolov8s (e) Yolov8m

Fig. 4 Results achieved with YOLO models : f1 confidence curve

respective model architectures. Where the YOLOv8s model architecture shows the best fit among all with 0.680 confidence and model YOLOv5s is performing 67% lower comparatively.

Figure 5 shows the Precision-Recall Curve with mAP@50 for all respective model architectures. Where the YOLOv8 model architecture shows the best fit among all with 0.985 confidence and model YOLOv5 is performing nearly 0.004% lower comparatively. The results of the predictions for palm recognition are visualized in Fig. 6.

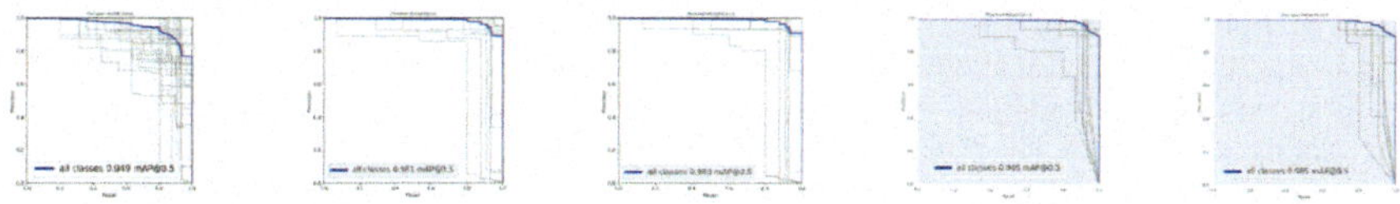

(a) Yolov5s (b) Yolov5m (c) Yolov5l (d) Yolov8s (e) Yolov8m

Fig. 5 Results achieved with YOLO models: precision-recall curve

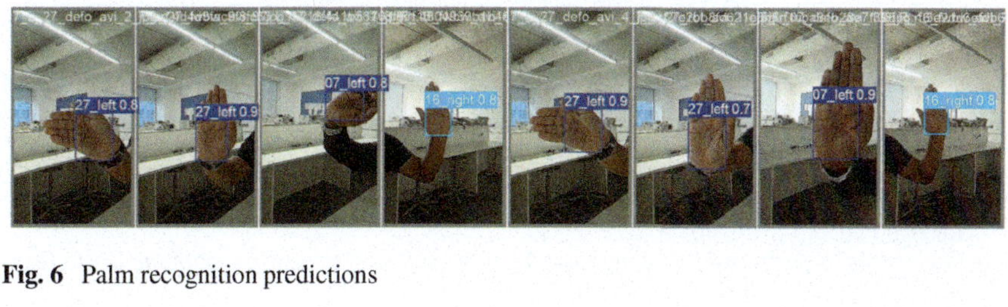

Fig. 6 Palm recognition predictions

5 Conclusions

This paper introduces a new palmprint smartphone-based video dataset to aid palmprint detection in real-world scenarios. The dataset encompasses significant variations in hand pose, orientation, illumination, and sensor proximity, accurately representing palmprint detection in unconstrained real-world acquisition setups. The study evaluates two widely used YOLO object detection families—version 5 and version 8—using standard performance metrics like IoU and mAP. The comparative analysis of these object detection models reveals YOLOv8 as the superior performer, achieving a mAP@0.5 of 0.985. The findings underscore the efficacy and robustness of the proposed palmprint dataset for training palmprint-based biometric systems in real-world conditions. Additionally, the paper outlines plans to process isolated regions of interest in the future, extracting distinctive features to enhance identification accuracy.

References

1. Yang Z, Leng L, Wu T, Li M, Chu J (2023) Multi-order texture features for palmprint recognition. Artif Intell Rev 56(2):995–1011
2. Liang X, Fan D, Yang J, Jia W, Lu G, Zhang D (2023) PKLNet: keypoint localization neural network for touchless palmprint recognition based on edge-aware regression. IEEE J Sel Top Signal Process
3. Zhu X, Lyu S, Wang X, Zhao Q (2021) TPH-YOLOv5: improved YOLOv5 based on transformer prediction head for object detection on drone-captured scenarios. In: Proceedings of the IEEE/CVF international conference on computer vision, pp 2778–2788
4. Zhao S, Zhang B (2020) Deep discriminative representation for generic palmprint recognition. Pattern Recogn 98:107071
5. Liang X, Zhang D, Lu G, Guo Z, Luo N (2019) A novel multicamera system for high-speed touchless palm recognition. IEEE Trans Syst, Man, Cybern: Syst 51(3):1534–1548
6. Chopade A (2019) Classification of skin lesions by using extended-incremental convolutional neural network. In: 2019 International conference on issues and challenges in intelligent computing techniques (ICICT), vol 1. IEEE, pp 1–7
7. Jia W, Zhang B, Lu J, Zhu Y, Zhao Y, Zuo W, Ling H (2017) Palmprint recognition based on complete direction representation. IEEE Trans Image Process 26(9):4483–4498
8. Xu Y, Fei L, Wen J, Zhang D (2016) Discriminative and robust competitive code for palmprint recognition. IEEE Trans Syst, Man, Cybern: Syst 48(2):232–241
9. Fei L, Zhang B, Xu Y, Yan L (2016) Palmprint recognition using neighboring direction indicator. IEEE Trans Hum-Mach Syst 46(6):787–798
10. Luo YT, Zhao LY, Zhang B, Jia W, Xue F, Lu JT, Xu BQ (2016) Local line directional pattern for palmprint recognition. Pattern Recognit 50:26–44
11. Nguyen BP, Tay WL, Chui CK (2015) Robust biometric recognition from palm depth images for gloved hands. IEEE Trans Hum-Mach Syst 45(6):799–804
12. Lu G, Zhang D, Wang K (2003) Palmprint recognition using eigenpalms features. Pattern Recogn Lett 24(9–10):1463–1467
13. Dai J, Zhou J (2010) Multifeature-based high-resolution palmprint recognition. IEEE Trans Pattern Anal Mach Intell 33(5):945–957
14. Hao Y, Sun Z, Tan T, Ren C (2008) Multispectral palm image fusion for accurate contact-free palmprint recognition. In: 2008 15th IEEE international conference on image processing. IEEE, pp 281–284

15. Shang L, Huang DS, Du JX, Zheng CH (2006) Palmprint recognition using FastICA algorithm and radial basis probabilistic neural network. Neurocomputing 69(13–15):1782–1786
16. Connie T, Jin ATB, Ong MGK, Ling DNC (2005) An automated palmprint recognition system. Image Vis Comput 23(5):501–515
17. Wu X, Zhang D, Wang K (2003) Fisherpalms based palmprint recognition. Pattern Recogn Lett 24(15):2829–2838
18. Connie T, Teoh A, Goh M, Ngo D (2003) Palmprint recognition with PCA and ICA. In: Proceedings image and vision computing. New Zealand, pp 227–232
19. Kung SY, Lin SH, Fang M (1995) A neural network approach to face/palm recognition. In: Proceedings of 1995 IEEE workshop on neural networks for signal processing. IEEE, pp 323–332
20. Glenn J (2023) Ultralytics, YOLOv8. https://github.com/ultralytics/ultralytics

Improved Localization of Knuckle Regions for Contactless Acquisition

Shreya Sidabache, Kruti Pandya, Toukir Sabugar, and Ritesh Vyas

Abstract In hand-based biometric identification and authentication systems, the localization of the knuckles is a crucial task. The accurate localization of knuckle regions in images has shown to have great potential in recent years thanks to deep learning techniques. The YOLOv5 algorithm, a cutting-edge object detection algorithm, has attracted a lot of attention in this regard because of its high accuracy and quick processing time. In this study, we use YOLOv5 to propose a novel method for knuckle localization. Training and testing are the two main phases of the suggested strategy. We trained the YOLOv5 algorithm using a sizable dataset of hand images during the training phase. To locate the knuckle regions in the images, the dataset was manually annotated. We then improved the pre-trained YOLOv5 model's localization of knuckles accuracy using our dataset. During the testing phase, we assessed the effectiveness of our strategy using a different test dataset. Performance was evaluated using the mean intersection of union (mIoU) and mean average precision (mAP) measures. Our recommended approach for knuckle localization using YOLOv5 demonstrates the strength and capability of deep learning techniques in solving knuckle localization issues. We use this as a future work, a comparative examination of the holistic (all twelve knuckles of 4 fingers) knuckle localization problem will be discussed.

Keywords Knuckle · Localization · YOLO · Mean average precision (mAP) · Mean intersection of union (MIoU)

1 Introduction

Hand Anatomy According to Brand and Hollister (1999; Kry et al. 2002), the bones, muscles, tendons, and skin that make up the complex anatomical architecture of the human hand are interconnected in a complicated way. Various areas, such as ergonomics, human-computer interaction, hand surgery, and computer animation,

S. Sidabache · K. Pandya · T. Sabugar · R. Vyas (✉)
Pandit Deendayal Energy University, Gandhinagar, Gujarat, India
e-mail: ritesh.vyas@sot.pdpu.ac.in

S. Chaudhury et al. (eds.), *Computer Vision, Pattern Recognition, Image Processing, and Graphics*, Lecture Notes in Electrical Engineering 1218,
https://doi.org/10.1007/978-981-97-5212-6_14

need an understanding of the anatomical structures of the human hand [7]. The hand consists of digital, carpal, and wrist bones, along with smaller bone groups. The digital bones in each finger are connected by three important joints: distal interphalangeal joint (DIP), proximal interphalangeal joint (PIP), and metacarpal phalangeal joint (MCP). These joints work in tandem to create the digital bones in each finger. The thumb's virtual bones consist of interphalangeal and carpometacarpal joints, the radius and ulna, and eight carpal bones. In biology, the terms "distal interphalangeal joint," "proximal interphalangeal joint," and "metacarpophalangeal joint" are used to refer to knuckle factors, labeled as major, minor, and base in the dataset [7]. The lack of detailed research on knuckles and their potential use in forensic investigations prompts further exploration, as no other publication specifically discusses this topic (Fig. 1).

Biometrics According to their unique physiological and behavioral traits, the field of "biometrics" predicts how people spontaneously become aware of themselves. The sectors of security and insurance have several uses for biometrics [1]. Biometric systems use physiological, behavioral, or both attributes to confirm and identify a person as a distinct user. This state-of-the-art technology validates and identifies the user as a distinct user, ensuring their identity remains secure and unique [4]. Researchers are exploring the use of hand knuckle patterns in personal spotting, using the YOLO algorithm to recognize and localize three knuckle points in human fingers. Object detection in computer vision involves locating and identifying objects using bounding boxes. Convolutional neural networks (CNNs) are deep learning approaches that achieve high accuracy in recognizing and localizing objects. Two-stage object detection algorithms involve Region Proposal Generation, generating candidate areas with interesting features, and Object Classification and Refinement. The first stage creates candidate areas and suggests objects, while the second step divides these regions into multiple object types and refines bounding box coordinates. Classifier networks categorize suggested areas, and bounding box regression networks adjust the bounding box coordinates to fit the objects.

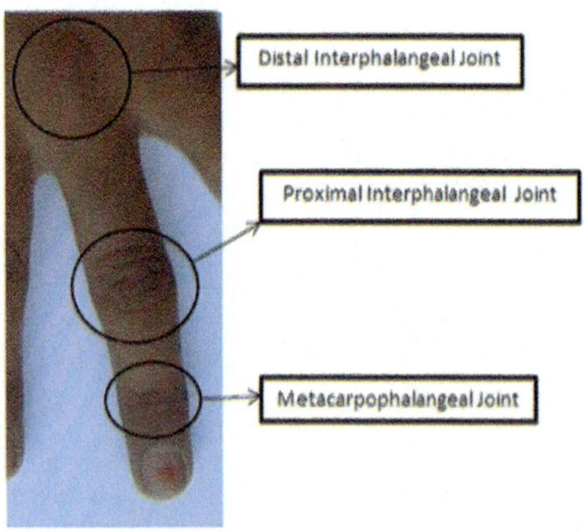

Fig. 1 Finger knuckle image with biological names [7]

You Only Look Once The YOLO algorithm, based on a regression problem, enables real-time object recognition in photographs. By glancing at a picture, humans can quickly identify its constituent parts, positions, and relationships. This quick and precise vision allows for easier tasks like driving. Adaptive robotic systems, assistive technologies, and computers that can drive without specialized sensors can benefit from quick, accurate object detection algorithms. Convolutional neural networks (CNNs) are used by the YOLO system to subtly honor details, requiring only one forward propagation through a neural network to detect objects. This method allows for simultaneous projection of bounding boxes and probability for multiple classes, enhancing the overall image quality.

2 Literature Review

2.1 Comparison Between R-CNN and YOLO

The R-CNN series is the most widely used object recognition algorithm for goal identification, offering greater accuracy despite its higher average speed [13]. YOLO, a popular object detection method, is known for its dynamism and accuracy. Introduced by Joseph et al. in 2016, it uses an end-to-end neural network to perform bounding box and class probability divination simultaneously. This approach outperforms traditional methods, which first processed data using classifiers and then detected objects. YOLO's accuracy is linked to Fast R-CNN, making it the fastest way to identify objects, unlike other modern algorithms like Fast R-CNN and R-CNN [5]. To finish the linked work segment, these models were just recently presented. Future comparisons are possible.

2.2 Personal Recognition Using Biometrics

Recent developments in MULTIMODAL biometric systems have drawn the interest of academics, and some work has already been published in the literature [2, 3, 10]. Bimodal biometric systems, including voice with face, palmprint with face, face with iris, fingerprint with face, or fingerprint with face, have been extensively researched. These systems use two separate sensors or pictures to perform tasks, with the exception of face and iris. These systems can recover information about hand shape and palmprint from a single medium-resolution photograph, aiding in palmprint recognition [12, 14], Researchers have developed biometrics techniques to help humans become aware of themselves based on their physiological and behavioral peculiarities. This phenomenon has applications in security and insurance industries [1]. A technique confirms a person's description based on intelligence or visible character traits, evaluating attributes such as physical characteristics like fingerprints, eye color, hair color, hand geometry, voice, tongue, signature, framework, or keyboarding technique [6]. Modern technology known as a biometric system helps to validate and identify a person as a distinct user by using their physiological, behavioral, or both, features as input.

2.3 Strategy of YOLOv3

YOLOv3 predicts a model using backbone, neck, and head criteria. The backbone extracts useful characteristics from input pictures, while the head connects the backbone and head. Higher-level features like object pieces and semantic information are extracted from deeper layers, while lower-level features like edges and textures are extracted from earlier layers [9]. The backbone and neck work together to enhance spatial and semantic information, often using convolutional layers or feature pyramid networks. The head, the final component, makes predictions based on the data, while task-specific subnetworks handle classification, localization, instance segmentation, and pose estimation. The head evaluates the neck's qualities to make predictions for each prospective item, and non-maximum suppression (NMS) eliminates redundant predictions for the highest detection certainty [9]. But the work of YOLOv5 model is comparatively better than the YOLOv3 model.

3 Methodology

3.1 Normalization

Normalizing data is a popular approach for data preparation, translating numerical columns to a common scale. It improves the dependability of machine learning models when features fall into discrete ranges, although it is not necessary for all available datasets.

3.2 Image Labeler

Image labeling assigns labels to images for recognition and classification, aiding tasks like object identification, picture classification, semantic segmentation, and machine learning model development. Open-source and paid applications provide an intuitive user interface, enabling features like pixel-level segment labeling, object class labels, and bounding boxes.

3.3 Ground Truth

Ground truth refers to precise and annotated information in images, serving as a benchmark for evaluating the YOLO paradigm's effectiveness. A dataset of photos and related annotations is necessary for training a YOLO model. Typical ground truth annotations consist of: **Bounding Boxes**: Picture depicts rectangular areas containing important subjects, with bounding boxes providing top-left corner, width, and height coordinates. **Class Labels**: Class labels are assigned to enclosing boxes to identify the item category or type, like "car" for an automobile. **Objective Score**: YOLO uses bounding boxes with objectness scores to determine object likelihood, aiding in distinguishing foreground and background areas. Human annotators create bounding boxes and class labels for each image, which are trained on the annotated dataset for item recognition and categorization.[1] Annotation process, bounding boxes, and associated class labels are manually created by human annotators to identify the objects in each image.

3.4 YOLOv5

YOLO, the original YOLO algorithm, has evolved with new categories since its release in 2015. In 2020, Ultralytics released YOLOv5, an open-source project that builds on past versions and introduces more functionality. Its Efficient-Det design, based on Efficient-Net network architecture, achieves exceptional accuracy and universality across various object types. YOLOv5 is trained on 600 item categories from the D5 dataset.

YOLOv5 algorithm employs single-shot object identification to predict object presence and placement in a single pass through an input image [11]. YOLO improves computational efficiency by processing the entire image in one step and applying a single CNN to divide it into grids [8]. In this study, YOLO version 5, also known as YOLOv5, offers four primary model types in YOLO. **YOLOv5s**: The lowest model in this family, with about 7.2 million parameters, is perfect for making conclusions on the CPU. **YOLOv5m**: A medium-sized model with 21.2 million parameters is the end result, offering a well-balanced speed and accuracy for various datasets and training. **YOLOv5l**: A massive 46.5 million parameter YOLOv5 family model is used. For datasets where we must find really fine details, it works wonderfully. **YOLOv5x**: The YOLOv5 model, a regression-based approach, is used in this study to detect outside hand knuckle prints, focusing on object detection in computer vision. With 86.7 million parameters, it is faster than other methods and requires more time. The YOLO algorithm generates classes and bounding boxes for the entire image in a single run, making it a highly regarded object detection method in computer vision.

[1] Available at http://wp.lancs.ac.uk/icvl/research/datasets/.

3.5 Performance Measure

Evaluation Metrics: Evaluation metrics measure a statistical or machine learning model's performance and efficacy, enabling comparisons and enhancing future results. This dataset will be utilized for future enhancements.
Precision: The categorization model's capability to only find important data pieces. In mathematics, precision is determined as the total number of true positives divided by the total number of false positives.
Recall: Recall is a statistic that measures the proportion of accurate positive predictions among all possible positive predictions.
AP: Average precision is a statistic that combines recall and accuracy for ranking retrieval results. It is calculated by averaging precision scores after retrieving relevant documents. The model's average precision for each class can be found by examining the region below the accuracy versus recall curve.
mAP: Mean Average Precision (mAP) is the average accuracy number across all classes in object detection class predictions. Positive predictions have an IoU value above 0.5, while negative predictions have an IoU value below 0.5. Three bounding boxes can be predicted for each grid cell in the input image [15].
IoU: The intersection over the union metric is essential for evaluating localization precision and identifying errors in object identification models. It involves computing the intersection of two matched bounding boxes for the same item, determining the IoU between predicted and ground truth bounding boxes. YOLOv5, which incorporates C IoU loss, improves model performance on unbalanced datasets. The intersection of both boxes detects knuckles, ensuring proper object identification output. Figure 2 describes the Intersection of Union [15]. The two boxes which are shown in Fig. 2 are the ground truth and prediction. And the intersection of both boxes is used to get the proper output in detecting the knuckles.
Intersection over union equation is shown below:

$$IOU = \frac{Area\,of\,Intersection\,of\,Two\,boxes}{Area\,of\,Union\,of\,Two\,boxes} \tag{1}$$

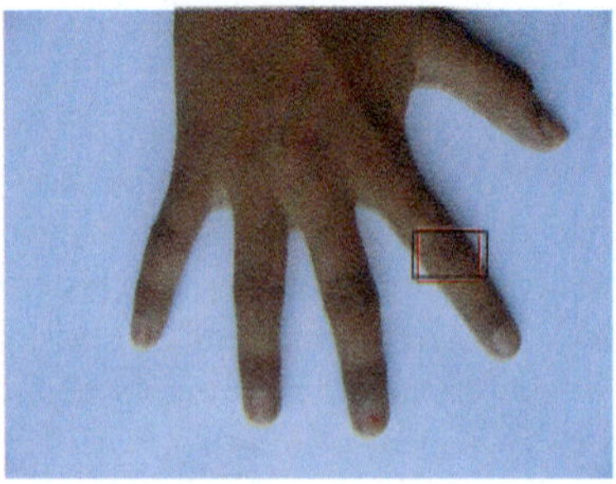

Fig. 2 Figure of IoU which represents two boxes; the Red box is for ground truth and the black box is for prediction [15]

4 Results and Discussion

4.1 Database

We are using the dataset of hand biometrics for detecting the knuckle https://www4.comp.polyu.edu.hk/~csajaykr/knuckleV2.htm.

Finger knuckle patterns have been a subject of research and development for human identification, with the primary and secondary minor finger knuckles being prominent locations. This database project aimed to investigate the potential uses of second minor finger knuckle patterns, which are located at the intersection of proximal and metacarpal phalanx bones, as standalone biometric IDs. The study involved over 500 people and involved an extensive library of hand dorsal photographs. The database contains 2505 images of the dorsal surface of the right hand from 501 unique subjects, with each finger having three distinct knuckle patterns. The database is open to the public and contains pictures of 712 different people's dorsal hands. The availability of two-session hand dorsal pictures facilitates the study on the longevity of knuckle patterns, and the images have undergone automated splitting and normalization using several YOLOv5 models. The output ensures accurate labeling of knuckle patterns. The database project focuses on using finger knuckle patterns for biometric applications, particularly when considering second minor knuckle patterns (Fig. 3).

4.2 Comparison of Models

The study utilized the YOLOv5 version to detect finger knuckles using four types: small, medium, large, and extra large. Evaluation metrics included mAP 50, mAP 50–95, Precision, and Recall. The model was trained for mAP values between 50 and 95%. Comparisons were made between all YOLOv5 models, as shown in Table 1.

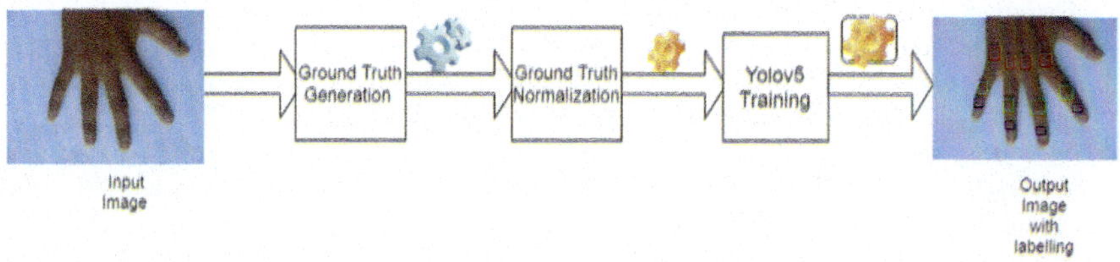

Fig. 3 Block diagram of knuckle localization using YOLOv5 model

Table 1 The results of different types of YOLOv5 models

Series model	mAP@50	mAP@50–95	Precision	Recall
YOLOv5s	0.717	0.334	0.638	0.686
YOLOv5m	0.833	0.432	0.765	0.826
YOLOv5l	0.87	0.462	0.801	0.855
YOLOv5x	0.863	0.439	0.78	0.826

5 Conclusion and Future Enhancement

The proposed approach for localizing knuckles using YOLOv5 demonstrates the effectiveness of deep learning methods in computer vision problems. This strategy can enhance hand-based biometric identification and authentication systems, improving their performance and accuracy. Accurate knuckle localization enhances security and dependability in these systems, making them more reliable and efficient.

Future enhancements for YOLOv5 localization of knuckles can improve accuracy and resilience. Future research should explore larger datasets, additional training methods, and optimizing model design. This approach advances computer vision and biometric identification, opening up new possibilities for user authentication and security processes in other sectors.

References

1. Bhaskar B, Veluchamy S (2014) Hand-based multibiometric authentication using local feature extraction. In: 2014 International conference on recent trends in information technology, pp 1–5
2. Hong Lin, Jain Anil (1998) Integrating faces and fingerprints for personal identification. IEEE Trans Pattern Anal Mach Intell 20(12):1295–1307
3. Jain AK, Ross A, Prabhakar S (2004) An introduction to biometric recognition. IEEE Trans Circuits Syst Video Technol 14(1):4–20
4. Kumar A, Wong DC, Shen HC, Jain AK (2003) Personal verification using palmprint and hand geometry biometric. In: Kittler J, Nixon MS (eds) Audio- and video-based biometric person authentication. Springer Berlin Heidelberg, Berlin, Heidelberg, pp 668–678
5. Mahalleh VB, ALQutami TA, Mahmood IA (2019) Yolo-based valve type recognition and localization. In: 2019 IEEE 6th international conference on industrial engineering and applications (ICIEA), pp 37–40
6. Oloyede Muhtahir O, Hancke Gerhard P (2016) Unimodal and multimodal biometric sensing systems: a review. IEEE Access 4:7532–7555
7. Rhee T, Neumann U, Lewis JP (2006) Human hand modeling from surface anatomy. In: Proceedings of the 2006 symposium on interactive 3D graphics and games, I3D '06, New York, NY, USA, 2006. Association for Computing Machinery, pp 27–34
8. Shinde S, Kothari A, Gupta V (2018) Yolo-based human action recognition and localization. Procedia Comput Sci 133:831–838. International Conference on Robotics and Smart Manufacturing (RoSMa2018)

9. Terven JR, Córdova-Esparza D-M (2023) A comprehensive review of yolo: from yolov1 and beyond
10. Toh K-A, Yau W-Y (2004) Combination of hyperbolic functions for multimodal biometrics data fusion. IEEE Trans Syst, Man, Cybern, Part B (Cybern) 34(2):1196–1209
11. Vyas R, Williams BM, Rahmani H, Boswell-Challand R, Jiang Z, Angelov P, Black S (2022) Ensemble-based bounding box regression for enhanced knuckle localization. Sensors 22(4)
12. Xiangqian Wu, Zhang David, Wang Kuanquan (2003) Fisherpalms based palmprint recognition. Pattern Recogn Lett 24(15):2829–2838
13. Yao J, Qi J, Zhang J, Shao H, Yang J, Li X (2021) A real-time detection algorithm for kiwifruit defects based on yolov5. Electronics 10(14)
14. Zhang Dapeng, Shu Wei (1999) Two novel characteristics in palmprint verification: datum point invariance and line feature matching. Pattern Recogn 32(4):691–702
15. Ćorović A, Velibor Ilić V, Đurić S, Marijan M, Pavković B (2018) The real-time detection of traffic participants using yolo algorithm. In: 2018 26th telecommunications forum (TELFOR), pp 1–4

NCVPRIPG 2023 Summer Challenge on Writer Verification

Gyan Prabhat, Abu Shahid, Prajwal Gatti, Manan Shah, Girin Chutia, Arvind Kumar Sharma, and Anand Mishra

Abstract This report presents the outcomes of the Summer Challenge on Writer Verification, hosted as part of the Eighth National Conference on Computer Vision, Pattern Recognition, Image Processing, and Graphics (NCVPRIPG) held at IIT Jodhpur on July 21–23, 2023. This challenge introduces a novel dataset comprising images of handwritten text contributed by 1,352 unique writers. Predominantly, these images feature handwritten Hindi text, but they also encompass a variety of elements such as numbers, mathematical symbols, and English text. Participants were tasked with developing a model capable of automatically determining whether the text in a given pair of images is authored by the same writer or different writers. The primary objective of this challenge was to advance research in the realm of handwritten text recognition. Throughout the competition, we registered 108 teams, with 18 teams submitting results for the validation dataset. Out of these, 13 teams provided submissions for the semi-final dataset. The top six teams from the semi-finals were subsequently invited to compete in the finals. Additional details about the challenge can be found at https://vl2g.github.io/challenges/wv2023/.

G. Prabhat (✉) · A. Shahid · P. Gatti · A. K. Sharma · A. Mishra
Indian Institute of Technology Jodhpur, Jodhpur, India
e-mail: prabhat.1@iitj.ac.in

A. Shahid
e-mail: shahid.3@iitj.ac.in

P. Gatti
e-mail: pgatti@iitj.ac.in

A. K. Sharma
e-mail: sharma.126@iitj.ac.in

A. Mishra
e-mail: mishra@iitj.ac.in

M. Shah
Cashfree Payments India, Pvt. Ltd, Bengaluru, India
e-mail: mt-shah@hotmail.com

G. Chutia
HCL Technologies Ltd., Chennai, India
e-mail: girin.iitm@gmail.com

S. Chaudhury et al. (eds.), *Computer Vision, Pattern Recognition, Image Processing, and Graphics*, Lecture Notes in Electrical Engineering 1218,
https://doi.org/10.1007/978-981-97-5212-6_15

Keywords Writer verification · Handwritten text · Indic language · Document analysis · Handwritten text recognition

1 Introduction

Handwriting comparison is a task to find the likelihood of similarity between the handwritten samples of the known and questioned writer [11]. The *Writer Verification* task originated as a signature verification problem [13] to identify potential fraud in the banking sector. It is the process of analyzing if the handwritten text in the given pair of images is written by the *same writer* or *different writers*. As the handwriting of different individuals can vary significantly, any writer verification model would need to learn the underlying variations of their handwriting. In the offline context, where dynamic information about the writing process is not available, unlike when working on electronic equipment, the writer verification becomes even more challenging.

Writer-independent verification is the task of measuring the similarity of two given handwritten samples as to how likely it is that the samples were written by the same writer, without having any knowledge of writer identity [12]. Handwriting experts or forensic document examiners (FDE) are people who are trained to do this task manually. They check various aspects of handwriting, like pen pressure, stroke patterns, letter formations, etc. FDEs are trained to identify unique characteristics in a person's handwriting that can serve as a basis for verification [4, 12]. Writer verification has found its application in various areas such as forensic analysis, identity verification [7], plagiarism detection, synthetic handwritten text generation, insurance, and banking. Such an important task stands to benefit from automation by using the advances in computer vision. Thus, to encourage research in this promising direction, we conducted the Summer Challenge on Writer Verification as part of the Eighth National Conference on Computer Vision, Pattern Recognition, Image Processing, and Graphics (NCVPRIPG 2023), utilizing a new dataset featuring handwritten Hindi text collected from 1, 352 unique writers. We believe that learning from this challenge will pave a new paradigm in the area of writer verification research.

2 Motivation

The Summer Challenge on Writer Verification aims to promote research in the area of *writer verification* by promoting the development of new and innovative methodologies and approaches. The images present in the dataset contain images of handwritten text, which can be a single or multiple word(s), sentence(s), paragraph(s), numbers, and other entities. Thus, it contains significant variations in the content and writing style for a single writer as well as for different writers.

This challenge prompts the participants to develop and implement new algorithms that have the capability to take a pair of images as input in order to detect if these texts were written by the same writer or two different writers.

3 Dataset

We formulated different question papers, which primarily consisted of short questions with one or few words of answers. In addition, a few questions were kept more subjective to collect long-form text. These subjective questions consisted of two to three questions, which can be answered in a short paragraph. A sample of duly filled-in question paper is shown in the Appendix (Fig. 5).

From these collected sheets, we extract data using the following steps:

1. *Extract answer boxes of every writer*: Given the images of answer scripts, detect and extract the answer boxes and store them in a folder where each folder contains the answers written by the same writer. There are different folders for different writers.
2. *Deleting empty answer boxes*: If questions were not attempted by the writer, the answer boxes are left blank. These empty answer boxes were removed.
3. *Deleting poor writers*: If a writer has very few images, it is considered noise. If answer boxes associated with a writer (after removing empty ones) were less than 4, they were removed from the dataset.
4. *Data Splitting*: After cleaning the data, train-validation-test split was made in the ratio $75:5:20$, such that writers in each split are disjoint.
5. *Anonymization of validation and test images*: Images in validation and test sets were renamed so that they cannot be traced back to their original writer.
6. *Ground Truth Generation*: While the training data structure did not necessitate ground truth labels, we created ground truth labels for the validation and test datasets.
7. *Unpacking test and validation sets*: Previously, the images were organized within individual folders for each writer. To eliminate inter-image relationships, we consolidated images from all validation and test set writers into single storage locations.

The train-validation-test datasets[1] consisted of handwritten images from 1,352, 92, and 360 unique writers, respectively. The number of available handwritten text images is not consistent for all the writers, and its distribution is shown in Table 1. We note that the dataset has been carefully processed to exclude any personal or identifiable information.

[1] For dataset access, please contact: prabhat.1@iitj.ac.in.

Table 1 Distribution of count of unique writers based on the number of images in the dataset

Number of images	Count of unique writers
4	180
5	102
6	133
7	144
8	107
9	150
10	179
11	204
12	153

4 Problem Statement

The problem of writer verification proposed in this challenge can be summarized as follows: *Given an image pair, identify if the text present in these two images is written by the same writer or different writers*. A few examples of such image pairs are shown in Fig. 1.

5 Evaluation Protocol

Given a pair of images containing handwritten text, the expected model output is a binary output depicting if the handwritten text present in the given pair of images is written by the same writer *Class-1* or different writers *Class-0*.

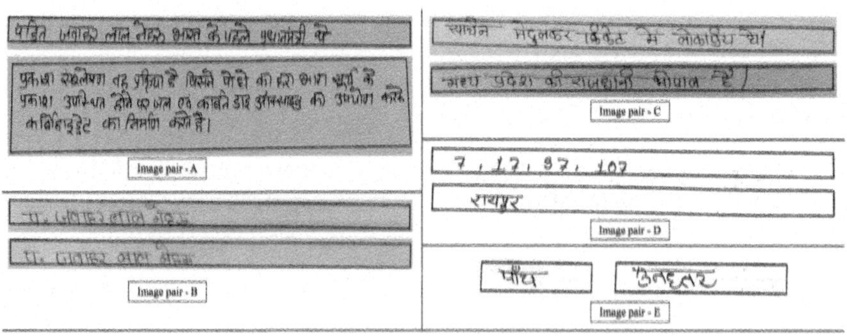

Fig. 1 Examples from our dataset. Can you identify the text in which image pair is written by the same writer? Answer: Image pairs A, D, and E are written by the same writers correspondingly

We employ evaluation metrics typical of binary classification problems, specifically the *F-Score* and the *AUC Score*. All the rankings in the challenge were decided based on the AUC score only.

5.1 *F1-Score*

Given a confusion matrix, the *Precision* and *Recall* can be defined as follows:

$$\text{Precision} = \frac{TP}{TP + FP} \tag{1}$$

$$\text{Recall} = \frac{TP}{TP + FN} \tag{2}$$

$$\text{Precision} = \frac{TP}{TP + FP}$$

$$\text{Recall} = \frac{TP}{TP + FN}$$

where *TP* is True positives, *FP* is False positives, *TN* is True negatives, and *FN* is False negatives. The F-Score is then calculated as follows:

$$F1 = \frac{2 \times \text{Precision} \times \text{Recall}}{\text{Precision} + \text{Recall}} \tag{3}$$

5.2 *AUC*

The Area Under the Curve (AUC) is a key metric used to evaluate binary classification models. It measures the area under the Receiver Operating Characteristic (ROC) curve, providing a score between 0 and 1. A score of 1 denotes a perfect classifier, while 0.5 represents random performance.

6 Details of Submitted Result

We divided the competition into two phases, namely *semi-final* and *final*. A dataset of 1, 383 images with handwritten text from 180 unique writers was released for the semi-final event. We received submissions from 13 teams for the semi-final event,

Table 2 AUC scores on the validation data from six finalist teams and the baseline

Team name	AUC score (%)	Leaderboard rank (↓)
Baseline	65.0	–
Word Detective	82.0	6
Alpha	87.8	5
Forza Code	91.2	4
Neural Survivor	91.5	3
InkSq	92.2	2
MaSha	97.6	1

and on the basis of the evaluation metric *AUC Score*, the top 6 teams were selected and invited to participate in the final event.

For the final event, a dataset consisting of 2, 926 images consisting of handwritten text from 360 unique writers was released, and all the 6 teams submitted their results on the final test data. The final leaderboard is shown in Table 2. The system descriptions of the top three teams (Masha, InkSq, Neural Survivor) are described below. Due to space limitations, solutions from the teams Forza Code (Rank-4), Alpha (Rank-5), and Word Detective (Rank-6) are not presented here. We also provide a baseline model that adopts SigNet [6] model for our dataset, using the original hyperparameter settings in our implementation.

6.1 Solution from Team MaSha (Winner)

We resized all images to dimensions of 224×224 before inputting them into a standard ResNet50 [8] architecture. Our choice of the ResNet50 backbone was based on its pre-training with DINO [2] on ImageNet [5], making it an excellent candidate for transfer learning and metric learning tasks.

Model architecture The original ResNet50 model concludes with a fully connected (FC) layer, generating 1000 output features for 1000 classes. In our implementation, we replaced this FC layer with a linear layer, reducing the output dimension to 64. We trained the network using a *triplet margin loss* [3], defined as $L(a, p, n) = \max d(a_i, p_i) - d(a_i, n_i) + \text{margin}, 0$. Here, *a* represents the anchor, *p* the positive image (from the same writer as the anchor), and *n* the negative image (from a different writer than the anchor). Triplets were mined using a *miner* function based on specific conditions. We employed the cosine similarity as our distance metric (d) and set the margin to 0.2 across all experiments. After triplet mining, the final batch loss was computed by averaging the losses of individual triplets. The architecture is depicted in Fig. 2.

Training strategy and conclusions Hyperparameters were tuned to optimize the AUC score on the validation set and minimize training time until AUC convergence.

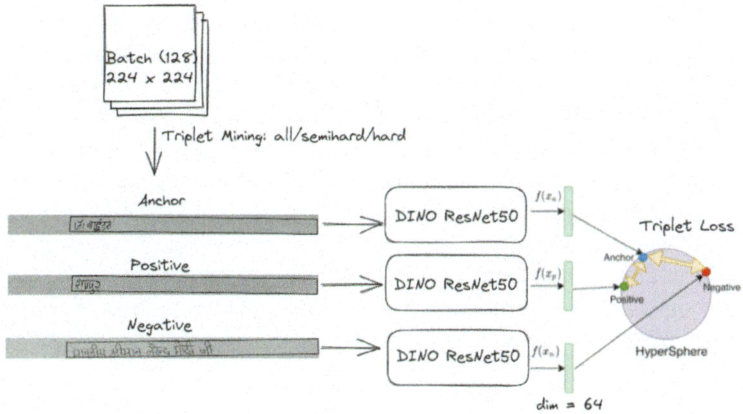

Fig. 2 Architecture diagram of the model presented by team-MaSha

A learning rate of 0.01 was used for the head (FC layer), 0.001 was used for the backbone, along with Adam [9] as the optimizer and an exponentially decaying lr scheduler. The lr decays every epoch according to $\text{lr} = \text{lr}_0(1 + 0.001 \times \text{lr})^{-0.75}$. The batch sizes were varied in {32, 128}, and the batch size of 128 significantly outperformed on the AUC as compared to 32. The models were trained till 80 epochs.

For the implementation of losses, miners, and samplers, the Pytorch-metric-learning [10] package was used. It was found that using an *MPerClassSampler* instead of the standard *RandomSampler* for sampling in the *Dataloader* provided extremely fast convergence in about 15 epochs. This sampler samples 4 images of every class in a batch of images, ensuring more number of triplets and thus a faster convergence. Mining of triplets was executed using the *TripletMarginMiner* with various strategies: *all*, *hard*, and *semihard*. Their respective AUC scores followed the order: *all* > *semihard* > *hard*. Intriguingly, in the case of hard mining, the loss function stagnated within a few epochs, leading to negligible learning progress.

The best AUC achieved on the validation set is 0.9775, with a batch size of 128, all mining strategy, *MPerClassSampler*, 0.2 margin, 64-dimensional output vector, and trained for 10 epochs.

6.2 *Solution from Team InkSq (First Runners-up)*

The dataset exhibited a median image height of 211 pixels and a width of 2, 789 pixels. To facilitate training, we resized all images to 200 × 2, 600 pixels. For data splitting, we employed a random 75 : 25 ratio to partition the dataset into training and validation sets. During training, we generated image pairs, both positive and negative, as required for the task.

Model architecture and training In the early 1990s, [1] introduced *Siamese* networks to tackle the signature verification problem by translating it as an image-matching problem. A Siamese neural network is made up of two identical networks which are connected by a loss function. Feature representations at the highest level from both these identical networks are passed to this loss function to compute the loss metric. The twin networks are tied via shared weights, ensuring consistency in learned features and preventing similar images from being mapped to significantly different locations in feature space. The Siamese network consisting of a backbone and a classification module was used for the challenge as shown in Fig. 3. The backbone module comprises layers extracted from *ResNet50* [8], up to layer 4. These layer weights are frozen and left unchanged during the model's training process.

6.3 Solution from Team Neural Survivor (Second Runners-Up)

The given dataset was processed to generate a new dataset containing 94, 800 pairs of images with nearly 48 percent positive labels (same writer for both images). Each pair of images is resized to 500 × 50 pixels.

Model architecture and training The feature-extracting block (FEB) is the first part of the model. FEB converts the images into features that capture visual characteristics of the handwritten text [6]. Figure 4 shows the structure of FEB. Images are passed to the FEB which encodes them into feature vectors of shape $\mathbb{R}^{1000}$. To train the FEB, it is connected via an absolution difference block to a fully connected layer. Adam optimizer with a batch size of 10 was used to train the model. After the model has been trained to its optimal state, the trained FEB is separated from the

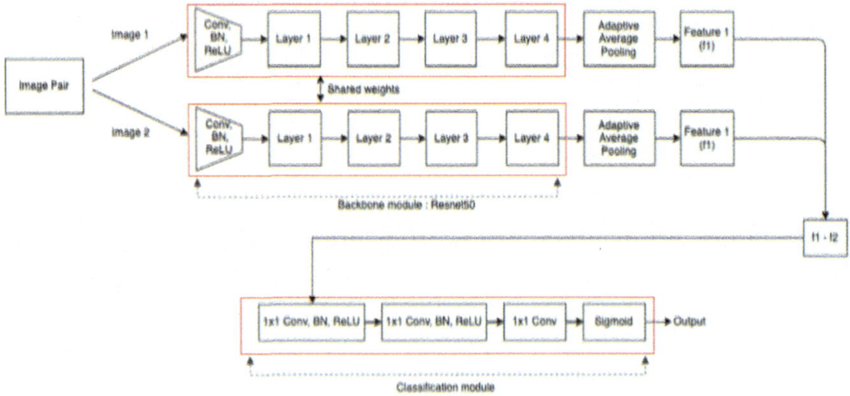

Fig. 3 Architecture diagram of the model presented by team-InkSq

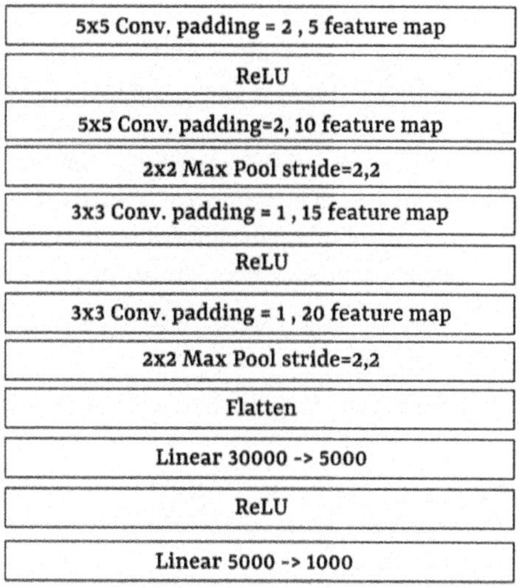

Fig. 4 Architecture diagram of the model presented by team-neural survivor

model, and the complete processed dataset is converted into a 1000-feature dataset. The KNN algorithm is applied to this dataset to generate the model.

7 Discussion and Future Work

Although the dataset provided in this challenge contained images with varying styles of handwriting and content, despite that, this dataset does not mimic the real world completely. We plan to modify and enlarge this dataset to capture the real-world nuisances of handwritten text.

The models submitted by the finalist teams perform significantly well for the test data. However, the generalization of these models is yet to be verified.

Additionally, we are yet to understand what exactly the model is learning to decide if the text is from the same writer or not. In this regard, we plan to implement an attention-based network to understand the features learned by the model for decision-making.

The dataset was originally collected for automatic reading and evaluation of handwritten answer sheets. We also plan to utilize the learning from this challenge to make further progress on this task.

8 Conclusion

In this paper, we have presented the overview of the *Summer Challenge on Writer Verification* which was organized in *NCVPRIPG 2023*. This challenge focused on the task of writer verification using offline text images consisting of handwritten text, primarily in the Hindi language. The task prompted the participants to build models and develop algorithms that have the capability to automatically identify if the handwritten text in the given pair of images has been written by the same writer or different writers.

We also presented the approach and results from the top three teams. We believe that the ideas and insights presented by these teams would serve as the stepping stone for future research in the area of writer verification. New challenges and competitions can expand on these ideas and can make use of the dataset prepared for this challenge.

Appendix: Sample Images of Duly Filled Question Papers

We have collected data in the form of answer sheets. A sample image of these answer sheets is shown in Fig. 5.

Acknowledgements This work was partly supported by MeitY, Government of India (Project Number: S/MeitY/AM/20210114) under NLTM-Bhashini.

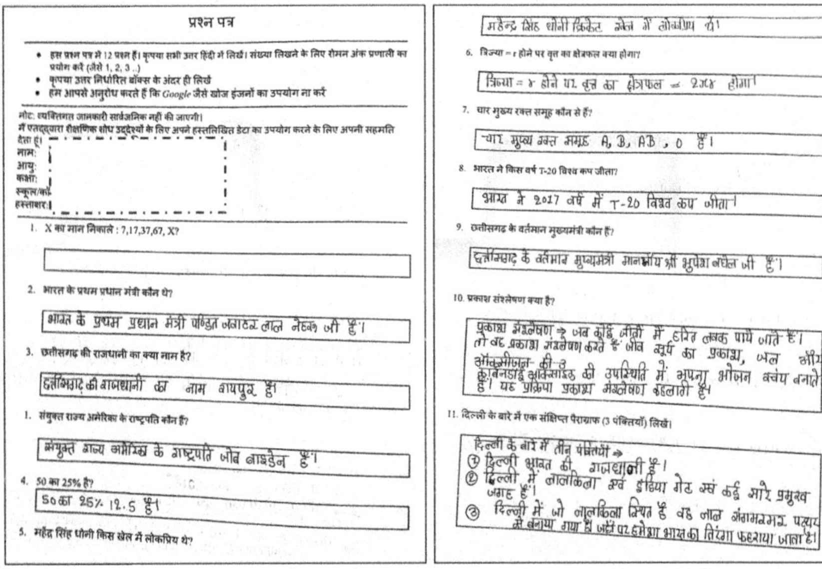

प्रश्न पत्र

- इस प्रश्न पत्र में 12 प्रश्न हैं। कृपया सभी उत्तर हिंदी में लिखें। संख्या लिखने के लिए रोमन अंक प्रणाली का प्रयोग करें (जैसे 1, 2, 3 ..)
- कृपया उत्तर निर्धारित बॉक्स के अंदर ही लिखें
- हम आपसे अनुरोध करते हैं कि *Google* जैसे खोज इंजनों का उपयोग ना करें

नोट: व्यक्तिगत जानकारी सार्वजनिक नहीं की जाएगी।
मैं एतद्द्वारा शैक्षणिक शोध उद्देश्यों के लिए अपने हस्तलिखित डेटा का उपयोग करने के लिए अपनी सहमति देता हूं।
नाम:
आयु:
कक्षा:
स्कूल/कॉ
हस्ताक्षर:

1. X का मान निकाले : 7,17,37,67, X?
2. भारत के प्रथम प्रधान मंत्री कौन थे?
3. छत्तीसगढ़ की राजधानी का क्या नाम है?
1. संयुक्त राज्य अमेरिका के राष्ट्रपति कौन हैं?
4. 50 का 25% है?
5. महेंद्र सिंह धोनी किस खेल में लोकप्रिय थे?
6. त्रिज्या = r होने पर वृत्त का क्षेत्रफल क्या होगा?
7. चार मुख्य रक्त समूह कौन से हैं?
8. भारत ने किस वर्ष T-20 विश्व कप जीता?
9. छत्तीसगढ़ के वर्तमान मुख्यमंत्री कौन हैं?
10. प्रकाश संश्लेषण क्या है?
11. दिल्ली के बारे में एक संक्षिप्त पैराग्राफ (3 पंक्तियाँ) लिखें।

Fig. 5 Sample image of a duly filled question paper. (Note that the personal information of the writer is intentionally omitted with a white block.)

References

1. Bromley, J., Guyon, I., LeCun, Y., Säckinger, E., Shah, R.: Signature verification using a" siamese" time delay neural network. Advances in neural information processing systems 6 (1993)
2. Caron M, Touvron H, Misra I, Jégou H, Mairal J, Bojanowski P, Joulin A (2021) Emerging properties in self-supervised vision transformers. In: Proceedings of the IEEE/CVF international conference on computer vision, pp 9650–9660
3. Chattopadhyay S, Manna S, Bhattacharya S, Pal U (2022) Surds: self-supervised attention-guided reconstruction and dual triplet loss for writer independent offline signature verification. In: 2022 26th international conference on pattern recognition (ICPR). IEEE, pp 1600–1606
4. Chauhan M, Shaikh MA, Srihari SN (2019) Explanation based handwriting verification (2019). arXiv:1909.02548
5. Deng J, Dong W, Socher R, Li LJ, Li K, Fei-Fei L (2009) Imagenet: a large-scale hierarchical image database. In: 2009 IEEE conference on computer vision and pattern recognition. IEEE, pp 248–255
6. Dey S, Dutta A, Toledo JI, Ghosh SK, Lladós J, Pal U (2017) Signet: convolutional Siamese network for writer independent offline signature verification (2017). arXiv:1707.02131
7. Engin D, Kantarci A, Arslan S, Ekenel HK (2020) Offline signature verification on real-world documents. In: Proceedings of the IEEE/CVF conference on computer vision and pattern recognition workshops, pp 808–809
8. He K, Zhang X, Ren S, Sun J (2016) Deep residual learning for image recognition. In: Proceedings of the IEEE conference on computer vision and pattern recognition, pp 770–778
9. Kingma DP, Ba J (2014) Adam: a method for stochastic optimization. arXiv:1412.6980
10. Musgrave K, Belongie S, Lim SN (2020) Pytorch metric learning. arXiv:2008.09164
11. Shaikh MA, Chauhan M, Chu J, Srihari S (2018) Hybrid feature learning for handwriting verification. In: 2018 16th international conference on frontiers in handwriting recognition (ICFHR). IEEE, pp 187–192
12. Shaikh MA, Duan T, Chauhan M, Srihari SN (2020) Attention based writer independent verification. In: 2020 17th international conference on frontiers in handwriting recognition (ICFHR). IEEE, pp 373–379
13. Wei P, Li H, Hu P (2019) Inverse discriminative networks for handwritten signature verification. In: Proceedings of the IEEE/CVF conference on computer vision and pattern recognition, pp 5764–5772

C4MTS: Challenge on Categorizing Missing Traffic Signs from Contextual Cues

Varun Gupta, Sandeep Nagar, Suman Paul Choudhury, Rohit Singh, Anandita Jamwal, Vibhu Gupta, Anbumani Subramanian, C. V. Jawahar, and Rohit Saluja

Abstract Traffic signs, despite being crucial for road safety, frequently remain absent. This challenge provides 200 scenes from a recent *Missing Traffic Signs Video Dataset* (MTSVD), distributed over four types of missing traffic signs: *left-hand-curve*, *right-hand-curve*, *gap-in-median*, and *side-road-left*, individually observed with their respective contextual cues. 2000 training images, each containing one of the four traffic signs with corresponding bounding boxes, are provided. Two tasks are proposed for the challenge: (i) *Object Detection*, wherein the model is trained using bounding-box annotations, and (ii) *Missing Traffic Sign Scene Categorization*, wherein the model is trained using road scene images with in-painted traffic signs, provided with the challenge dataset. Baselines were provided to the participants for both tasks.54 teams registered for the challenge. Overall, the participants could improve the top-1 accuracy significantly by a margin of 31.5% over the baseline. This work presents the MTSVD in detail, challenge baselines, and the methodology undertaken by the top 2 teams.

Keywords Missing traffic signs · Missing objects · Context · Object detection · Scene categorization

---

Challenge organizers.
Joint report with coordinators and invited contributions from the challenge winners.
https://cvit.iiit.ac.in/ncvpripg2023/c4mtschallenge.

V. Gupta (✉) · S. Nagar · A. Subramanian · C. V. Jawahar
IIIT Hyderabad, Hyderabad, India
e-mail: gupta.varun@research.iiit.ac.in

A. Jamwal · V. Gupta · R. Saluja (✉)
IIT Mandi, Mandi, India

S. P. Choudhury · R. Singh
SAHAJ AI, Chennai, India

S. Chaudhury et al. (eds.), *Computer Vision, Pattern Recognition, Image Processing, and Graphics*, Lecture Notes in Electrical Engineering 1218,
https://doi.org/10.1007/978-981-97-5212-6_16

1 Introduction

Global Autonomous Vehicle (AV) market is projected to reach 2162 Billion by 2030 [1]. Around 1.3M lives are lost yearly in road accidents [2], with traffic sign violations contributing significantly to this number [3]. The traffic signs are generally installed at the side of the road to control traffic flow or convey information about the road environment to Vulnerable Road Users (VRUs). Often, the information is also available in the form of cues present in the context around the traffic signs (*obstacle-delineator* in Fig. 1) or in the cues away from it (*pedestrian-crossing* in Fig. 1), which we refer to as *contextual cues*.

The Missing Traffic Signs Video Dataset (MTSVD) [4] is the first publicly accessible data for missing traffic signs. The dataset contains 4000 missing sign intervals, the first of its kind, covering more than 500 K frames across 30 traffic sign categories for which visual context exists. The MTSVD further contains bounding-box annotations of existing traffic signs on the road along with their context-interval markings, if present. Exact details are quantified and visualized in Sect. 2.

The C4MTS challenge of Categorizing Missing Traffic Signs provides 200 natural scenes from MTSVD uniformly distributed over 4 types of missing traffic signs. The traffic signs are common but individually observed with contextual cues (see samples in Fig. 1). In the given examples, contextual cues like *rumble strips*, *side roads*, etc., are present, but the traffic signs are missing, perhaps due to improper planning, etc. To learn the relationship between the traffic signs and the contextual cues, 2000 training images (similar to those in Fig. 1 with single traffic signs), each containing one of the 4 traffic signs (commonly and individually visible with con-

Fig. 1 MTSVD [4] samples having traffic signs with contextual cues. **Anti-clockwise from top-left**: a *left-hand-curve*, *obstacle-delineator*, *gap-in-median*, and *right-hand-curve*. The red markings are added for visual emphasis

textual cues) and corresponding bounding boxes are also provided. The following tasks are proposed for the challenge: (i) Object Detection and (ii) Missing Traffic Sign Scene Classification. The details of the individual tasks are given in Sect. 4.

2 Missing Traffic Signs Video Dataset

Prior missing object datasets either had the cue in their immediate vicinity or had a consistent relationship between the missing object and the corresponding cue [5, 6]. However, the MTSVD contains multiple cue contexts and complementary cue-object relationships, making MTSVD the most challenging and diverse, publicly accessible missing objects dataset. To ensure privacy, human-faces and vehicle-license-plates have been blurred in the dataset using [7]. This section primarily describes the dataset in detail.

2.1 MTSVD in Numbers

The various traffic signs present in the dataset are illustrated as a word cloud in Fig. 3. The traffic signs in the MTSVD are spread across 74 types of traffic signs like *signboard*, *speed-limit*, and *chevron-left/right*, covering the significant spread. Sample annotations from the MTSVD are exhibited in Fig. 2. Figure 5a illustrates the

Fig. 2 Frame-level traffic sign annotations in the MTSVD [4]. The dataset contains bounding-box track annotations with multiple attributes like *tilted*, *occluded*, etc., and is captured in diverse weather and lighting conditions

top-30 most frequent traffic signs in the dataset by the number of tracks annotated. *Signboard* primarily contain, but are not limited to, the overhead direction markers on the roads and other informatory markings, for example, *CCTV Surveillance*, *National-Highway* marking, etc. Further, *other* category comprises the signs that either do not fit well in the rest of the types or are challenging to define precisely. Moreover, MTSVD contains context frame annotations for various traffic sign categories, which can be identified by the corresponding scene context and are made available for existing traffic signs and, importantly, missing traffic signs. Figure 5b highlights the missing signs categories and the corresponding interval counts identified. Finally, Table 1 mentions a precise qualitative overview (Fig. 4).

Pie chart containing information about the categories in the MTSVD is split into two halves: context and no-context.

3 Challenge Impact and Significance

The challenge is proposed to boost the research on missing objects, which is exciting but is being studied by only a handful of groups. Till now, the problems related to the missing object are studied for identifying missing barricades [5], missing curbs [6], or locating potential positions for non-existing pedestrians [8]. Such works and related models are specific to the task and do not involve multiple classes. However, missing traffic signs is a reality and of great practical importance in the Indian scenario and similar countries lacking road infrastructure. Moreover, the variety of traffic signs that are found missing is more than the previous missing object-related works. Classifying scenes with missing traffic signs can help the government install them at appropriate locations, enable vehicle companies to include dash-cams with adequate warnings even in case of missing signs, and have the potential to help autonomous vehicles follow applicable rules even in the absence of traffic signs. Thus, it can significantly impact the industrial community, government, and smart-city planners.

4 Participation Rules and Evaluation Criteria

The challenge consists of the two tasks mentioned below:

- **Task 1**: Traffic Sign Detection: Localization and classification of traffic signs in the road scenes.
- **Task 2**: Classifying missing traffic sign scenes.

Both tasks involve four types of traffic signs: *left-hand-curve, right-hand-curve, gap-in-median*, and *side-road-left*. These traffic sign types are chosen based on two factors; firstly, their frequency is high among the missing traffic sign scenes in the MTSVD dataset [4]. Secondly, they are commonly observed without interference

Fig. 3 Various context categories in the MTSVD, where the corresponding traffic sign remains absent in the scene. The contexts may slightly differ from one scene to another, as it's a real-world artifact, but they remain fairly consistent and follow an observable pattern

Fig. 4 Word-cloud of the traffic sign categories in the MTSVD [4]

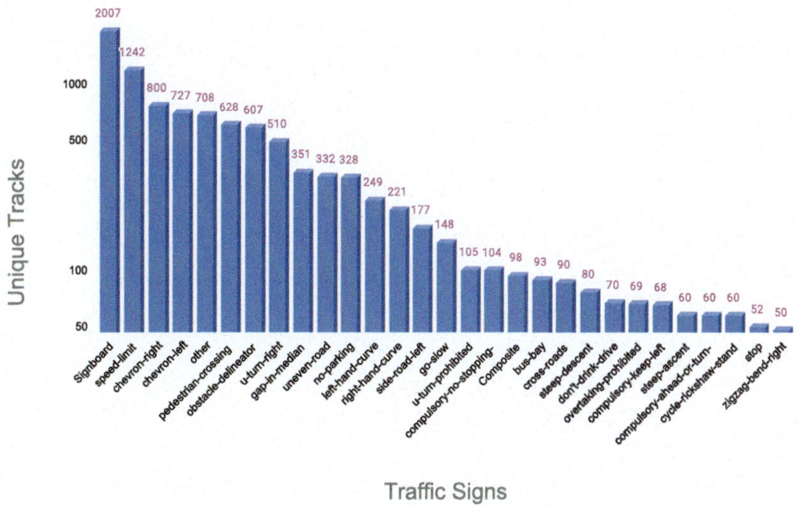

(a) Top 30 of the most frequent traffic signs in the MTSVD by the number of unique tracks annotated.

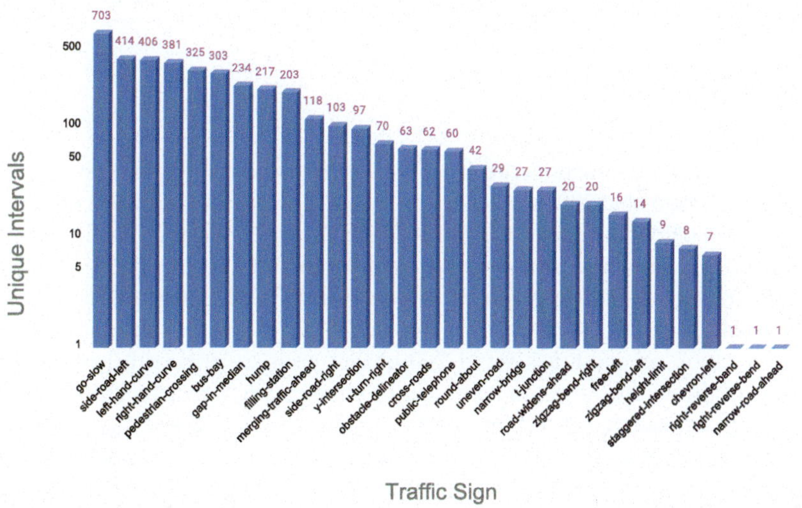

(b) Missing traffic sign categories marked in the MTSVD. The annotations are made available as frame intervals, where the context for the corresponding *missing* traffic sign remains visible

Fig. 5 Annotated and Missing traffic signs in the MTSVD [4]

Table 1 Overview of the MTSVD. † Each frame has dense attributes for shape, category, tilt, etc., along with the bounding box and belongs to a corresponding track, identified by a unique video-level track ID

Type	Count
Unique videos	1,590
Traffic sign categories	74
Missing signs categories	30
Unique traffic sign tracks	10,510
Annotated frames †	1,200,0658
Existing traffic signs context intervals	3,470
Missing traffic sign context intervals	3,977
Missing traffic sign context frames	573,441
Existing traffic sign context frames	839,172

from other traffic signs or contextual cues, possibly avoiding over-complicating the task and encouraging more participation.

4.1 Evaluation Criteria

Separate data and evaluations are proposed for the two tasks. For the first task, 2000 in training images and 200 in validation images will be provided. 200 test images will be provided before the end of the competition. The mean Average Precision (mAP) score will be considered for evaluating the different detection methods. To train the models for task 2, the 1000 images with in-painted traffic signs will be provided, in-painted using a SoTA in-painting method [9]. To evaluate the methods for task 2, a validation set and a test set of 200 images each are provided (test set before the end of the competition). In both sets, 100 frames are from actual missing traffic sign video sequences, and 100 frames are from images with traffic signs in-painted. The actual missing sign images are included to encourage participants to create in-painting agnostic solutions. Standard error rates will be considered to evaluate different methods for the classification task [10].

4.2 Participation Rules

The participation rules are established as follows:

1. Any individual or group can use email to create a participation ID for the competition.
2. Making multiple IDs of the same group or individual is prohibited.

3. No restriction exists on the number of groups from an institute or organization, but common group participants are not allowed.
4. The groups or individuals must upload the obtained results in the specific format to the challenge website, which organizers will verify.
5. Automated scripts will calculate the scores for the proposed task and display the results on the leaderboard.
6. The group members or individuals can update the results on the leaderboard, with a limit of 5 per day per group, after the test data release and before the end of the competition.
7. To verify the results and ensure fair participation, the participants or top teams will be told to reproduce them at the event (or before) using the trained models. If the submitted results are mismatched, the participants will be disqualified, and their results will be removed from the leaderboard.

The winning teams are Sahajeevi (Suman Paul Choudhury, Rohit Singh) and IAMG-ROOT (Sandeep Nagar). The baselines are created by Anandita Jamwal and Vibhu Gupta for task 1 and task 2, respectively.

5 Methodology

This section describes the baseline methodology, along with the approach of the winning teams, for both the tasks of the C4MTS challenge.

5.1 Task 1: Traffic Signs Detection

The task is to train a model to detect traffic signs using the provided bounding-box annotations. The output expected for evaluating this task is the (*class name*, *x center*, *y center*, *width*, *height*, *prediction score*) for each frame. The *Mean Average Precision* (mAP) is used to evaluate the output.

5.1.1 Baseline Method

Considering its light and efficient architecture, this approach uses the YOLOv8n [11] model. The challenge dataset is divided into a 90 : 10 train-validation ratio. The SGD optimizer is used to train the model for 100 epochs with a batch size of 16, and the prediction is made on the test data.

5.1.2 Sahajeevi's Method

First, the following data augmentation methods [12] are applied: ShiftScale, random brightness-contrast, changing saturation level, and mosaic data augmentation [13]. The SoTA YOLOv8 [11] object detection model is trained on an NVIDIA A100 GPU, taking about 40 minutes to train 60 epochs. For post-processing and inference, SAHI [14] detects small traffic signs. Evaluation plots are given in Fig. 6.

5.1.3 IAMGROOT's Method

The IMAMGROOT team applied the following data augmentation techniques from Roboflow: random rotation, and mosaic data augmentation, horizontal flip, and vertical flip, and generated 8000 extra samples from the task-1 dataset, resulting in total 10000 instances. It is observed that adding Dropout also improved the results. The small footprint of the traffic sign in the images suggests that this is a fine-grained detection task. Given the relatively limited samples in the dataset, small-to-medium models are considered to avoid possible overfitting. The task-1 dataset is split into train and validation, with an image size of 720×720. Existing SoTA models: YOLOv8n, YOLOv8s, YOLOv8m, and YOLO8l are fine-tuned using pre-trained weights, with the YOLOv8s model being optimal. The models are trained on the NVIDIA A100 for 80 epochs with the following hyper-parameters: $1e-4$ learning rate, $2e-4$ weight decay, 0.982 momentum, and 0.25 Dropout.

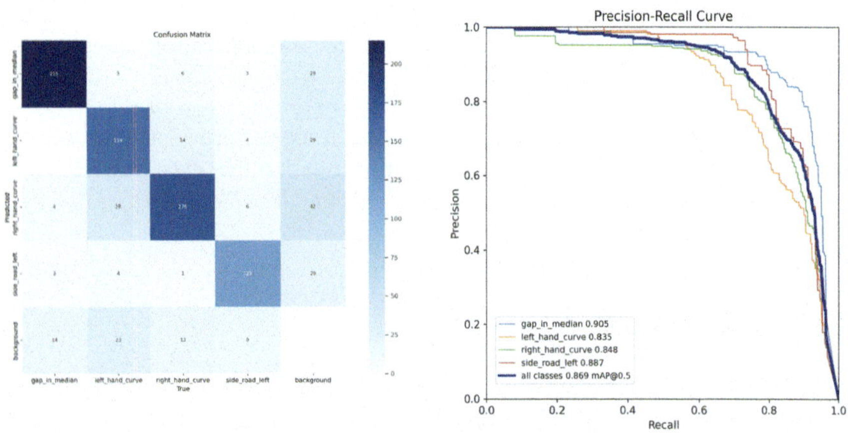

Fig. 6 Sahajeevi's method confusion matrix and PR curves for task 1

5.2 *Task 2: Traffic Sign Scene Categorization*

The aim of Task 2 is to train a model wherein model training happens using road scene images with in-painted traffic signs spread over four traffic sign categories: *left-hand-curve*, *right-hand-curve*, *gap-in-median*, and *side-road-left* for scene categorization. The evaluation for task 2 is done by comparing the predicted labels submitted by participants to the test labels of the 200 test images, with top-1 accuracy as the chosen metric to evaluate the models. The test set contains a proportionate combination of real and in-painted images to ensure that the model doesn't favor the in-painting artifacts and performs poorly on real scenes.

5.2.1 Baseline Method

For the second task, the ResNet-18 [15] model is chosen. The following hyper-parameters are employed for the experiment: 20 batch size, 100 epochs, 0.01 learning rate, $1e-4$ weight decay, and momentum of 0.9. However, the following hyper-parameters were observed to be optimal: 2 batch size, 100 epochs, 0.008 learning rate, $1e-6$ weight decay, and a momentum of 0.9, with the SGD optimizer used throughout. The model with the optimal parameters is further tested on the CIFAR-10 dataset, resulting in an impressive 0.91 accuracy. All models are trained on Google Colab, following a reference code.[1]

5.2.2 Sahajeevi's Method

No data augmentations are performed, and the preferred model is the ResNet50 [15], which is fine-tuned on the challenge dataset for 10 epochs. The confusion matrix is shown in Fig. 7.

5.2.3 IAMGROOT's Method

The IAMGROOT team improved the SoTA performance by conducting fine-tuning on the ResNet-18 architecture for four-class classification. To further improve the model, the team utilized data augmentation techniques. For model training, the task-2 dataset was split in $90:10$ train-validation ratio, and images were normalized using the following mean and standard deviation values: $(0.4914, 0.4822, 0.4465)$, $(0.2023, 0.1994, 0.2010)$, respectively. The model is initialized using pre-trained weights and fine-tuned for 60 epochs with the following hyper-parameters: $8e-4$ learning rate, 0.9 momentum, $1e-6$ weight decay, and the SGD optimizer. The

[1] ResNet-18 reference code link.

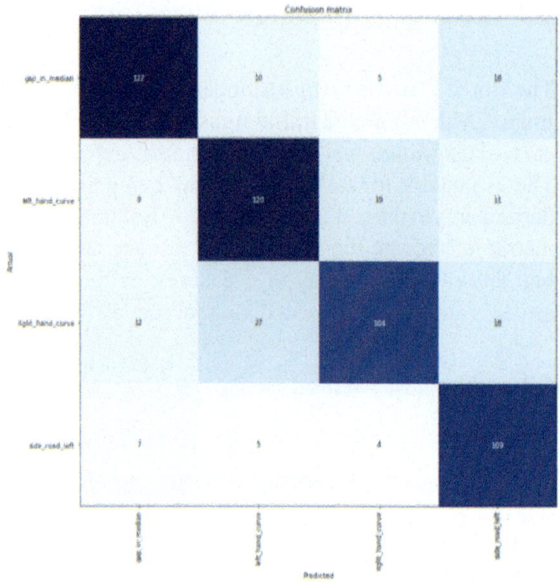

Fig. 7 Sahajeevi's method confusion matrix for task 2

Table 2 Tasks 1 and 2 results

Method	mAP (Task-1)	Top-1 accuracy (Task-2)
Baseline	0.88	0.290
Sahajeevi	0.84	0.514
IAMGROOT	**0.90**	**0.605**

model is evaluated using the Cross-Entropy loss. Results are described in Table 2, and the code is made available.[2]

6 Results

The results are elaborated in Table 2. The IAMGROOT's method outperforms the baselines with a mAP of 0.90 in task 1, while Sahajeevi's method under-performs the baseline by 4.76%. This happens perhaps because the baseline is trained for 40 more epochs than Sahajeevi's method (refer Sect. 5). For task 2, both teams significantly outperformed the baseline, with IAMGROOT being the best overall, with a top-1 accuracy of 0.605.

[2] github.com/Naagar/Missing_Traffic_Sign.

7 Session Held During the Event

We thank IHub-Data, IIIT Hyderabad (https://ihub-data.iiit.ac.in/), for sponsoring the awards. We had a dedicated two-hour session at NCVPRIPG to highlight the importance of the problems related to missing objects and provide the winning teams with a platform to showcase their work. The session included the presentation of the challenge, award ceremony, three oral presentations, and a keynote talk on *Recognition of Modern Indian Signboards and License Plates* by Prof. Ganesh Ramakrishnan (IIT Bombay).

8 Conclusion

We conducted the C4MTS challenge on Categorizing Missing Traffic Signs to gather interest in an exciting and equally important task of improving road infrastructure. For this, the challenge was designed to contain two tasks: Traffic sign detection and Traffic scene categorization, focusing on four categories of traffic signs from the recent Missing Traffic Signs Video Dataset. Methodologies explored by the winning teams who beat the baseline top-1 accuracy by a significant margin of 31.5% were also discussed. We encourage others to research and explore the publicly released Missing Traffic Signs Video Dataset.

References

1. Jadhav A (2018) Autonomous vehicle market by level of automation (level 3, level 4, and level 5) and component (hardware, software, and service) and application (civil, robo taxi, self-driving bus, ride share, self-driving truck, and ride hail)-global opportunity analysis and industry forecast, 2019–2026. Allied Market Research
2. World Health Organization. Road traffic accidents (2022)
3. Petrovic D, Mijailovic R, Pesic D (2020) Traffic accidents with autonomous vehicles: type of collisions, manoeuvres and errors of conventional vehicles' drivers. Transp Res Procedia 45:161–168
4. Gupta V, Subramanian A, Jawahar CV, Saluja R (2023) CueCAn: cue driven contextual attention for identifying missing traffic signs on unconstrained roads. In: IEEE international conference on robotics and automation (ICRA)
5. Chian E, Fang W, Goh YM, Tian J (2021) Computer vision approaches for detecting missing barricades. Autom Constr 131:103862
6. Sun J, Jacobs DW (2017) Seeing what is not there: learning context to determine where objects are missing. In: Proceedings of the IEEE conference on computer vision and pattern recognition, pp 5716–5724
7. Gupta V (2023) Dashcam anonymizer. https://github.com/varungupta31/dashcam_anonymizer
8. Chien JT, Chou CJ, Chen DJ, Chen HT (2017) Detecting nonexistent pedestrians. In: Proceedings of the IEEE international conference on computer vision workshops, pp. 182–189

9. Suvorov R, Logacheva E, Mashikhin A, Remizova A, Ashukha A, Silvestrov A, Kong N, Goka H, Park K, Lempitsky V (2022) Resolution-robust large mask inpainting with Fourier convolutions. In: Proceedings of the IEEE/CVF winter conference on applications of computer vision (WACV), pp 2149–2159
10. Krizhevsky A, Sutskever I, Hinton GE (2017) Imagenet classification with deep convolutional neural networks. Commun ACM 60(6):84–90
11. Jocher G, Chaurasia A, Qiu J (2023) YOLO by ultralytics
12. Jung AB (2018) Imgaug. https://github.com/aleju/imgaug. Accessed 30 Oct 2018
13. Bochkovskiy A, Wang CY, Liao HY (2020) Yolov4: optimal speed and accuracy of object detection
14. Akyon FC, Altinuc SO, Temizel A (2022) Slicing aided hyper inference and fine-tuning for small object detection. In: 2022 IEEE international conference on image processing (ICIP). IEEE
15. He K, Zhang X, Ren S, Sun J (2015) Deep residual learning for image recognition

DePondFi'23 Challenge Summary

A. Sasithradevi, R. Suganya, P. Prakash, S. Mohamed Mansoor Roomi, M. Vijayalakshmi, Sabari Nathan, P. Kasthuri, J. Persia, L. Brighty Ebenezer, Sparsh Jain, Sshubam Verma, S. Balasubramanian, M. Sai Subramaniam, T. Sai Sriram, M. Pranav Phanindra Sai, Chandan Raj, Amandeep Yadav, and Ritik Payak

Abstract Aquaculture is now a significant part of the country's economy, but fish infections are a serious threat to its success. Industry experts are burdened with spotting sick fish based on their behaviour. Therefore, there is an urgent need for an intelligent system that stops the spread of disease while enhancing aquatic well-being. Fish recognition in underwater photography, in particular, is essential for vision-based fish health analysis. Aquaculture could benefit from the combination of vision-based fish health analysis and intelligent technology, allowing for non-invasive monitoring, early disease identification, and enhanced fish population health. DePondFi'23 dataset will support vision-based fish health analysis, and the event highlighted its potential to transform the aquaculture sector in line with current environmental and financial concerns. Our DePondFi'23 challenge provides a forum for inter-disciplinary discussion, which aids fish farm decision-making and ecosystem health maintenance. This article discusses the details of the dataset developed for the DePondFi'23 challenge and provides the extensive results attained by the Top 3 winners of our challenge event.

Keywords DePondFi · Fish detection · Pond aquaculture · Underwater images

A. Sasithradevi (✉) · R. Suganya · M. Vijayalakshmi · J. Persia · L. B. Ebenezer
Vellore Institute of Technology, Chennai, India
e-mail: devisasithra@gmail.com

P. Prakash
Madras Institute of Technology, Chennai, India

S. M. M. Roomi · P. Kasthuri
Thiagarajar College of Engineering, Madurai, India

S. Nathan
Couger Inc, Shibuya, Japan

S. Jain · S. Verma
Maharaja Agrasen Institute of Technology, Delhi, India

S. Balasubramanian · M. S. Subramaniam · T. S. Sriram · M. P. P. Sai
Sri Sathya Sai Institute of Higher Learning, Anantapur, Andhra Pradesh, India

C. Raj · A. Yadav · R. Payak
IIT, Roorkee, India

S. Chaudhury et al. (eds.), *Computer Vision, Pattern Recognition, Image Processing, and Graphics*, Lecture Notes in Electrical Engineering 1218,
https://doi.org/10.1007/978-981-97-5212-6_17

1 Introduction

In today's era, characterized by a prominent blue hue, aquaculture assumes an integral role within the economic landscape of our nation [1]. The problem of fish disease significantly negatively impacts aquaculture businesses' profitability and productivity, from small-scale operations to large ones [2]. The ability of industry experts to spot ailing fish by their unusual behavior increases the workload on labor forces [3]. Therefore, an intelligent and perceptive system that can prevent the spread of fish diseases while promoting the wellbeing of aquatic life is desperately needed in the field of aquaculture [4]. The introduction of intelligent systems becomes crucial to meet this urgent need [5]. The initial and vital stride towards achieving fish health monitoring automation hinges on the precise and automated identification of fish within underwater images and videos [6]. This undertaking, marked by its complexity, becomes the cornerstone for ushering the advancements in fish disease detection [6]. Our Challenge focuses on primary phase in detection of fish disease. This serves as the launchpad for creating automated workflows within the fish disease detection process. Also, complimentary nature between performance and time complexity is pivotal in this task [7]. Detecting fish within underwater images is difficult, owing to the intricate and ever-changing subaquatic milieu [5]. The issues in the detection of fish from underwater images include the volatility of lighting conditions, the turbidity of water, and obstructions posed by other objects [5]. Thus, creating an effective algorithm for fish detection is of utmost importance. Given that it is the first stage in the vision-based fish health analysis domain, its successful implementation can significantly impact the aquaculture industry's productivity [8]. Vision-based fish health analysis involves several steps to accurately assess the health and well-being of aquatic organisms through image and video data. The first step in this process [9] is Image and Video Data Collection, Gathers underwater images and videos of the fish species. This can be done using cameras placed within the aquaculture environment, underwater drones, or other imaging methods. We used an efficient underwater camera for the capturing process. Next is the Preprocessing step, which involves removing noise, correcting lighting conditions, and enhancing image quality to improve the accuracy of subsequent analysis. The following step is fish Detection, which employs object detection techniques to identify and locate fish within the images or video frames. This step involves isolating fish from the background and other objects present in the aquatic environment. The next step is Feature Extraction, in which relevant features from the detected fish, such as size, shape, colour patterns, and texture, are derived. These features will serve as inputs for the subsequent analysis. Following this step, the disease/anomaly is detected through behaviour analysis. It involves machine learning or deep learning algorithms to detect signs of diseases, anomalies, or deviations from healthy fish behaviour. This step often involves training models on labelled data that indicate healthy and diseased fish. After detecting fish, the potential issue is classifying and diagnosing the specific health condition. This could involve categorizing diseases, identifying parasites, or assessing stress levels. Based on the analysis results, we can determine the overall health status of the fish. This assessment could support an evaluation of the severity of detected issues and estimate the impact on the fish population. Thereby continuously monitor the fish population to track changes in health conditions. Regular monitoring helps in identifying early signs of diseases or stressors. We can integrate the analysis results into a comprehensive report or dashboard. This allows aquaculture operators and researchers to understand the fish population's health status easily. Finally, a feedback loop where the analysis results and assessments contribute to the management and decision-making processes within the aquaculture facility can be implemented. This will involve adjusting feeding schedules, environmental conditions, or treatment plans based on the health analysis outcomes. The regular refinement improves the analysis models based on new data and feedback. This iterative process enhances the accuracy and effectiveness of the vision-based fish health (VFH) analysis system. In conjunction with intelligent technologies, the vision-based fish health analysis system holds immense promise for the aquaculture industry, contributing to economic sustainability and marine ecosystem protection [10]. VFH facilitates early fish detection, minimizes the use of antibiotics, and ensures non-invasive monitoring, ultimately enhancing the overall health and productivity of fish populations. It's a critical tool for the modern aquaculturist, aligning the industry with contemporary environmental and economic imperatives. Hence, our DePondFi'23 dataset provides a good platform for AI and robotics teams to work on eco-health systems. Our Challenge focuses on the first step, called fish detection, on which the accuracy of the entire VFH relies. It allows collaboration from various multi-disciplinary fields to make informed decisions in fish farms to make the entire ecosystem efficient and healthy. This article is organized as follows: Sect. 2 details the background genesis of our challenge event. Section 3 describes the image acquisition process and details about the DePondFi'23 dataset. Section 4 discusses the summary of results attained by the participants in our challenge. Section 5 concludes our challenge "DePondFi'23" event.

2 Background

There might be a lack of specific earlier datasets focused solely on the detection of pond fish. Datasets for fish detection in various aquatic environments, such as rivers, lakes, and oceans, might exist, but finding datasets specifically tailored to pond environments could be a challenge. The most commonly used datasets are the Fish4knowledge dataset, AquaCrop pond fish dataset, FishNet dataset, Underwater Fish Detection dataset (UW-FDD) and YOLOv3 Fish detection dataset. Working with the above-mentioned real-world datasets can sometimes present challenges, such as variations in lighting, water conditions, and fish behaviour. Preprocessing and augmentation techniques are often required to improve model robustness. The availability of datasets tailored explicitly to the detection of pond fish remains limited, as most existing datasets focus on aquatic environments like rivers, lakes, and oceans. While various datasets hold relevance for fish detection, challenges unique to pond environments can still arise. Notably, the Fish4Knowledge Dataset offers annotated underwater footage of fish in diverse habitats, including ponds, enabling tasks like species classification and tracking. The AquaCrop Pond Fish Dataset is designed for pond fish detection, featuring images from aquaculture settings with annotations aiding object detection. Similarly, the FishNet Dataset contributes to fish species classification and detection research, although it's not exclusively pond-centric. The Underwater Fish Detection Dataset (UW-FDD) provides annotated underwater images adaptable for pond fish detection tasks, despite its broader scope. Custom datasets using YOLOv3 for object detection, including fish in pond settings, are also valuable resources, typically accompanied by annotations suitable for training YOLO-based models. However, even with these datasets, the intricacies of pond environments present challenges such as lighting variability, water condition fluctuations, and diverse fish behavior. Adapting models to these challenges through preprocessing, augmentation, and fine-tuning is pivotal for achieving accurate and robust fish detection results within pond environments.

The existing datasets for pond fish detection provide valuable resources but have certain limitations. These include a potential lack of representation of diverse fish species found in ponds, mainly small-scale or rare species. Some datasets might not cover many pond environments, overlooking unique conditions and seasonal variations. Annotations might be sparse over time, and there could be a lack of augmentation scenarios that mimic real-world challenges like varying lighting and water turbidity. Multi-modal data sources, such as depth and water quality information, might also be missing. Furthermore, the datasets might not address challenging conditions like low-light environments or extreme water murkiness, and benchmarking protocols could be insufficient. Addressing these gaps requires creating more diverse and comprehensive datasets, collaborating with experts, and emphasizing standardized evaluation practices. To improve existing datasets, it's crucial to enhance species representation, capture temporal variability, and incorporate challenging conditions. Augmentation techniques should be developed to simulate different lighting and water conditions accurately. Expanding annotations to cover every frame in video sequences and including multi-modal data can create more realistic scenarios for fish detection models. Standardizing benchmarking protocols will ensure consistent evaluation and comparison of detection algorithms, fostering pond fish detection technology advancements.

3 Challenges

* Complex underwater environments, diverse fish species, and varying lighting conditions complicate fish detection accuracy in aqua-farms.
* Limited availability of annotated underwater images tailored to the Indian context hinders the development of robust detection models.
* Adapting international fish detection approaches to India's unique aqua farming conditions demands consideration of regional species and water variables.

* Collaborating with aqua farmers, researchers, and domain experts is crucial to address challenges and tailor solutions for effective disease prediction in Indian aquafarms.

4 Origin of DePondFi'23 Dataset

Data collection lays the groundwork for research. This executive summary report highlights the extensive DePondFi'23 Dataset collection journey that we undertook for our challenge, presenting details about the Camera used and the pond details. The specification of the underwater camera used is shown in Table 2 (Table 1).

The dataset is collected from four coastal districts of Tamilnadu namely Cuddalore, Chennai, Kanchipuram and Tanjore. At first the district choosen was Cuddalore, there were ponds with dimension 10 K sq.m each 4 m deep with approximately four thousand fish species. The species cultivated are Carp, Rogu, Catla, Mrigal, Silver carp, rupchanda, Tilapia, and Grass carp. Video is captured considering both high

Table 1 Details of DePondFi dataset

Parameters considered	Description
Types of image	Low resolution RGB underwater images
Number of images	8150
Modality of dataset	Extracted images from 60 fps videos
Split-up of dataset	70:15:15 (train:test1:test2)
Augmentation	Resizing
Obstacles taken into account	Water absorption and scattering losses
	Color distortion
	Turbulence
	Lighting conditions
	Depth and pressure
Resolution	640p at 60 fps

Table 2 Specification of camera used

Model	CT9000
Resolution	4K (25 fps), 2.7 K (30 fps), 1080p (60 fps)
Pixel	16 MP, 12 MP, 8 MP, 5 MP, 4 MP
Lens	170° wide-angle lens
Storage	Support Class 10 TF card up to 32 GB
Battery	Rechargeable 3.7V 1050 mAh
Weight	64 g/2.240z (with battery)
Dimensions	59×41×25 mm/2.33"×1.61"×0.97"

and low resolution specifications. Moving on to Tanjore district, there are so many ponds located mainly focused for fish cultivation. Among them, one pond housed a mix of common carp, catla, rohu, mrigal, grass carp, and silver carp. There were also ponds allocated for male and female fish, including other fish species, as well as separate ponds for catla, rohu, mrigal, and rupchanda. Additionally, three ponds accommodated mixed varieties of fish of varying sizes. Fertilization was aided by fermented cow dung, and different feed types were provided for various fish species. Pond dimensions varied from 50 to 100 * 100 to 200 * 4 to 5 in Wide*Length*Height. In Chennai, aquaculture farm is located near by Kolathur tapped into nearby water resources, particularly from Red Hills Lake. Fish species cultivated includes Catla, Rohu, Tilapia, Catfish, and Pangasius, chosen for their fast growth, adaptability, and market demand. Videos were recorded within tanks at a depth of 1 m and wide-angle (135°) using low-resolution settings, with each video lasting approximately 1 min. Lastly, In Kancheepuram, ponds near Brahmadesam were surrounded by cultivated lands, and the fish were ready for harvest. These fish primarily consumed an oil cake-based diet and included Catla, Rogu, and Mrigal species. Pond dimensions in this area ranged from 50 to 100 m wide and 100 to 200 m long, with depths of 4 to 5 m. We captured videos from these pond and cleaned the data. We converted it into frames and removed the frames without fish. We selected keyframes from the video through manual inspection and checked it vigilantly twice to ensure the benchmark of our dataset. Once we filtered the keyframes, the next step is data annotation.

5 Data Annotation

Data annotation is paramount in detecting pond fish, as accurate and detailed annotations lay the foundation for training effective machine learning models. In this context, annotating images with bounding boxes around fish instances facilitates the learning process for detection algorithms. Precise annotations enable models to recognize fish with varying environmental conditions, sizes, orientations, and potential occlusions. Moreover, annotated datasets reflect the complexities of pond environments, helping models generalize to real-world scenarios by accounting for challenges like lighting changes, turbidity, and different fish behaviors. We used Roboflow tool for annotation process. Roboflow plays a crucial role in simplifying and enhancing the data annotation process for pond fish detection. Roboflow can efficiently label fish instances in images as an annotation platform, ensuring high-quality annotations. It's features streamline the labeling workflow, enable consistency among annotations, and provide options for managing complex labeling tasks. Furthermore, Roboflow's capabilities extend beyond annotation, encompassing data preprocessing, augmentation, and integration with various machine learning frameworks. By expediting the annotation process and offering a comprehensive suite of tools, Roboflow contributes to the development of accurate and robust pond fish detection models, fostering advancements in aquatic research and aquaculture management. A collaborative effort involving students, research scholars, and fac-

Fig. 1 A glimpse of our dedicated team's collaborative annotation work

ulty members resulted in meticulously annotating a substantial dataset comprising 8,150 frames/images. This endeavor was marked by a commitment to accuracy and precision throughout every phase of the annotation process. Training sessions were conducted to ensure that the team was well-prepared for the task at hand, led by recognized experts in the annotation field. These sessions equipped participants with the necessary knowledge and skills to carry out the annotations effectively. The actual annotation process was executed with a high degree of diligence and systematic organization. Each image was meticulously examined, and the relevant objects or features were annotated with great care. The team adhered to established best practices, ensuring uniformity and consistency in their annotations across all images. Following the initial annotation phase, an equally rigorous validation process was undertaken. To verify the accuracy and quality of the annotations, two rounds of cross-checking were conducted by expert validators. This meticulous review process was critical in ensuring that the annotated dataset was reliable and of the highest possible quality. Figure 1 provided below serves as a visual representation of the extensive work invested in this annotation project, showcasing the dedication and expertise of the team involved. The result is a valuable dataset that can be utilized for various research and applications.

6 Results and Discussion

In this study, we extensively evaluated various fish detection models for underwater environments. The goal was to develop a robust and accurate system for the automated detection of fish species in challenging underwater conditions. The results of our experiments are summarized in Table 3, which displays the mAP (mean Average Precision) scores achieved by different teams and methods.

The mAP metric is a crucial indicator of the detection performance in object detection tasks, including fish detection. It combines precision and recall to provide a single numerical value representing the quality of the detection results. The mAP is calculated as follows:

$$\mathrm{mAP} = \frac{1}{N}\sum_{i=1}^{N} \mathrm{AP}_i$$

Where:

- N is the total number of classes (in our case, fish species).
- AP_i is the Average Precision for class i.

The mAP values obtained by the participating teams showcase the effectiveness of their respective approaches. Detectron secured the top position with an mAP of 38.93%, indicating superior accuracy in fish detection. DMACS_SAI and PondVision also performed commendably with mAP scores of 36.65% and 31.63%, respectively. Figure 2 shows the sample predicted images of top two teams in comparison with original prediction.

The highest mAP team, Detectron, achieved an impressive score of 38.93% using the YOLOv8n+Sahi technique, highlighting the advancements in computer vision techniques for underwater fish detection. These results hold great promise for applications such as marine ecology monitoring, fisheries management, and biodiversity research, where accurate fish detection is crucial. Furthermore, the success of these models underscores the potential for further research and development in underwater object detection. Future work could focus on enhancing the robustness of these systems in varying underwater conditions, including low visibility and diverse fish species.

Table 3 Fish detection performance

Position	Team	mAP (%)
1	Detectron	38.93%
2	DMACS_SAI	36.65%
3	PondVision	31.63%
4	Sahajeevis	29.06%

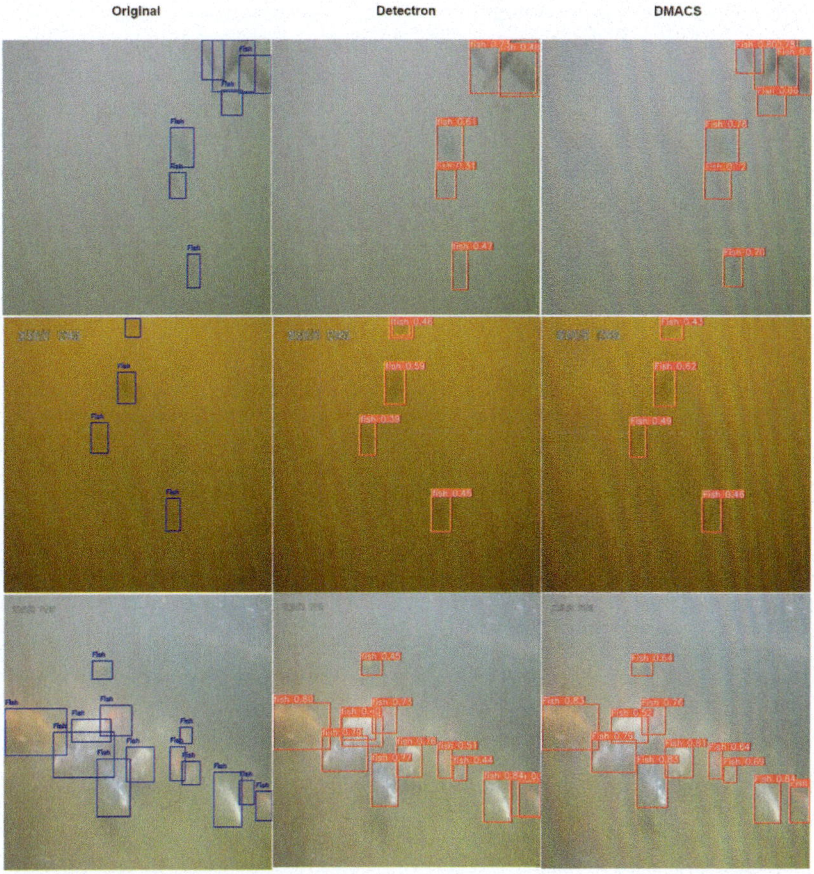

Fig. 2 Sample visual results from top two submissions

In conclusion, the mAP metric is a valuable tool for quantifying the performance of fish detection models in underwater environments. The results presented here demonstrate the potential of computer vision technologies to contribute to underwater research and conservation efforts.

7 Conclusion

The multi-stage process of encompassing data collection, preprocessing, fish detection, feature extraction, disease/anomaly detection, classification/diagnosis, continuous monitoring, and result integration, has the potential to revolutionize aquaculture.The development of intelligent systems integrated with vision-based fish health analysis using underwater photography, offer non-invasive monitoring, early disease detection and overall fish population health, aligning with current environmental and economic concerns. Our DePondFi'23 Challenge facilitated interdisciplinary collaboration, enhancing decision-making in fish farming and fostering healthier ecosystems within the aquaculture sector, making it an essential tool for the industry's future success. The team "Detectron" outperformed the competitors and attained the highest mAP of 38.9%.

References

1. Naylor R, Hardy R, Buschmann A, Bush S, Cao L, Klinger D, ..., Troell M (2021) A 20-year retrospective review of global aquaculture. Nature 591(7851):551–563
2. Mohsan S, Li Y, Sadiq M, Liang J, Khan M (2023) Recent advances, future trends, applications and challenges of the internet of underwater things (iout): a comprehensive review. J Mar Sci Eng 11(1):124
3. Ahmed M, Aurpa T, Azad M (2022) Fish disease detection using image-based machine learning technique in aquaculture. J King Saud Univ-Comput Inf Sci 34(8):5170–5182
4. Shreesha S, MM M, Verma U, Pai R (2020) Computer vision-based fish tracking and behavior detection system. In: 2020 IEEE international conference on distributed computing, VLSI, Electrical circuits and robotics (DISCOVER). IEEE, pp 252–257
5. Wang H, Zhang S, Zhao S, Wang Q, Li D, Zhao R (2022) Real-time detection and tracking of fish abnormal behavior based on improved yolov5 and siamrpn++. Comput Electr Agr 192:106512
6. Pai K, Shenoy K, Pai M (2022) A computer vision based behavioral study and fish counting in a controlled environment. IEEE Access 10:87778–87786
7. Petrellis N (2021) Fish morphological feature recognition based on deep learning techniques. In: 2021 10th international conference on modern circuits and systems technologies (MOCAST). IEEE, pp 1–4
8. Schellewald C, Stahl A, Kelasidi E (2021) Vision-based pose estimation for autonomous operations in aquacultural fish farms. IFAC-PapersOnLine 54(16):438–443
9. Sun M, Yang X, Xie Y (2020) Deep learning in aquaculture: a review. J Comput 31(1):294–319
10. Wu Y, Duan Y, Wei Y, An D, Liu J (2022) Application of intelligent and unmanned equipment in aquaculture: a review. Comput Electr Agr 199:107201

A Challenge on 3D Reconstruction and Restoration of Indian Heritage from Partial and Noisy Scans

Atharva Pandey, Vishal Yadav, Akash Karthikeyan, Deepanshu Solanki, and Rajendra Nagar

Abstract The problem of 3D Reconstruction and restoration of Indian heritage sites is a classical 3D computer vision problem which has been addressed in the Indian vision and graphics research communities. The major focus of these approaches has been to reconstruct a point cloud model of the heritage sites from multiple colored images captured from different viewpoints. This essentially requires solving the structure from motion problem to be solved. This becomes a challenging problem to solve for large scale architectural sites. With the emergence of 3D scanners, we can obtain partial 3D scans of a site from different viewpoints. Then, the main problem to solve is to fuse these noisy and partial 3D scans to obtain the complete 3D model of the underlying surface of the heritage site. The problem of reconstructing the complete 3D model from the partial 3D scan can be solved using classical approaches as well as learning based approaches. Using machine learning based approaches in the context of Indian heritage may suffer from the limited training dataset availability. Also, the order of points representing the 3D model of such sites can be in millions. Therefore, reconstructing such high resolution 3D models using neural network may demand high-end parallel computing facility.

Keywords Heritage site restoration · Point cloud registration · Feature based registration

A. Pandey (✉) · V. Yadav · D. Solanki · R. Nagar
IIT Jodhpur, Jodhpur, Rajasthan, India
e-mail: pandey.19@iitj.ac.in

V. Yadav
e-mail: yadav.40@iitj.ac.in

D. Solanki
e-mail: deepanshu.1@iitj.ac.in

R. Nagar
e-mail: rn@iitj.ac.in

A. Karthikeyan
Thiagarajar College of Engineering, Madurai, India

S. Chaudhury et al. (eds.), *Computer Vision, Pattern Recognition, Image Processing, and Graphics*, Lecture Notes in Electrical Engineering 1218,
https://doi.org/10.1007/978-981-97-5212-6_18

1 Problem Definition

In this challenge, our main focus is to encourage participants to propose novel and efficient classical algorithms to solve this problem. We describe the actual problem to be solved as follows. Let $\{\mathcal{Y}_i\}_{i=1}^{k}$ be a set of partial 3D scans of a heritage site obtained through a D scanner. Then, find the 3D model $\mathcal{Y}$ that represents the complete 3D model of the underlying 3D surface of the considered site. The reconstructed 3D model $\mathcal{Y}$ should be as close as possible to the actual 3D model of the building. For validation of the algorithms, we provided partial 3D scans and respective ground truth 3D models for some of the architectural sites. For the testing phase, we only provided partial 3D scans and asked the participants to submit the reconstructed 3D models. In Fig. 1, we represent the problem description for $k = 3$.

2 Performance Evaluation

In order to rank the submitted algorithms for this challenge, we will use the point cloud distance as a ranking metric. In specific, let $\mathcal{X}$ be the ground truth point cloud and let $\mathcal{Y}$ be the reconstructed point cloud. Then, the Chamfer distance between $\mathcal{X}$ and $\mathcal{Y}$ is defined as below.

$$d_{CD}(\mathcal{X}, \mathcal{Y}) = \frac{1}{|\mathcal{X}|} \sum_{x \in \mathcal{X}} \min_{y \in \mathcal{Y}} \|x - y\|_2^2 + \frac{1}{|\mathcal{Y}|} \sum_{y \in \mathcal{Y}} \min_{x \in \mathcal{X}} \|x - y\|_2^2$$

Lower the value of this metric better would be reconstruction performance. This metric accounts for both 3D reconstruction and restoration performance since the

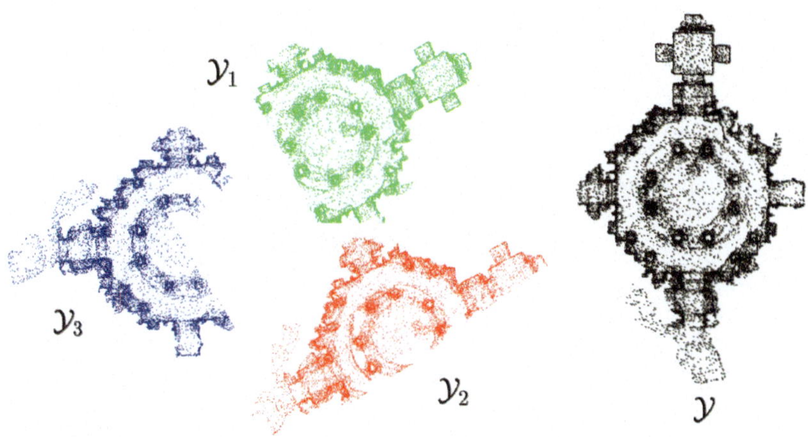

Fig. 1 Problem description for $k = 3$

Table 1 CD for the baseline approach, winner approach, and the runner-up approach

	T1	T2	T3	T4	T5	T6	T7	Mean CD
ICP	55161.9	33283.6	5069.7	89534.3	7397.9	36226.9	25662.4	36048.1
Runner-up	126.35	47.19	3.41	15.87	198.21	2332.18	44.05	47.19
Winner	0.74	0.12	0.098	0.16	0.22	0.16	0.38	0.16

terms $\min_{y \in \mathcal{Y}} \|x - y\|_2^2$ and $\min_{y \in \mathcal{Y}} \|x - y\|_2^2$ would higher for incomplete and noisy reconstruction.

For this challenge, the top two teams are the following.

- Atharva Pandey and Vishal Yadav, IIT Jodhpur, Rajasthan 342030, India (**Winner**)
- Akash Karthikeyan, Thiagarajar College of Engineering, India (**Runner-up**).

For evaluation purpose of these winners, we used seven test cases and the test Chamfer Distance (CD) scores are given in Table 1. We have used the dataset of Bishnupur group of Temples provided by ISI Kolkata and Archaeological Survey of India.

We now, discuss the algorithms submitted by these two teams.

3 Winner Algorithm

3.1 Introduction

Preserving and restoring cultural heritage sites is of utmost importance to safeguard their historical, cultural, and architectural significance for future generations. With the emergence of advanced digital technologies, three-dimensional (3D) laser scanning has become a key ally in the field of cultural heritage conservation. This paper presents a comprehensive comparative analysis of prominent point cloud registration algorithms used in the context of heritage site restoration. Point cloud registration involves aligning multiple scans acquired from different positions or time frames into a coherent 3D representation, enabling a comprehensive understanding of the site's current state and supporting the restoration process. Through the evaluation of the strengths and limitations of these algorithms, including performance, accuracy, computational efficiency, and applicability to various heritage sites, this research aims to provide valuable insights that can aid preservation efforts and ensure the continued conservation of these invaluable landmarks. Heritage sites hold invaluable historical, cultural, and architectural significance, representing the roots of civilizations and acting as a bridge between the past and the present. However, the passage of time and exposure to various environmental factors often lead to the degradation and deterioration of these precious landmarks. To preserve and restore these iconic sites for future generations, advanced digital technologies have emerged as a key ally in the field of cultural heritage conservation. Among these digital technologies, three-dimensional (3D) laser scanning has gained considerable attention due to its ability to create highly accurate and detailed point cloud representations of heritage sites. A point cloud is a vast collection of 3D data points acquired through laser scanning or photogrammetry, capturing the spatial coordinates and surface information of objects and structures in the real world. To achieve complete and precise 3D models of heritage sites, the process of point cloud registration becomes paramount. Point cloud registration involves aligning multiple scans acquired from different positions or time frames into a single, coherent 3D representation. This critical step ensures that all the individual scans are spatially aligned, thus enabling a comprehensive understanding of the site's current state and supporting the restoration process.

Point cloud registration aims to find the optimal transformation $\mathcal{S}$ that aligns two or more point clouds together in a common coordinate system. Let $\mathcal{X} = \{\mathsf{x}_i\}_{i=1}^n$ represent the source point cloud and $\mathcal{Y} = \{\mathsf{y}_i\}_{i=1}^m$ represent the target point cloud. The goal of registration is to find the transformation $\mathcal{S}$ that maps the points in $\mathcal{X}$ to their corresponding points in $\mathcal{Y}$. The transformation $\mathcal{S}$ is typically represented as a combination of translation, rotation, and scaling parameters. The objective of registration is to find the transformation $\mathcal{S}$ that minimizes the discrepancy between corresponding points in the two point clouds. This discrepancy is often measured as a distance metric, such as the Euclidean distance, between the transformed source point $\mathcal{S}(\mathsf{x})$ and the corresponding target point y.

$$\mathcal{S}^* = \arg\min_{\mathcal{S}} \sum_{\mathsf{x}\in\mathcal{X}} \|\mathcal{S}(\mathsf{x}) - \mathsf{y}\|_2^2$$

The objective of this report is to conduct a comprehensive comparative analysis of several prominent point cloud registration algorithms in the context of heritage site restoration. By evaluating the strengths and limitations of these algorithms, we aim to provide valuable insights into their performance, accuracy, computational efficiency, and applicability to different types of heritage sites.

3.2 *Related Works*

The registration problem has been extensively studied, and various approaches have been proposed to tackle the challenges associated with aligning point clouds. In this section, we present a concise overview of the key methodologies used in the field, including optimization-based methods, feature-based learning, and end-to-end learning.

Optimization Based Registration Methods: Optimization-based techniques form the foundation of point cloud registration algorithms, aiming to find the optimal transformation parameters that minimize the discrepancy between two or more point clouds [1, 2, 4–6]. Once the 3D correspondences between the two points clouds are found, the rigid-transformation can be obtained using a closed formed solution [2].

Feature Based Registration Methods: Feature-based point cloud registration methods utilize higher-level geometric features or key points from the point clouds to establish correspondences and perform the registration. These features can be found using Neural Networks [1] or by classical methods [7]. Then, the transformation between the point clouds can be estimated directly through an optimization-based approach after establishing correspondences using features.

Learning-based Rigid Registration Algorithms End-to-end learning-based point cloud registration methods [1, 9] refer to techniques that use deep learning models to directly learn the registration process from raw representations of point clouds. These methods aim to find the optimal transformation between two or more point clouds by training a neural network to predict the transformation parameters, without relying on traditional intermediate steps such as feature extraction or correspondence estimation.

3.3 *Methodology*

The methodology adopted for comparing point cloud registration algorithms for restoring heritage sites is tailored to address the specific challenges posed by the limited dataset and memory constraints. Given the scarcity of ground truth odometry information and the small number of available partial point clouds (only 7 sets), the use of deep learning-based end-to-end methods is not feasible. Consequently, the study focuses on optimization-based (ICP) and feature-based (HKS [3], GCNet[9]) registration approaches in a multiway registration fashion. Additionally, due to the high point density in each ground point cloud (approximately 25k to 30k points), downsampling techniques are employed to alleviate memory issues during experimentation.

Dataset Description: The dataset used for this study consists of a very limited number of partial point clouds from heritage sites. Only 7 sets of partial point clouds are available, making it challenging to train deep learning models effectively. Each partial point cloud in the dataset represents a specific portion of the heritage site and contains approximately 10,000 points.

Limitations for Deep Learning: Due to the limited data and absence of ground truth odometry information, the application of deep learning-based end-to-end registration methods is not viable. Deep learning models often require large amounts of labeled data for effective training, and the lack of sufficient ground truth data hinders their practicality in this context. Considering the characteristics of our dataset, which consists of only six heritage sites and lacks ground truth data, it is difficult to employ end-to-end learning methods for our problem statement. End-to-end learning approaches often require a substantial amount of labelled data to effectively learn complex registration functions directly from the input data.

Downsampling of Point Clouds: We conducted all our experiments on downsampled point clouds. The downsampling was performed due to the large number of points present in each point cloud. This allowed us to achieve faster computations and analysis while still obtaining meaningful insights and results.

Optimization-Based (ICP) The Iterative Closest Point (ICP) algorithm [2], a fundamental optimization-based technique, serves as one of the main benchmarks. ICP iteratively aligns two or more point clouds by minimizing the distances between corresponding points, seeking the optimal transformation parameters. Given two set of points $\mathcal{X} = \{\mathsf{x}_i\}_{i=1}^n$ and $\mathcal{Y} = \{\mathsf{y}_i\}_{i=1}^n$, where y_i is the corresponding point of x_i, we find a rigid transform $\mathcal{S} = (\mathsf{R}, \mathsf{t})$ to align $\mathcal{X}$ with $\mathcal{Y}$:

$$\mathsf{R}^*, \mathsf{t}^* = \underset{\mathsf{R}\in\mathbb{R}^{3\times3}, \mathsf{t}\in\mathbb{R}^3: \mathsf{R}^\top\mathsf{R}=\mathsf{I}, \det(\mathsf{R})=+1}{\arg\min} \sum_{i=1}^{n} \|\mathsf{R}\mathsf{x}_i + \mathsf{t} - \mathsf{y}_i\|_2^2, \tag{1}$$

Given the correspondences between the two point clouds, it is simple to find the optimal $\mathsf{R}^*, \mathsf{t}^*$ using the SVD algorithm. However, we are not given an initial set of correspondences. Therefore, the ICP algorithm [2] solves this problem using an iterative approach that alternates between the following two steps. First it initializes R and t use nearest neighbour approach to find initial correspondence. Then, it update the transformation using the found correspondences. It iterate between the two steps till the convergence.

- *Correspondence step*: find the closest point $\mathsf{y}_{\sigma(i)}$ in $\mathcal{Y}$ for each point $\mathsf{x}_i \in \mathcal{Y}$ based on the current estimated transformation R and t.

$$\mathsf{y}_{\sigma(i)} = \underset{\mathsf{y}\in\mathcal{Y}}{\arg\min} \|\mathsf{R}\mathsf{x}_i + \mathsf{t} - \mathsf{y}\|_2^2, \tag{2}$$

- *Alignment step*: update the current estimated transformation R and t using the current correspondences $(\mathsf{x}_i, \mathsf{y}_{\sigma(i)})$.

$$\mathsf{R}^*, \mathsf{t}^* = \underset{\mathsf{R}\in\mathbb{R}^{3\times3}, \mathsf{t}\in\mathbb{R}^3: \mathsf{R}^\top\mathsf{R}=\mathsf{I}, \det(\mathsf{R})=+1}{\arg\min} \sum_{i=1}^{n} \|\mathsf{R}\mathsf{x}_i + \mathsf{t} - \mathsf{y}_{\sigma(i)}\|_2^2, \tag{3}$$

Feature-Based Two feature-based learning methods are evaluated in this study. The first method employs the Heat Kernel Signature (HKS) descriptor [3], a distinctive local feature that captures geometric properties of point clouds. The second method explores the use of GCNet, a Graph Convolutional Network-based approach, which effectively learns local and global features to facilitate point cloud matching.

Heat Kernel Signature: The Heat Kernel Signature (HKS) is a widely used descriptor for characterizing the geometric properties of 3D point clouds and shapes. It is particularly effective in capturing local geometric information and has found applications in various fields, including shape analysis, point cloud registration, and object recognition. The HKS is derived from the concept of heat diffusion on the surface of a shape or point cloud. The HKS measures the amount of heat at each point and records how it changes over time. The HKS is computed based on the eigenvalues and eigenvectors of the Laplace-Beltrami operator, which describes the geometry of the shape or point cloud. The resulting HKS function provides a compact representation of the local geometric properties of the point cloud.

Geometry-guided Consistent Network (GCNet) Proposes techniques to enhance feature-learning-based point cloud registration by leveraging inlier correspondences proportion. These techniques include a pyramid hierarchy decoder for multi-scale point feature characterization, a consistent voting strategy for maintaining reliable correspondences, and a geometry-guided encoding module for considering geometric characteristics. These advances address challenges posed by partial and indistinguishable surfaces, leading to improved registration performance with broader applications in 3D reconstruction and object recognition. Since we do not have sufficient data to train or fine-tune the model we use the model used for inference is pre-trained on the task of registration on 3DMatch dataset [8].

3.4 Results and Evaluation

The shortcomings of GCNet become evident in scenarios where there are similar local structures in the point cloud data. This similarity can lead to false correspondences being established, which, in turn, causes erroneous registrations. On the other hand, HKS faces challenges in performing well due to the downsampling of the point cloud data. The downsampling process results in a significant loss of information, which negatively impacts the ability of HKS to capture distinctive features across the entire point cloud. Consequently, the limited variance in features over the downsampled

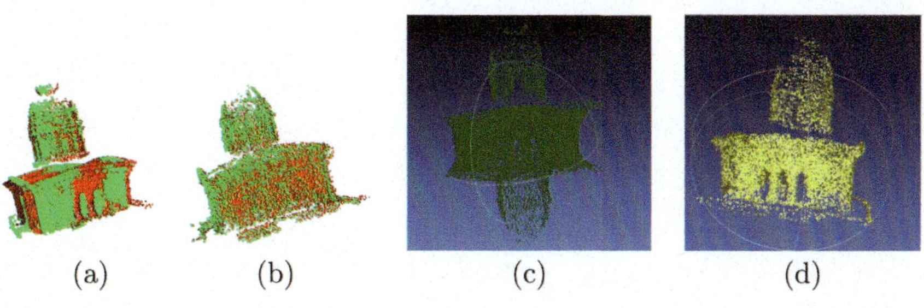

(a) (b) (c) (d)

Fig. 2 Qualitative Results of GCNet: **a** & **b** represents registered point cloud overlayed over the ground truth (Red is the Ground Truth point cloud & Green is the registered point cloud). The bottom rows show an improper registration via GCNet. **c** is the registered point cloud, **d** is the Ground Truth

point cloud hampers the registration performance of HKS-based methods. Figure 2 shows the results of this approach.

References

1. Ao S, Hu Q, Yang B, Markham A, Guo Y (2021) Spinnet: learning a general surface descriptor for 3D point cloud registration. In: Proceedings of the IEEE/CVF conference on computer vision and pattern recognition, pp 11753–11762
2. Besl PJ, McKay ND (1992) Method for registration of 3D shapes. In: Sensor fusion IV: control paradigms and data structures, vol 1611, pp 586–606. SPIE
3. Bronstein MM, Kokkinos I (2010) Scale-invariant heat kernel signatures for non-rigid shape recognition. In: 2010 IEEE computer society conference on computer vision and pattern recognition, pp 1704–1711. IEEE
4. Forstner W, Khoshelham K (2017) Efficient and accurate registration of point clouds with plane to plane correspondences. In: Proceedings of the IEEE international conference on computer vision workshops, pp 2165–2173
5. Iglesias JP, Olsson C, Kahl F (2020) Global optimality for point set registration using semidefinite programming. In: Proceedings of the IEEE/CVF conference on computer vision and pattern recognition, pp 8287–8295
6. Kezurer I, Kovalsky SZ, Basri R, Lipman Y (2015) Tight relaxation of quadratic matching. In: Computer graphics forum, vol 34, pp 115–128. Wiley Online Library
7. Salti S, Tombari F, Di Stefano L (2014) Shot: unique signatures of histograms for surface and texture description. Comput Vis Image Underst 125:251–264
8. Zeng A, Song S, Nießner M, Fisher M, Xiao J, Funkhouser T (2017) 3DMatch: learning local geometric descriptors from RGB-D reconstructions. In: Proceedings of the IEEE conference on computer vision and pattern recognition, pp 1802–1811
9. Zhu L, Guan H, Lin C, Han R (2022) Leveraging inlier correspondences proportion for point cloud registration (2022). arXiv:2201.12094

Author Index

S. Chaudhury et al. (eds.), *Computer Vision, Pattern Recognition, Image Processing, and Graphics*, Lecture Notes in Electrical Engineering 1218,
https://doi.org/10.1007/978-981-97-5212-6

The manufacturer's authorised representative in the EU is Springer Nature Customer Service Centre GmbH, Europaplatz 3, 69115 Heidelberg, Germany. If you have any concerns regarding our products, please contact ProductSafety@springernature.com

Printed and bound by CPI Group (UK) Ltd, Croydon, CR0 4YY

29/07/2026

02180508-0008